MW01699299

Waking Up Dying

CAREGIVING WHEN THERE IS NO TOMORROW

Waking Up Dying

CAREGIVING WHEN THERE IS NO TOMORROW

ROBERT A. DUKE

Good Enough Publishing
BELLINGHAM

Copyright © 2014 Robert A Duke

All rights reserved. No part of this publication may be reproduced, distributed, or transmitted in any form or by any means, including photocopying, recording, or other electronic or mechanical methods, without the prior written permission of the publisher, except in the case of brief quotations embodied in critical reviews and certain other noncommercial uses permitted by copyright law. For permission requests, write to the publisher at the address below.

Good Enough Publishing
4949 Samish Way, No. 8
Bellingham, WA 98229
www.robertaduke.com

Printed in the United States of America

First Printing, 2014

ISBN 978-0-9753286-1-3

The article "Scholarship helps keep Shearlean Duke's memory alive" appeared in the March 2011 issue of the WWU Department of Journalism's "Alumni News" publication. It is reproduced here with permission of the reporter and WWU's Department of Journalism.

COVER DESIGN: Robert A. Duke
COVER IMAGE: Copyright © 2014 by Robert A. Duke
EDITING: Cami Ostman author, editor and writing coach at Camiostman.net
BOOK DESIGN AND PRODUCTION: K.M.Weber, www.ilibribookdesign.com
PHOTOS AND ILLUSTRATIONS: Copyright © 2014 by Robert A. Duke

For Shearlean with gratitude to:

Dr. Daniel Silbergeld, Surgeon, who inspired confidence when it was so vital.

Dr. William Hall, Radiologist, whose care soothed and comforted a blighted patient and encouraged a beleaguered caregiver.

Table of Contents

Illustrations

EXHIBITS

PHOTOGRAPHS

Introduction

THE FOUNDATION for this book is 22 Updates written to keep 17 relatives, friends and colleagues informed of Shearlean (pronounced Shurleen) Duke's experience with treatment for terminal brain cancer. The diagnosis was stage IV glioblastoma.

Updates are mingled with personal journal entries, letters and emails to doctors and nurses, memos to myself, records of telephone conversations and notes from ever-present notebooks. A narrative spanning 18 months ties together all of these pieces to answer the who, what, when, where, why and how of care and treatment.

I structured the book this way to let you experience what we experienced as patient and caregiver just as we lived it, just as we shared our experience with others. My purpose is to provide you with rare insight into events few have access to unless it happens to them.

All of the Updates were written spontaneously and quickly for the practical purpose of informing an audience I knew well, about a person we all cared deeply about. They are all just straightforward and raw life-and-death *news*. Shearlean read and approved each update—except for the last one—because, after all, it was her story.

The reason I think these Updates are valuable and needed to

be rendered in their original form was best stated by Mark Twain on page 281 of volume one of his 2010 autobiography: "When an eyewitness sets down in narrative form some extraordinary occurrence which he has witnessed, that is *news*—that is the news form, and its interest is absolutely indestructible." I hope Twain was right and that my Updates retain their news value.

In this same journalistic vein, none of this material was tampered with for the sake of this book. No drama was added, history revised, or spin attempted to make a point. For example, Shearlean and I had to learn as we went. We made assumptions, committed mistakes, and were often confused and frequently misinformed. So the reader will come across inconsistencies, errors and omissions. But that is part of the story. In fact, it is one of the reasons for telling the story, as you will find.

Some may say this story raises more questions than it answers. You can judge for yourself after reading it. The questions though, I think you may agree, turn out to be more important than any answers.

By most standards, Shearlean and I were well prepared for our experience. We certainly thought we were. But even being well prepared in the conventional sense proved to be grossly inadequate. Being adequately prepared for the end of life is far more complex and challenging than we realized. What do I mean by that? Read.

I

Cancer Diagnosis and Surgery

CHAPTER ONE

Waking Up Dying

"I will be a miracle."

WAKING UP DYING was how every day began for the past 18 months.

Diagnosed with a malignant stage IV glioblastoma brain tumor on August 21, 2009, Shearlean Duke could die any day.

The immediacy of the original 12-month death sentence had withered after 18 months and optimism had bloomed profusely. Though she was too weak to walk, and had worrisome blood chemistry, that tiny bright dot of cancer on her brain magnetic resonance imaging (MRI) picture was unchanged.

Despite last week's scare that sent us to the emergency room, the MRI signaled our cancer battle was stalemated. A stalemate was a victory in this war. And if anyone could beat this, her many supporters said Shearlean could.

Except me.

It would take a miracle, and I didn't believe in miracles. I believed the numbers, the odds, and the data. As a life-long technical writer, I'd worked too long with too many scientists and engineers to not believe the numbers.

A stage IV glioblastoma is one of the deadliest cancers known. Doctors tick off on their fingers the months of life afforded by each method of treatment: six months for surgery, three months for radiation and three months for chemo. Patients with good health at onset and a little luck may have more time. At 18 months (versus a 12-month prognosis) Shearlean already had her miracle.

I'd often told her as much, reminding her of her amazing quality of life and freedom from tumor symptoms.

Over the months we had discussed our divergent outlooks about her illness and were reconciled to our differences. Shearlean was a fighter. As a teenager, she used to take a shotgun with her when she drove from home to pick up her mother, who worked as a strike-breaking scab at the local Tennessee Levi's factory, at the end of each day's shift.

Shearlean put everything she had into beating this cancer and she succeeded for a long time. No one could have worked harder or embraced the treatment process more than she did. I'd told her she *should* deny the diagnosis and cling to every positive finding, but I didn't think we should both be doing that. "One of us," I said near the beginning of her treatment, "*must* take the doctors seriously and act accordingly, and that's my job. You mustn't be burdened with it. When the doctors no longer know what to say or do, I will abandon them and jump on your bandwagon," I'd said. "Until then, you should fight it for all you are worth, and I will make sure you get the best of care and do everything the doctors say."

I could see then that she was disappointed in my attitude, and I was slightly ashamed of my pragmatism, but I believed this was the most effective way to handle the biggest battle of our lives. I felt it was the best I could do for her.

~

On Wednesday, February 2, 2011, there would be no tomorrow.

It was 5:30 a.m.

The sound of a wracking cough jolted me awake.

I looked at the glowing blue digits of the alarm clock. Shearlean had had a quiet night. We'd both slept soundly for a change.

I looked at her hospital bed in the corner of our winter-dark bedroom that was eerily lit by the green light of the humming oxygen generator. The cough was coming from under a pile of blankets and pillows, inclined 30 degrees to help her breathe.

"Did you sleep well, sweetie?" I asked, hoping I was loud enough to be heard over the oxygen generator.

No answer.

"Sweetie?"

More coughing and wet, gurgling, strangling sounds.

I raised myself on my elbow and blinked to clear my vision for a better look. But it was too dark to see anything. I threw myself out of bed and in two staggering steps crossed the bedroom to the light switch.

I was blinded momentarily. With each thick cough, bright red fluid surged through Shearlean's lips and then receded, like a wave on the beach.

"Oh honey. Oh honey," I said as the red surged and receded. It was so bright and vivid against her pale skin. I had to fight off the hypnotic effect of the sight and will myself to look at the whole situation to determine what to do. If I didn't get hold of myself I was going to be a mere bystander at her death.

This is it, I thought, as I grabbed a towel from the adjacent bathroom, intent on stopping the flow of blood. I wiped the stream trickling from the left corner of her mouth because her head was turned slightly left. Irresistibly my eyes drifted back to the surging red wave at her mouth. It was so red, so bright and so startling.

As I dabbed at the blood, repeating "Oh, honey," I remembered a nurse's warning that if a hemorrhage occurred, I should use dark towels to wipe up so as not to alarm the patient at the sight of blood. I swapped out the towels I was using for the black ones that were part of our black and white bathroom décor.

This is it, I repeated silently to myself. *So this is how it ends.* I was shocked. I had imagined that death from a brain tumor would be some sort of seizure and coma, a bloodless death. But here was blood.

I ran to the kitchen phone and dialed the 24-hour hospice phone number. A woman answered. I explained what was happening. "Do you want me to call 911?" she asked. I think I held my breath. The silence was incredible. My own silence!

"No," I said finally. I was swamped by a wave of relief at breaking my silence. *This is it*, I said again to myself. More felt than said, I acknowledged to myself that I knew this was the end. This was where we had been heading for so long. The waiting and wondering were over. *It's over. It's over.*

Only seconds passed and the woman on the phone was talking. "Crush two 5 milligram oxycodone tablets and give them to her through her stomach tube," she said. "I will call the duty nurse, and she should be there in about 20 minutes. She is coming from Blaine. Are you okay?"

"Yes," I answered, marveling at my composure, but wondering if it was real or imagined.

I stepped back into the bedroom and saw Shearlean was still breathing and the flow of blood had decreased. I went to the head of the bed to adjust her oxygen tube but couldn't get it to stay in place. My hands were shaking and I couldn't think. I stepped into the bathroom and crushed the two oxycodone tablets and mixed them with a little water and then sucked them up in a syringe. Going back to her, I lifted the bedding to expose her stomach feeding tube and emptied the syringe's content into the tube. Though she didn't seem to be in pain, I didn't want to take any chances.

She was gagging now. The renewed coughing jarred me. The blood was no longer receding, but running onto her left shoulder and the pillow. I couldn't stop it or soak it up with towels.

While I tried to think of something more to do, I continued studying her. Bright red blood was arterial, I knew. Had she suffered a massive hemorrhage? At the hospital I had overheard something about potassium, blood chemistry and clotting. The nurse's comment about dark towels now seemed portentous. She had suspected this might happen, but I failed to comprehend its significance.

I looked closely at Shearlean's face, particularly her eyes. I understood much more now than I had at the beginning.

While I watched, I realized that Shearlean wasn't frightened or struggling. There was no terror there. Her expression was calm and pain-free. It began to dawn on me that the flood of bright red blood probably meant that the blood pressure in her brain had dropped so quickly she didn't have time to sense that she was dying. She basically woke up dead. She practically died in her sleep.

I felt a surge of joy and deep peace at this. She was in bed, at home, with me sleeping beside her. She had a restful and quiet night while I attended her as she died. It was a good death. And I was able to share it.

"Oh, honey," I heard myself still saying.

Shearlean's expression continued to be tranquil, even peaceful. Her eyes closed; blood stopped flowing. Soon she was no longer breathing.

I became very still, holding my breath and watching her intently. I moved closer. She was paler. There was no movement under her eyelids. Putting my hand under the blanket over her left breast, I felt for a heartbeat. There was none. I leaned down with my ear near her nose and listened. No breathing. I stepped back. She was motionless.

Should I be doing something else, something more? *Is this all there is to do? Is this death? Is it this simple and absolute?*

I put my hand on her forehead and was startled by how cool it felt.

I sat on a dressing stool next to the closet at the foot of her bed. There was nothing to do now. Just sit and let myself absorb this. *Don't turn away*, I cautioned myself. *Don't get busy with distractions.*

As I sat still, 42 years of memory became a torrent and then abated. I felt empty and just sat and stared at Shearlean until I felt satisfied that I had fully and permanently absorbed this most important moment of my life.

Now what? I found myself wondering.

I'd better get dressed, I realized. And with that thought the practical me magically materialized and I found myself back from wherever I had gone mentally. Hospice would arrive any minute and there would be questions to answer and forms to complete and decisions to make. While my world had frozen briefly in time, the rest of the universe hadn't noticed.

I roused myself to gather up the blood soaked towels and to straighten the bedding and wipe a final trickle of blood from the corner of her mouth.

After dressing I estimated the time she died: 5:50 a.m. I must have been motivated by what I knew was the first question in every movie, TV show or book about dying: "Time of death?"

It was over in 20 minutes. So little time.

Next I thought of Archie, Shearlean's cat. He needed to know. I wondered whether her silver tabby American shorthair would know death when he saw it. I brought him from the living room to her bed and said to him that she was gone. I set him on her chest and he simply jumped off onto the floor, showing no reaction. I was disappointed. I wanted him to understand.

Next, I got the camera and took three photos of Shearlean. No close-ups, just an overall view of her deathbed. I thought that if I didn't do this now, there would never be an opportunity. I wanted a picture—wanted the means to study the scene in case I might have missed something in witnessing her death.

The hospice nurse arrived at 6:30 a.m. I described the past hour for her and watched as she checked Shearlean to confirm her death. She checked her irises for response to light, which would indicate brain activity, and she listened for a heartbeat with a stethoscope. She nodded at me and then asked me to step out of the bedroom, saying she would clean up the room and body.

I sat quietly in the living room. I had to remind myself to breathe and let it all start to settle in: A lifetime, a marriage, and 42 years of loving someone. I was supposed to die first. Men always die first. Shearlean was to live 20 years more. She was eight years younger. She was in wonderful health, took good care of herself and should have lived a long and happy life. It was thanks to her good health that she survived treatment so well and lived six months longer than predicted. Still, she shouldn't be dead. I never expected to be here without her.

When the nurse came out of the darkened bedroom she phoned the cremation mortuary service I had selected and said that they would arrive in about 45 minutes. And then she left.

I returned to the bedroom that was now illuminated by the pallid early dawn light, which matched the blue-gray pallor of Shearlean's face. The light created the effect that she was slowly fading away, blending seamlessly into the ether. I sat with her, urging my mind back over the months to the beginning of the end.

CHAPTER TWO

Snake Bite?

"Bob suggested I had a pinched nerve, so I did not panic, but the pain was very intense: burning, numbness, electrical sensations as if I were going to be paralyzed."

AUGUST 2009. We were eager and excited to be going on our first Maasai Mara game drive. We dressed in the dark and used our flashlights to follow the path through the savanna grass to the dining tent for breakfast. After breakfast, Shearlean noticed a phone booth-sized green tent latrine on our way to the reception area. It was her last chance to relieve herself in private before our daylong adventure. I said she could meet me out front with our guide when she was done. Kenya's equatorial sun was rising quickly, and I was glad for the shade of the thatched roof over the reception benches.

A handsome Maasai youth in full regalia, including the ever-present spear (and cell phone) greeted me. "Mister Willis is at the safari wagon," he said.

Before I could answer, a scream—a real, full-force, serious prolonged scream—silenced the cheerful bird songs. It was Shearlean. The Maasai youth immediately ran off toward the scream, but I remained seated momentarily, knowing that if I went to her breathless and panicky, it would only add to her terror. Shearlean and I were independent people, each of us. We didn't take on one another's anxiety, so I fought the urge to run to her. *A lion?* I thought, but that was absurd—too many people around the camp's dining and office area. Something harmless, I hoped, had spooked her terribly. Whatever it was, a lot of people were around there and it was already over. When I got there my job would be to take charge and calm her down. Now I got up and, resisting the urge to run, walked quickly the 100 feet or so back down the path. I forced a smile onto my face and controlled my breathing.

Shearlean stood on the path in the midst of several Asian women tourists and camp employees. Her eyes were wild with terror. She was hyperventilating and sobbing. Her T-shirt hung off of her left shoulder, her bra dangled uselessly and her right breast was exposed. My will to stay calm was challenged as I watched the people around her examine her breast and arm, while others knelt on the ground looking searchingly at her foot and right leg.

I walked directly up to her with my arms open and wrapped her tightly against me and asked as calmly as I could, "What happened, sweetie?" She was shaking as I pulled her T-shirt back over her head and worked her arm through the sleeve to cover her.

"I was bitten by a snake in the toilet," she said. But a chorus of "Nos," said otherwise. There were no fang marks and no viper had been found in the latrine. I kept up a running murmur of endearments and reassurances.

She argued that she felt a stinging bite in her right leg followed immediately by a hot and painful sensation that traveled up her body and into her right breast and arm. She conceded the feeling had disappeared quickly and she felt fine now. Someone suggested fire ants, but there was no sign of them or their bite. I thanked everybody for their concern as they dispersed. Shearlean, much calmer now and a little embarrassed by her outburst and subsequent exposure, walked on to reception with me. Willis was waiting for us and we left for our game drive. We thought that was the end of the episode.

We traveled nine more days, including a stay on Lamu, a Kenyan island in the Indian Ocean near Somalia. Shearlean and I did a lot of adventure traveling and had developed the philosophy that short of a fatal threat, we would never turn back, so we didn't even consider returning home immediately.

But similar painful attacks occurred throughout the trip, though they were never more severe than this first one. Shearlean could feel an attack coming and would step in close to me and ask me to hold her tightly until it passed, usually in under a minute. No fuss, no drama. We carried on, enjoying each day and blaming each attack on a nerve pinched in her back.

Because Shearlean had traveled to Kenya for her job at the university and I had joined her later at the end of her work there, we traveled home separately. She arrived in Bellingham a day before me, no longer worried by the attacks when they happened. She recognized their onset and knew they would pass quickly without becoming debilitating.

Shearlean made an appointment with her primary care physician, Dr. Brockman, as soon as she got home. Dr. Brockman ordered a brain MRI for August 20, 2009. The day before the MRI, Shearlean said to me *(honest)*: "You don't think I have a brain tumor, do you?"

How absurd, I thought. "No way," I said.

Later on, the same day of the MRI, Dr. Brockman's office called to say that they were ordering a second MRI for the next morning, and Dr. Brockman wanted to see Shearlean at her office at 1 p.m.

Shearlean was puzzled and concerned.

I dismissed the whole thing, saying they had probably screwed up the first imaging and now had to do it all over again to get it right. *What a bother*, I thought.

I dropped Shearlean at Dr. Brockman's office so I could do a quick errand and then waited in the car for her to finish her appointment. I hated doctors' waiting rooms. From the parking lot, I could see through the lobby windows to the door of Dr. Brockman's office and watched it intently as more and more time passed. I saw a flash of reflected light when the office door opened and then Shearlean pushed open the lobby door and stepped into the bright afternoon sunlight, clutching a fistful of tissues and obviously crying. She saw I was looking at her and waved to me to come in as she let the door swing closed. I was startled at her appearance.

When I entered the lobby, I saw Shearlean was already at the far end of the office hall and I hurried after her. We entered Dr. Brockman's examination room nearly together, and Shearlean broke down sobbing. Shearlean and I took the only two chairs while Dr. Brockman leaned against the examination table.

"I have a brain tumor," Shearlean said, choking on the words as she succumbed to a flood of tears.

I was stunned. Suddenly, I felt trapped and threatened, even defensive and desperate, without knowing what we were up against.

Determination and resolve surged from deep within me and washed away ordinary sensations. It settled behind my eyes, which now bored mercilessly into the doctor's bland expression. I wanted to hear how to quickly and decisively solve this problem—this "tumor" Shearlean and the doctor were informing me about.

I instantly felt I had to take charge, take control and not lose it. In those moments as Dr. Brockman stared back at me—maybe she was even talking—all I could think was that I had to muster everything and be at my very best, my strongest and most capable. This was the biggest thing we had ever faced. It could be life-altering. Nothing might ever be the same again for either of us.

Just as I really felt my adrenaline amping up and I was preparing a deluge of questions, statements and accusations for the doctor, Shearlean glanced at me, and I realized I needed to slow down. She, of course, could read my expression, body language, and even my pent-up silence and didn't want to be a casualty of the explosion about to be unleashed. *Back off. Pay attention. Listen. Don't talk too much*, I counseled myself. And I regulated my breathing so I could stay present.

Dr. Brockman was clearly uneasy and nervous. I resented this. I wanted her to be direct and definitive, to be strong for Shearlean and for me.

Dr. Brockman explained the situation. She said Shearlean had something called glioblastoma, but I was distracted by what she didn't say. She omitted two critical words. Dr. Brockman never uttered the words "cancer" or "malignant."

There were tumors and there were Tumors, I knew this. A friend's wife had had a huge tumor removed from her brain many years ago. It had been benign and she continued to live normally. I needed to know what kind of tumor we were talking about here.

I finally spoke. "This is cancer, correct?" I asked.

"Yes," Dr. Brockman answered.

"Malignant?" I said.

"Yes," Dr. Brockman answered flatly. She was giving me a look like I was unusually dense.

I looked at her with all the contempt I could muster, wondering why I had to say these words. Why did I have to say these ugly and vulgar words in front of Shearlean?

This is the end of Dr. Brockman, I vowed to myself. Neither Shearlean nor I had been very pleased with Dr. Brockman's treatment and conduct over the years. But since Shearlean had needed only routine treatment, she felt it wasn't worth finding a replacement.

After sitting a while longer and exchanging a few more repetitive and meaningless words, we left. As we walked out, I sensed that Shearlean's diagnosis had gotten around the office; the staff was looking at us sympathetically. Outside, we stood on the sidewalk, getting our bearings. I was dazed. Where were we parked?

The sun was still high and bright in the August sky and, strangely, everything going on around us was so normal. Cars pulled to the curb to pick up and drop off patients; sullen teenagers were accompanied by harried parents; shuffling elders pushed their walkers; and a former cheerleader (I assumed), now a drug company rep (much too pretty and seductively dressed) hurried to call on a doctor with the latest silver bullet cure.

The world looked the same, but felt foreign. Yesterdays—all of them—had evaporated. There was only a chain reaction of *nows* that vaporized and materialized moment to moment. Tomorrow was unknowable. Shearlean was different. I was different. Why wasn't the world different?

We sleepwalked along the sidewalk, picking our way through the landscaped parking lot median to our car. Even it looked different. I paused a moment to decide if it was mine. Before I got in, I looked back at the door to the doctor's office and visualized again the Shearlean of a half-hour ago, bunched tissues to her face, waving at me.

I slumped into the driver's seat and began composing myself to start the engine and drive home. I looked over at Shearlean and watched as a familiar expression of resolve began to replace the stricken look that had recently masked her face. I studied her.

She looked far younger than her 63 years, thanks, she would have told you, to good genes and using a sunscreen foundation makeup since she was a teen. Her features were compact. Her eyes, nose and mouth were tightly grouped on her narrow face displaying a small chin and a high brow framed by blonde hair cut to an inch or two above her shoulders. She was attractive without being especially pretty because she was well groomed, smartly dressed with a slim well-proportioned figure. Tall at five feet, six inches, she exuded a presence that was the result of her demeanor, tranquil expression and alertness.

The set of her eyes and mouth always revealed what she was thinking or feeling, if you knew what to look for as I did. Her narrowed eyes, pursed lips and rigid posture declared an aloofness that warned, "Don't mess with me."

She is angry. Good, I thought. *Let's be angry.*

"She started off saying I had maybe a year to live. What a horrible thing to say to somebody," she said. "That's awful. I hate her. I've never liked her."

I rested my hand on her knee and waited to see if she would erupt or subside. Dr. Brockman had made a bitter enemy.

Of course, I didn't know the exact context of the upsetting remark and this was no time to disagree, but I thought that if it were me, I would just as soon hear it straight out, unvarnished and up front. But I wasn't Shearlean and had no relationship with Dr. Brockman—though my opinion of her "bedside manner," if she had one, was low.

We both took slow, deep breaths as we searched in our own ways for something ordinary to focus on. I started the engine and reminded myself to be extra careful driving because I probably should not be on the road in this mental condition in the first place. But as soon as I backed out of the parking space I felt my instincts slide comfortably into place and I was calmed a little.

As we got up to full speed on the freeway, Shearlean transformed from someone who had just received a devastating diagnosis into the Los Angeles Times reporter she had been—one who had just been assigned an important breaking story. I glanced over at her and knew she was on the hunt, on the clock, and unwilling to take no (or a death sentence) for an answer. She was planning, I could see, taking charge of herself. I heard her wheels turning: *We need a second opinion. We need to know what treatment options are available. We must identify the best institutions with the most skilled doctors. We must research this disease. We must look into our insurance coverage. We must find out about the university's sick leave policy.*

As Shearlean enumerated the steps she was contemplating, my mind wandered to Senator Ted Kennedy. On May 20, 2008,

Kennedy was diagnosed with the same brain cancer in the same area of the brain: a glioblastoma in the left parietal lobe. Kennedy suffered a seizure on May 17, 2008, had a biopsy, and three days later revealed the tumor diagnosis to the world. News coverage frequently described the prognosis as "grim."

Recent reports indicated he was near death 15 months after his diagnosis. Kennedy, I thought, had access to the best possible treatment and care but couldn't beat the disease. Realistically, what could Shearlean and I expect?

That night Shearlean sat up past 1:30 a.m. watching consecutive reruns of "Cheers" and writing in her journal about what she titled: The Most Important Day of My Life.

August 21

I am in shock. I am angry. I am terrified. I am profoundly sad. I am confused.

It just is not fair.

Why me?

So many decisions to make. Part of me wishes I DID NOT KNOW. *That I just had treatment for my symptoms and did not know.*

What can I do?

Feel the pain and fear.

The day after the diagnosis the world hadn't stopped turning. The sun rose, yet things felt different. Shearlean and I went shopping for self-help books about cancer and dying. It was the most macabre book shopping we'd ever done. Over large mochas (who's worried about calories now?) she wanted to talk about what to do with her body. Also, she wanted a cat, so I said I would try to borrow one from a breeder we knew that had a house full of cats.

As soon as we returned home from the coffee shop, she started clearing away closet clutter and bagging up clothing for donation to save me "the trouble." But she filled only two shopping bags with business clothes before losing interest in the effort.

She settled in the living room and we talked about assisted suicide. We logged onto the Internet and found that there were

ARCHIE GOODWIN DUKE, CAT

It turned out the cat breeder we knew had no spare cat to lend us because it was between breeding seasons. She doubted we could find what we wanted, but I thought that if I looked hard enough I could find one. I knew sometimes there was a leftover or returned kitten available, usually at a bargain price, because most buyers wanted the youngest kittens and shunned older kittens. Breeders didn't want to waste money advertising discounted cats.

We agreed we didn't want a kitten and all the work that would entail, and we didn't want a mature cat that someone else had trained. We were certain we wanted an American short-hair under a year old and preferably a pure bred so we could be guaranteed it would have the qualities we prized: a sweet voice, good disposition, and eager to please.

I got on the Internet and contacted every American and British short-hair breeder within 250 miles of Bellingham to find a kitten under one year old. Within a month a breeder south of Seattle who had one male and one female American short-hair silver tabby, seven months old, contacted me. The brother and sister had developed eye infections that caused buyers to reject them and before they were cured they got too old for most buyers. That was exactly the situation I was looking for. Instead of $600 apiece, they were both available for $100 each. We chose Big Boy (his litter name) and brought him home on November 7, 2009. We named him Archie, after a British blue short-hair we had for 16 years. Shearlean was overjoyed and Archie immediately began his comfort and play duties with enthusiasm. He will be five years old on April 23, 2014.

Web sites that would connect interested persons with "amenable" physicians. We didn't know brain cancer was painless, so we seriously considered it an option. We were comforted to know we could pursue it as a means of ending pointless suffering. It was an option we could hold in our back pockets.

That night, while Shearlean slept soundly, I was awakened by my own runny nose and sat on the edge of the bed, my elbows on my knees, worrying there was too little to do to help her. A big part of me was dying too. I thought, *A large part of who I am is who she is.* But she was now in her world, and I was in mine, and we would never share the same world again. Our life paths had now diverged after merging 40 years ago. She would be the patient; I would be the caregiver.

The next morning, the second morning after diagnosis, Shearlean woke up a different person. She was loud, energetic and talkative, not her usual calm, quiet and purposeful self. She was agitated and fighting to maintain control. She wanted to send money to our Kenyan safari guide because she was suddenly worried she'd wronged him with a too-small tip. She was frightened he was thinking bad thoughts about her that could affect her condition. She didn't want anyone thinking negatively about her. She was afraid, worried about her karma. She wanted only positive thoughts from everyone, and so she set about sending thank you notes to anyone and everyone she might owe gratitude. As the day went on, her thoughts grew scattered, and she verged on hysteria over little things.

I watched, telling myself that she was rattled by the diagnosis, but a part of me knew it was more than that. I felt increasingly susceptible to her emotional unraveling, and I had to work hard to resist falling into the same quagmire.

I tried to make sense of what was happening. In the early morning when she had trouble changing styling tips on her curling iron, I reminded myself that that wasn't new for her because she was never mechanically adroit. But then in the late morning, when she filled the dishwasher racks in strange ways, I worried. She wanted help making the bed because of arm pain I'd never heard of before. And in the car that afternoon she couldn't put the GPS in its storage sleeve. Still, none of this (except the arm pain) was new, exactly—or was it, I wondered? Maybe her irritation with herself was new. Was this the brain tumor? Was it nerves? Maybe it was just me and not her at all. I grew increasingly uncomfortable with what felt like spying as I watched her every move, growing more and more concerned.

Each passing day I was saddened to see what she was going through to adjust to her new condition and status. Every day I wondered whether she was changing—being changed. It was terrible to be wary of her actions when maybe she was as normal as ever and the problem was with me. Maybe I was the one changing.

CHAPTER THREE

Tumor Board: And So It Begins

"I am going into this with all my heart and soul with an expectation of absolute belief. I will be strong and know I can succeed."

SHEARLEAN DECIDED she wanted to be treated by University Medical's Brain and Spinal Cord Tumors Center in Seattle, Washington.

From somewhere, however, she got the idea that she might not qualify as a surgery candidate with University's tumor board. Thinking she needed to convince the board she was worthy of its consideration and help, she wrote the following letter to the board, marshaling her journalism and public relations skills in a heartbreaking plea calculated to gain its agreement to treat her:

> Dear University Tumor Board:
>
> Friday, Aug. 21, 2009, when my doctor told me I had a brain tumor, that it was brain cancer, and that I may be dead in a year, I went home, cried for two days, bought books on dying and put my affairs in order.
>
> Sunday I awoke, dry-eyed and with a fierce determination to do everything in my power to prolong my life. I believe a patient is more than a chart, a diagnosis and an MRI report. I am a unique individual who has overcome great obstacles, beat tremendous odds, and accomplished the impossible.

So, this is not my ego, but my heart trying to offer you evidence of my drive and determination to continue to meet challenges—even this, the most terrifying challenge I have faced in my 63 years. This is my way to help you see me as more than the medical charts you have before you in the meeting you are having today that may decide my fate.

I got to where I am by doing the impossible, and beating the odds in my life. So, even though these new life-and-death odds are terrifying, to me they are not impossible.

I grew up in Appalachia. My father was a copper miner and my mother worked at the Levi's factory. Neither finished high school. But I learned the values of education, self-reliance, hard work, positive thinking and self-determination. Such determination has helped me accomplish the impossible. Examples:

- As a 22-year-old college graduate from an unknown state university in Tennessee, my dream was to work at the Los Angeles Times. At age 24, I applied with just two years experience. Impossible. Getting hired at the Times took a minimum of five years, a prestigious degree and connections. I never had a chance. The Times hired me.

- As a mid-life Times newspaper editor, I wanted to teach journalism. Never, people said. Not when I had only a bachelor's degree. The University of California hired me. I was the only non-Ph.D. in my department.

- At 50 while still working full time, I decided to earn a master's so I could become a full-time tenured professor in journalism. Impossible. I was too old. No one would hire me without a Ph.D. Today, I am a tenured associate professor and chair of the Journalism Department at Western Washington University. In fact, until I got this news Friday, Aug. 21, I was busy preparing my dossier to apply for professor.

I am healthy, active, have lots of stamina, a positive outlook on life. In short, I have never had serious health problems, which is why this diagnosis came as a shock. My first symptoms occurred Aug. 3, 2009, while I was in Kenya as part of a WWU faculty group that took students to help work with high school girls orphaned by AIDS.

So this is who I am and where I am. I have a wonderful life, and if I die tomorrow, I have no regrets. I have:

- Everything I want and am thankful every day for my life and the people I love.
- A husband of 39 years who loves me and whom I love with all my heart.
- A sister I love and treasure, of whom I am proud and derive great strength.
- A beautiful nephew, who is like a son to me, his loving wife, and two great nephews whom I adore.
- A brother-in-law to bring happiness to my sister and a smile to my face.
- A home in beautiful Bellingham, where we love to live.
- A job I love, where I work with young people who inspire and ennoble me.
- So even though I am not wealthy in terms of money, I am rich. I love my life.

Please understand that I am not in denial of this diagnosis, but based on lifetime experience, I see it as a challenge. And I would like your help in meeting it.

Sincerely,
Shearlean Duke

I don't know where she got the idea she had to bargain for treatment. We never saw any evidence that the board functioned as she presumed. On the other hand, we had no direct and easy way to find out how the board *did* function. I assumed that Shearlean knew what she had to do through her contacts and connections through the media and academia. Considering that we viewed the board's acceptance as a matter of life and death, anything she had to say or do to get the treatment she wanted was fine by me. This was a no-holds-barred desperate appeal for help. It was the first such act of desperation, but not the last. Facing what she was facing, nothing was too humiliating to do. Judging by the results, her letter was potent and, besides, the presumed requirement for her to do some persuasive writing played to her greatest strength.

The tumor board accepted her for surgery subject to a personal interview and diagnostic testing. They offered her an immediate evaluation appointment on August 26, 2009 (five days after diagnosis) to meet with a surgeon. We were both nearly panicked by how soon she might be in surgery. We hadn't even digested the suddenness of the diagnosis, and here we were faced with scheduling a date and time for brain surgery. We wanted speed but this was too fast. Still, we were pleased that the system was able to respond so quickly and it boosted our confidence.

Shearlean had intended to consult with two different surgeons to get more than one opinion. Her appointment with the brain surgeon we expected to meet with first was for August 31, 2009–10 days after diagnosis. Much to our surprise and relief, though, University Medical's tumor board offered her the earlier appointment with its surgeon on August 26; we could get started right away. Shearlean had told me the tumor board met only weekly and was always backlogged. We presumed her letter must have arrived at the perfect time and hit just the right nerve. True or false, Shearlean felt that her letter had earned her immediate consideration because (one way or another) she was an outstanding candidate.

We both broke into wide grins at the news. *We're already on a roll,* our expressions seemed to say.

Because we started out wanting two opinions—just to be prudent—we would keep the August 31 appointment we'd made and use it for our second opinion about the surgical procedure. It was just as well that we went to University Medical first though (the August 31 surgeon was in Bellingham) because our local surgeon told us this type of surgery was too specialized for him or any local surgeon. He said he would have sent us to Seattle had we seen him first anyway.

I didn't know how or why Shearlean had set her sights on being treated by University Medical, but she had instantly named it as her choice. This was part of the Shearlean mystique. She had always been a superlative networker (part, I thought, of what made her a good journalist) and she continually amazed me with who and what she knew. That she knew about University Medical and its tumor board was nevertheless surprising.

But there was a critical matter to be attended to before we could move forward with Shearlean's treatment: payment. We had insurance, but insurance is tricky. You don't know what you've got until it is tested and often, by then, it is too late. As it would turn out, we had very good insurance, but that wasn't clear up front. Our insurance's role was not obvious or practical. As the insured, we were consistently kept at arm's length and left on the outside of the insurance process. That was going to be problematic. I had a lot to figure out. Right away I called our insurance company to get answers.

Looking for Community Help

After Shearlean's diagnosis on August 21, 2009, I floundered about seeking a path to organized and directed care that we could follow through the looming healthcare maze. I didn't know where to turn or where to start, and began to panic. We needed help but I didn't know whom to ask and didn't want to burden Shearlean with helping me solve the problem.

Clearly I was going to have to confide in someone. Shearlean's doctor had offered nothing and had been relegated to the

Duke family shit list after her diagnosis performance. My own doctor was part of the same practice as Brockman and I was afraid professional loyalty would trump any ethical obligation to me. Besides, what doctor wants to be involved in another doctor's messy situation?

Racking my brain reminded me of an acquaintance who had long been active in the local Alzheimer's support community. Alzheimer's was connected to nearly every entity of Whatcom County healthcare and government so my acquaintance likely knew a lot about what was generally available.

Trembling with real fear of speaking for the first time about Shearlean's diagnosis outside a doctor's office, I steeled myself for the phone to be answered. "Hello," answered her familiar voice and I spoke with such choked-back emotion I doubted she recognized who was calling. I began with my name and hurried through the reason I was calling and didn't slow down until I'd asked her for a promise of secrecy. Calmly and smoothly she sympathized and launched right into a list of organizations and people I might want to talk to. She ended with the caveat that there was probably nothing available suitable to our needs, at least not at this stage of Shearlean's condition.

Undeterred by her warning, I hung up the phone convinced that with enough digging and persistence I could uncover something helpful. Surely there was something useful out there for us.

What I learned at the outset of becoming a caregiver, and it was reinforced throughout my experience, was that there was generous assistance at many levels of care for what I learned to call "legislated rights" and "organized diseases." This was where resources were directed because this was where they would do the most good and funding was available. And that was the way it should be: the greatest good for the greatest number of people.

I made appointments all around Whatcom County and visited every office I'd been told about and followed up on every referral, all in a few days. I met a lot of nice, sympathetic people and learned about many valuable and helpful services and programs, but there were none for Shearlean and me.

The explanation was the simple socio-economic facts of life. Shearlean and I didn't fit into any category of need for which aid was available and her disease was minor: hers was a rare form of cancer claiming 13,000 victims annually compared with 160,000 lung cancer deaths in the United States. (Figures were from 2007, the latest year for which statistics were available.)

Another factor was that lung cancer is treatable, with a good survival rate. Brain cancer is nearly always fatal.

With little counseling and no advice, questions kept piling up and answers were not materializing.

Listing my questions had been a good start because it focused my thinking, but what I needed desperately were some answers. Here we were financially, treatment- and disease-wise past the point of no return with brain cancer and our list of questions was growing longer, not shorter.

What does brain surgery cost? Is it negotiable? Are there brain surgery or cancer treatment options that we can elect or cancel to save money? Whom do I ask? Whose job is it to answer my questions?

The questions alone sound crazy. The answers must be even crazier, I guessed.

What do I do? What I *don't* do is bring up any of this to Shearlean. She's got too much to handle as it is. This is my responsibility. I feared I was letting her down.

We were about to accumulate such huge costs already, I speculated, that we may be bankrupt already and didn't know it.

I had to have answers. I couldn't go on like this. With so much treatment ahead, big costs were looming. Could we afford further treatment? Everyone acted like cost was not an issue. There were even hints that if we couldn't pay, arrangements might be made, but nothing explicit was said. I should have faith apparently.

We had savings, but for all I knew, they were wiped out by treatment already pending. What continuing income was Shearlean eligible for, and on what terms? And with whom did we discuss her employment options? Exactly what benefits was she eligible for that could be used for her medical care? How were benefits determined and by whom? And when? We were falling off a cliff and spectators were standing around chatting about how and when we might land.

On August 26, 2009, we met as scheduled with Dr. Steinberg, professor and chief, at University Medical in Seattle. Dr. Steinberg was board-certified in neurological surgery and specialized in tumors of the central nervous system. His research focused on glioma brain tumors and on methods to break the blood/brain barrier to deliver chemotherapy to malignant brain tumors.

The medical center where we met with him had the feel and look of a university campus rather than the institutional gloom of a big city hospital. The familiar collegiate feel had an immediate calming effect on Shearlean, which eased my apprehension about how the meeting would go.

Floor to ceiling windows and contemporary interior design gave the neurosurgery floor the appearance of a hotel lobby, except that many guests looked afflicted or disabled or distressed to various degrees. This was our first introduction to the somber population of patients and caregivers we were soon to join and associate with daily.

Before we could see the surgeon, a University Medical financial services representative greeted us with a folder of forms to sign. After signing, I asked whether we were covered for Shearlean's scheduled tests and procedures, and to what extent. I had not yet heard back from our insurer, Uniform Medical Plan; I hoped the medical center would have an answer about our coverage.

"The way insurance works is that it never approves anything prior to it being submitted, but they have always covered this sort of thing," the financial representative said.

In other words we were not to be told we were covered until after the fact. Yet, University Medical's written notice to patients stated, "... the patient must confirm coverage prior to surgery." How confusing, since apparently that was impossible. We could only *suppose* we were covered because we hadn't been notified that we were not covered.

After finishing with financial services, I telephoned Uniform again to confirm coverage, but was again unable to speak with anyone and had to leave a message.

After checking Shearlean's weight, temperature, blood pressure and pulse, and list of medications, a nurse had us wait in a small consultation room with an examination table, a computer, a sink and two chairs. We sat silently, holding hands and feeling grim. I marveled at how ordinary and routine it all was. We were here to discuss cancer and brain surgery; it shouldn't be so mundane—so like waiting for our annual flu shots.

While we waited we each reviewed our separate lists of questions and considered whether to add to the list or play it by ear. Some of our questions overlapped, some did not.

- Should we delay surgery until symptoms worsen?
- How many surgeries were possible?
- What was the likely time between surgery and re-growth of the tumor to its pre-surgery size?
- What could we do to help control costs?
- What was likely to be Shearlean's post-surgery condition and how much time would it take to return to "normal"?
- What medications might be employed for pain and disease?
- Because the diagnosis was fatal, what would ultimately cause her death?
- What were the typical stages of the disease as it advanced?
- How many such surgeries did Dr. Steinberg perform annually?
- Did the same team perform each surgery?

Dr. Steinberg was on time and accompanied by a tall, handsome, younger doctor who displayed all the deference of an understudy to a virtuoso. Both smiled, introduced themselves and got down to business. I had my notebook out, wrote down their names, and prepared to document what was said.

Dr. Steinberg turned on his computer and brought up Shearlean's brain MRI images on the monitor before launching into a smooth and even toned explanation of brain cancer and glioblastoma while he pointed out relevant features on the MRI. We both listened in silence. Dr. Steinberg rose up from the computer and leaned back against the edge of the examination table without interrupting his monologue. He folded his hands at his lap and showed a warm gap-toothed smile while his eyes maintained an intense focus on Shearlean, trying, I thought, to read how she was taking his words. By now she had donned her reporter's persona, was alert and intent, and had her own notebook out, though I noticed the page was blank.

Shearlean's tumor, Dr. Steinberg told us, was located in an area of the left brain that was the confluence of several vital functions. In particular, the Broca and Wernicke language areas were involved. The two areas were adjacent to each other, on the outer left side of the brain extending from above the ear to above the left eye, a distance of approximately five inches.

Pierre Paul Broca (1824–1880) identified this area in the brain where the ability to understand and express speech is located. Loss of that ability is termed *aphasia*. Carl Wernicke (1848–1905) identified the site for understanding written and spoken language. Besides the risk of losing all forms of language, symptoms of a tumor in this area could include convulsions, loss of right-side motor skills, and changes in personality or behavior. Soon we were to learn that Shearlean's optic nerve was directly in the path of radiation treatment of the tumor area. A slight miscalculation or misalignment of radiation targeting could blind her.

Dr. Steinberg explicitly explained that Shearlean's right-side episodes of pain—which we thought were pinched nerves in her back—were actually seizures caused by the tumor's effect on her brain.

So she was already suffering seizures. How bad might they become? To me brain seizures meant uncontrollable rolling-on-the-floor, epileptic-type fits; crippling of hand, arm and leg functions; alarming personality aberrations; and destruction of any means of communication to or from her. I hadn't imagined that a seizure could feel more like a snakebite, as Shearlean's did.

Progress of the disease and the results of surgery and other treatment could mean being afflicted with any or all of the symptoms Dr. Steinberg was describing—or none of them. Overall, however, Shearlean's condition, he said, should be very good after surgery.

"But inevitably she will likely decline with time," he finally said.

I almost audibly groaned when I heard this and resisted taking a sidelong look to see her reaction when Dr. Steinberg delivered this news. She seemed calm.

Most alarming to me, aside from the knowledge that her condition was terminal, was the possibility of personality changes. Could I care for her if she was no longer the person I knew and loved? I hoped so, but I wasn't sure.

I pushed this ugly, devastating thought away and tuned back into Dr. Steinberg's insistent voice.

He explained that we could do a biopsy first to confirm the diagnosis if we preferred that route to moving directly into surgery. Or we could do a biopsy of the removed brain matter after the major surgery was over. The risks of brain surgery were huge because every brain, patient and cancer is unique.

"There has never been a brain cancer exactly like yours and there has never been nor will there ever be another person like you, Shearlean," the doctor said. "You are unique, your cancer is unique and so your surgery will be unique."

We both fished for a hint of whether he preferred to biopsy the tumor before or after surgery, but found no clues. There was no reading between the lines with Dr. Steinberg's expression, voice, manner or tone. He was even, objective and stayed exactly on message.

Dr. Steinberg repeatedly emphasized that there were many choices open to Shearlean and that it was important for her to participate in her care. He wanted to be certain that we both understood what we were getting into: that we were facing life-changing problems, and that there were many risks, rewards and options to be weighed in choosing treatment.

He held up his left hand and with his right hand he gripped one finger at a time as he summarized treatment. "Surgery is the most effective treatment and can increase longevity by about five months; radiation combined with surgery can add three or more months; and chemotherapy combined with radiation can add another three months," he said clutching the three fingers in his fist. "Beyond that, it's hard to say," but he emphasized that Shearlean's excellent health and good attitude and outlook were pluses. "There are patients who have survived beyond 18 months. Four years and more," he said. And some patients had multiple surgeries—up to 14.

"Everyone and every cancer are unique. No one can predict your outcome," he said in conclusion.

Though Shearlean and I were both experienced interviewers, neither of us could expose a chink in Dr. Steinberg's professional armor. He wasn't going to tell us what to do. It was up to us.

I was worn out from being on mental high alert for so long—though the meeting had lasted all of 30 minutes. I could see that Shearlean's intensity was subsiding too, so we both settled back in our chairs and grew silent. I was unable to speak. I was choking on words and images that were too vulgar to be voiced about my beloved's brain. Shearlean sat beside me alternating between weeping quietly and suddenly finding a strong clear voice for another question.

In the end we were handed attractive colorful brochures as though we had just booked a cruise or vacation with a pair of somewhat grim travel agents. Titles included: "About Your Surgery Experience," "Understanding Treatment for Glioblastoma Multiforme (GBM)," "Conventional Radiation Treatment," and "Brain Tumors: Understanding Your Care." A DVD was added to our pile with the explanation that it showed an actual craniotomy performed by Dr. Steinberg on a University Medical Center nurse with GBM.

As Dr. Steinberg gripped the door handle, he summarized the essence of our consultation. He suggested Shearlean and I talk it over and let him know how we wanted to proceed.

~

Driving the 90 miles back to Bellingham on Interstate 5, we were ahead of the northbound afternoon traffic. I could let my mind roam back over our meeting with Dr. Steinberg. He was a big hit with Shearlean (thank God). She enthused over his frank and direct presentation. She felt relieved at the sense of comfort and confidence she experienced in his presence. With him, she was certain she would be in good hands.

He performed approximately 250 such operations per year and worked with a regular team of doctors, nurses, technicians and specialists, rather than whoever was available at the time of surgery. He was confident and assertive, but not cocky. He was not the gunslinger sort of risk-taker that some surgeons exemplify.

As we drove, we sporadically interrupted our respective reflections to compare notes about what we'd heard or gathered from the consultation, and then lapsed back into thoughtful silences. Shearlean flipped through pages of her reporter's notebook, making remarks without any context:

"Motor paralysis."

"Aphasia, no speech."

"Sensation changes."

"Open the outer coating of brain."

"Damage spinal cord."

"Bleeding and infection."

"Coma and death."

"Transfusion okay."

"Two weeks pain and headaches."

"Take it easy for two weeks."

"Seven to 10 days, more treatment."

She had managed to take notes after all, possibly the grimmest interview notes of her career as a journalist.

I was on guard against revealing any prejudice or conclusion I came away with. This had to be Shearlean's decision every step of the way. I didn't want to interject my thoughts or influence her. I would offer my analysis if asked, but would avoid initiating any opinion until she revealed her thinking.

Still, I did have an opinion, and I silently prayed that Shearlean and I would think and feel the same way about her treatment. I hoped she would ultimately arrive at a conclusion we could share. After 38 years of marriage, I felt comfortable about the route she would take. I believed that even this devastating disease would not alter her outlook and action. She was strong. I admired her strength and resolve.

She obviously concluded this was no time to cower, hide or be timid. She had already done the impossible many times in life already, she felt, so why not try for the impossible once more? She knew how to do it, as she expressed in her letter to the tumor board. Before we went to bed, we agreed to thoroughly consider our choices and not be hasty. We both realized it would be a relief to make the decision and move on to the next step. Time, we had been warned, was critical, but we could take one night to think it over.

Cancer never sleeps, however.

Shearlean didn't sleep that night either. While I slept, she was writing in her journal:

> *So today I went to the University neurosurgery clinic and then spent hours talking about my options. The tumor is plum size and bigger than I thought. I can do nothing, or have a biopsy, or have full surgery—a craniotomy—wide-awake with a big chunk of my brain exposed.*
>
> *They take out the tumor and parts of my brain. The big risk is that I may lose my ability to read, write and speak. How ironic!*
>
> *If I do nothing I die in a year.*
>
> *For me the decision is easy. I am having the surgery. There is no question that this is the risk I would choose. I am afraid but not terrified. I like my doctor, and I am in good hands.*
>
> *This is an adventure and a challenge I feel in my heart I can meet.*
>
> *I have hope. I really do. I think I am the luckiest person in the world. I have found a great doctor and he will help me—a whole team of doctors. And I will be the best, most optimistic patient in the universe. I will be a miracle.*
>
> *I have told no one else yet and the hard part will be figuring out how to tell my sister on Friday.*

The next morning she told me of her decision while she reviewed and analyzed Dr. Steinberg's remarks. She reacted as I did to the idea of a biopsy (I didn't want her to go that route), and I was now free to show my whole-hearted agreement with the choice to do surgery.

"A biopsy of the brain *is* brain surgery," I said. "Why elect brain surgery twice when once would be better?" Ted Kennedy had had a biopsy, but Shearlean Duke would not. Any doubt that Shearlean had a glioblastoma stage IV cancerous brain tumor was so tiny that, to my way of thinking, to do a biopsy was just engaging in wishful thinking. I viewed wishful thinking and looking for miracles as a waste of precious time that would merely delay the inevitable. I was confident in the best practitioners' abilities to interpret MRIs, diagnose disease and prescribe the best course of treatment. Besides, a biopsy delayed the most beneficial treatment available for her tumor: surgery. And the sooner the best treatment was applied, the better the prognosis.

CHAPTER FOUR

Breaking the News

"I am going to let more people into my life and feelings. Bob, of course, and I am working on that. Be more honest with them on the good and bad."

On August 27, Shearlean called Dr. Steinberg's nurse to tell her she had decided to go ahead with surgery as soon as possible. The nurse suggested Tuesday September 8, 2009. "So soon," I heard Shearlean say. Then she listened for a long while and said, "How about Thursday, September 10? I want to visit my sister and family one last time—I don't mean last time—but you know, I don't know how I will be after surgery."

I muted the TV and sat very still trying to parse every utterance, seeking a clue about how she was holding up. She sounded so business like—efficient—as if she were talking about somebody or something else. She sounded so ordinary, but knowing what she was talking about made her sound all the more *extra*ordinary. *Can she sustain that? I asked myself. Or is she going to break down?* I found myself growing tense as I listened.

"Well, I've done it," she said grimacing after hanging up the phone. She looked worried. The nurse had explained that there would be a lot of tests that needed to be done before surgery. "She was able to schedule them while we were on the phone. Some will be at Metropolitan Hospital and the last one will be the day before surgery." She paused. "I guess we better start telling people what's happening."

I discovered I was holding my breath as I thought of how much more real this was becoming. Putting Shearlean's condition into words and telling others would make it more tangible. How would we say it? What words would we find? How would we react when the words came tumbling out? And how would our friends, family and colleagues react?

We were suddenly confronted again by the urgency and reality of this cancer, this tragedy. Ironically, shortly before Shearlean's diagnosis, I'd read Joan Didion's book, "The Year of Magical Thinking," about the death of her husband John Gregory Dunne. What I remembered best was the unreality of his death, her inability to accept it as permanent. Long after he died, Didion kept one of his suits, just in case he wasn't really dead and decided to come back. I understood that instinct now.

While Shearlean called her sister, Janet, and nephew, Jeff, to tell them the situation, I phoned my sister, Jean. I don't recall the actual words I chose as I spoke, but I do remember long pauses on Jean's end of the phone as I blurted out the news.

I remembered 10 years earlier calling Jean from a pay phone in a mall to tell her how our 1999 trailer camping trip across Canada was going. She listened until I finished and then told me she had been diagnosed with breast cancer. I had managed a few sympathetic words and then said I couldn't talk and would call her back. I realized in that moment that my generation and I had now crossed a threshold that I had only associated with my parents. Now it was us who were dying, succumbing to crippling or killing disease, and making and receiving unimaginable calls about life's inevitable abominations. I felt very, very old.

Shearlean spoke softly in the other room, and I could only hear murmurs and silences. When we were both off the phone, she reappeared with tears in her eyes, looking downcast and exhausted—and, for the first time in my eyes, she looked old, too.

We'd told the most crucial people, but how to tell everyone else? Who to tell immediately? The phone was out of the question; it was too hard, as we'd just discovered. We weren't phone people and, besides, there was too much to cover. The first seizure had occurred nearly a month ago and a lot had happened since then.

We came up with 17 people who needed to be kept in the loop. We decided I would write an announcement at some point in the near future (it would become the precursor of 22 email reports over 18 months). We would rely on these 17 people to tell others. We didn't use Facebook or want to start a blog because we didn't want to have to address and satisfy a large and public audience. We wanted to set an optimistic tone for our situation and control the information that we put out and took in. At the outset, people should know we were coping and seeing this as an adventure for us both. I would title our first email "How Shearlean and Bob Spent Their Summer Vacation" so not to alarm or shock anyone and to ease readers into our message. I would send it when we knew Shearlean had survived surgery.

Owning Your Cancer

SHEARLEAN AND I valued self-sufficiency. We had both risen by our bootstraps. We possessed great confidence in our abilities to solve problems and achieve goals. Some might describe us as "self actualizing." In so far as anyone can, we made our own world or tried to.

As soon as we were told of her brain cancer, we took possession of it. We owned it. It was ours and we would deal with it. Of course we couldn't cure brain cancer. We could barely even treat any part of it ourselves. But we weren't just going to throw ourselves on the mercy of the healthcare system or some higher power (insert the name of your higher power here).

Regardless of our limitations, we thought there was a lot we could do to affect the outcome of the disease and treatment. For one thing, we would not be passive; we would be proactive. We would not meekly submit, but would be equal partners within our care team. We would participate in all decisions and we would critically question what we didn't understand. We would set standards for care, not be afraid to say no or to disagree.

We would be constantly on guard and expect to be treated like intelligent fully functional adults. Just because Shearlean was sick and we were in a terrible predicament did not mean that we had lost all of our faculties. We would not allow ourselves to be transformed into objects of medical practice, but would retain our individuality and personhood.

Shearlean instantly took charge of finding treatment and in particular a surgeon to remove her tumor. She immediately began assessing her strengths and weaknesses to decide what she thought she could and couldn't do. She began working on her nutrition and exercise. She chose and began studying spiritual and meditative resources she thought would bolster her mental and emotional condition. She began researching authors and titles of books that told inspiring and instructive stories of what others had learned in similar situations. She "went into training" to begin conditioning her mind, body, spirit and emotions to the new reality of her life. Almost immediately she began receiving the strength and benefits she hoped for. She began to speak of calm, acceptance, hope, gratitude and determination. In all sincerity she celebrated how cancer brought her life into sharp focus, and how keenly she felt and saw things compared to the routine of life just a few weeks ago. Over the next few months she often mentioned how cancer was an awakening. She was seeing life as she had never seen it before and marveled at her new awareness. (This wasn't original with her. Many before her had similar experiences from life-altering afflictions and she was now learning the reality of other people's' stories.)

As quickly as Shearlean took control of herself and her situation, I jumped at the chance to be a part of her care and treatment. As mentioned earlier, I saw this as an interesting and vital project. It was something I could sink my teeth into and provide important skills and care. My areas of concern were insurance, benefits, finances, communications, and organization. I focused on studying medications, treatments and the disease. It was I who would deal with the healthcare system and organize bill paying. I would see to changing our housing, selling one home and finding and buying another.

Within two days of diagnosis neither of us had much time to worry about cancer. While it was never very far from our minds, it was not foremost in our daily thoughts or actions. We were far too busy. We were looking forward, making plans, digging into new fields of study, reassessing our life up to this point and thinking very specifically about our future. Everything was in sharp focus and of critical importance. Life was extraordinary, vigorous and exciting. Every thought, feeling and action was every bit as exhilarating as any of the many other adventures we had sought out and relished. Our experience could have been different if we had let it or if we were someone else.

The possible adverse results of brain cancer and surgery are infinite. They are too horrible to contemplate, but contemplate them we did. Shearlean wanted her family to see her one last time alive, loving and functioning, if the worst happened. If their memory of her was all that was left after surgery, then she wanted it to be positive. Plus, she wanted to show them she was prepared and confident, and they should be too. Everything would be all right.

Shearlean's mother and father were both dead. She had only her younger sister, Janet Jones, Janet's husband Martin, and Janet's son, Jeff Bain, and his family—his wife Kristin and sons Jake and Ryan. They all lived in southern California, near where Shearlean and I lived until 1997.

In early September, she flew to Orange County, California, to spend the 2009 Labor Day weekend with everyone gathered at her nephew's home in Rancho Santa Margarita. I stayed home.

Every moment for the past two weeks had been intense. Our behavior around and toward each other as we struggled with our feelings was making us both irritable. Shearlean was over-explaining trivial things, which annoyed me, which, in turn, made me feel guilty. When she was frightened, she wanted to control everything. She kept finding busy work to feel she was doing something but would overdo and get exhausted and frustrated. She couldn't put in her pierced earrings and when I tried to help, I didn't do it well and it annoyed her. We were both trying to work out our proper roles in the new context of her disease. I thought we could use a break from each other.

After taking her to the airport for her 7 a.m. flight, I returned to a silent, empty house. Was this how it would be all the time soon? Empty? Would I be empty, too?

While she was gone, one night I watched the DVD of the nurse's craniotomy that we were given at our consultation with Dr. Steinberg. While I am not particularly squeamish, I've always been obsessively curious. I was intensely interested in how the procedure would be done, but when I watched the video, I could not help but see Shearlean lying on that table. It was tough to watch.

For a craniotomy your head is shaved on the side where the surgery will be done. This is the side opposite of the symptoms (the right brain controls the left side and the left brain controls the right side of your body). You are anesthetized while your scalp is cut and folded out of the way. A series of small holes are drilled to outline the section of skull to be removed. A saw is then guided by the holes to cut out a section of skull bone, which is set aside until you are reassembled. Removing the skull exposes the dura, a tough protective membrane covering the brain. A section of the dura is moved out of the way to provide access to the brain itself.

Rita Carter, in her excellent book, "Mapping the Mind," describes the brain this way: "The human brain is as big as a coconut, the shape of a walnut, the color of uncooked liver and the consistency of chilled butter. It has two hemispheres, which are covered in a thin skin of deeply wrinkled grey tissue call the cerebral cortex."

When the brain is exposed, the anesthesiologist awakens you so you can name pictures of objects and speak with the surgeon and his assistants while he stimulates your brain with an electrode to determine where eloquent functions are relative to the cancer.

Glioblastoma is cancer of the astroglial cells. Carter explains: "Zoom in close enough on a section of brain and you will see a dense network of cells. Most of them are glial cells— relatively simple-looking structures whose main purpose is to glue the whole construction together and maintain its physical integrity."

Cancer and brain cells are intermingled. The goal in Shearlean's case, as in all cases, would be to remove as much of the cancer as possible. Watching the video, I understood that as the surgeon stimulated her brain and her responses were monitored, a tiny paper number would be placed at the site of stimulation and logged to map the location of her brain functions. Eventually, a group of numbers would outline the areas of the tumor and the surgeon would know where to excise the cancerous matter that must be removed. Unavoidably, normally functioning brain cells would be removed with the cancerous ones. Disturbing as this was to me, I was glad to see how it all worked. I felt a lot of emotional resistance to associating this procedure with Shearlean because I didn't want it to happen to her. Intellectually, I owed it to her and myself to learn all I could about what she was going to face; she needed and deserved a surrogate to bear some of the burden for her. I wanted to spare her all I could.

Shearlean's cancer tissue would not be cut out with a knife, but rather it would be sucked out with a hollow ultrasound wand. Since the viscosity of the cancerous brain is different from the viscosity of normal brain matter, suction could discretely differentiate between good and bad tissue to minimize damage to good tissue.

This comforted me. But it was very small comfort, indeed, as I watched the end of the video. I was grateful to that anonymous nurse for sharing her experience—for touching my life and Shearlean's life. A wave of sadness swept over me at the thought of that nurse, about 20 years younger than Shearlean, and most likely long dead of her merciless cancer, as would be Shearlean in a matter of months. I sagged under the weight of sadness upon sadness for everyone stricken with this thing.

I watched to the finish of the surgery. The patient was put back to sleep and her dura was sewn closed. Her skull was reattached to her cranium with titanium screws and brackets (which we were later assured wouldn't set off airport metal detectors). Her scalp was smoothed back in place and closed with layers of absorbable sutures. The skin was closed with staples.

A post-surgery MRI image was compared with the pre-surgery MRI and the removed tissue was sent to pathology for biopsy.

Because Shearlean was too squeamish to watch forensic and pathology crime shows on TV, I thought she would find the nurse's craniotomy video too vivid. I hadn't wanted her to see it and thought watching it would do her more harm than good. Once I'd seen it myself, I knew I'd been right.

When she returned home from her family visit, I told her I'd watched the video and recommended that she not watch it. I added that I also hoped she would not research glioblastoma on the Internet because there was no good news there and it would just undermine her optimism and confidence. She agreed to both of my suggestions and said that she had already received enough information; more was not going to help. Between reading Science of Mind's monthly guide to spiritual living and books by Norman Cousins, Deepak Chopra, Bernie Siegel MD and Shakti Gawain—plus listening to her numerous meditation CDs—she had enough to keep her busy.

She'd been busy in California, too. I noticed right away that while visiting her sister, Shearlean had her hair cut quite short. She said that Kristin, a former hairdresser, had cut and styled it in preparation for surgery so she wouldn't have to have a hospital orderly do it. Her hair had always been one of her prettiest features and though she had worn it shorter as she got older, I was sad to see it so ravaged. It was another stark reminder of the coming changes.

CHAPTER FIVE

Testing, Testing, Testing

"I believe I am part of the universal mind, that I am healed, that my body knows how to heal itself. I believe that I am worthy to be healthy and am truly blessed."

EXTENSIVE TESTS AND REHEARSAL for the role Shearlean would have to play during the procedure were prerequisites for participating in the surgery. Shearlean would be awake during surgery (there are no pain nerves in the brain) so she could be asked to identify objects in pictures and to answer questions to aid the surgeon in mapping her brain in the area of her tumor. She practiced taking a test with the technician who would administer it during surgery, under conditions simulating the actual procedure, so as not to be alarmed by the sight of a stranger or surprised by being interrogated in the midst of the real thing.

Her intellectual capacity would be benchmarked as a diagnostic tool for measuring any lost functionality should that situation arise. Because of her high IQ and 18 years of education, the test had to be rigorous. At first we thought the testing process was done for research (University Medical being a research-oriented institution) but later learned it was only diagnostic with clearly ominous implications.

Shearlean's last test was on September 9, the day before surgery. The hospital where the testing was conducted was also Seattle's trauma center, so we were warned that Shearlean's treatment could be interrupted by an emergency.

This final test was to see whether Shearlean was among the 10 percent of the population with some language ability in her brain's right hemisphere. To find this out, a catheter had to be inserted from an artery in her groin and routed up to her brain to deliver anesthesia to the left side of her brain's language center (where her tumor was), leaving the right side conscious while she was asked to identify words and answer questions.

But before her test could be completed, a heart attack victim required the catheter team to insert a heart stent to keep him alive. Shearlean had to wait in the procedure room, sedated, while the team attended to their new patient. I sat on pins and needles in the waiting room knowing she was in limbo. Finally, after a couple of hours, the catheter team was able to resume Shearlean's test.

They found no right-brain language faculty; she was entirely dependent for language where her tumor was centered on the left side.

Exhausted from the drawn-out ordeal, we didn't get to our Seattle hotel until 8:30 p.m., where Janet and Jeff, who had come up to be present for the surgery, were waiting to hear how everything had gone. We visited briefly and then went to bed, setting the alarm clock for 4 a.m. in order to be at the surgery pavilion for our 5:15 a.m. check-in. Surgery was scheduled to start at 7:30 a.m. and Janet and her son Jeff would meet me then.

~

That either of us could sleep at all the night before surgery was testimony to how tired we were. The sound of the alarm was shocking, but we got up immediately and dressed quickly. Anticipation of what we were going to do today was high and the prospect of confronting Shearlean's cancer in this all-or-nothing battle filled us with excitement. In just 20 days we had turned the tables on cancer and had taken the offensive with the ultimate weapon of surgery. We weren't going to let even cancer frighten us into cowering, hiding or retreating. We drove less than a mile to the hospital and parked in the underground garage. We took an escalator up to a brightly lit glass cubicle that was the reception area. An elderly security guard and half-awake receptionist gave us vague directions to the surgical unit.

The surgery pavilion was in a distant wing across the campus.

The campus was dark, chilly and deserted, but as we walked toward the only lighted entry, people began to emerge from every direction. Pushing through the doors, we joined a noisy, milling crowd. Three uniformed women behind a counter shouted out patients' names and waved file folders in the air. People pushed up to the counter but were turned back by sharp commands we couldn't make out from where we stood watching the scene. The atmosphere felt more like we were among bargain hunters at a Black Friday sale than patients seeking life-saving surgery.

"Duke! Shearlean Duke!" came a cry. I raised my arm and pulled Shearlean toward the desk as an Asian couple stepped in front of us. The nurse said to them, "No, only 5:15 now. 5:30 is next. Please step away from the counter."

"Duke?" she asked.

"Yes," I answered.

"That will be $600 cash, check or credit card," she said.

I thought I misheard and tried to guess what she must have actually said. I gave her a quizzical expression. I flashed on the bizarre impression that this whole pre-dawn event had actually been staged as an elaborate hoax to extract a last minute bribe for admittance to surgery.

"Six hundred. Your insurance deductible," she enunciated clearly.

And good morning to you too, I thought.

As I fumbled for my wallet and credit card, I felt irritated that this financial and administrative transaction should take precedent at such a moment. *Why wasn't the sum collected days earlier? Or why didn't any of the half-dozen people I talked to about insurance and payments ever mention this?* But this was no time or place to start a dispute, which certainly wouldn't do Shearlean any good. Still, what a poor reception at such a crucial point in the process.

We signed several forms including the Uniform Medical Plan Statement of Patient's Rights, a full-page, two-column, densely printed sheet that we seem to have been expected to read, and the Patient Information for University Medical Inpatient Facility Directory and the Care Agreement. (We had already signed these and other forms twice, on August 26 and September 3. These forms had been proffered by our healthcare providers and signed by Shearlean, yet no one ever discussed them. Nor did any of the various receptionists we encountered seem competent to do so. Many months later, this would come back to haunt me.) This repetitious ceremonial capitulation required of all patients for all treatment at every step never failed to infuriate me, but yielding to the impulse to complain now could only harm Shearlean.

After signing without either reading or caring, we found a seat among others who had been "processed." I certainly felt "processed." Shearlean and I held hands. She was quiet and calm with a pleasant near-smile gracing her face.

I didn't want to look directly at Shearlean for fear of the emotional reaction that eye-to-eye contact might produce. Rather, I settled for the indistinct but safe peripheral view I could get if I scooted my chair back a couple of inches so she was slightly forward of me. It was the first I was able to appraise her since our pre-dawn walk here to surgery reception. She reminded me of a vagrant. She was wearing non-descript loose clothing. Her hair was unnaturally short on one side, making her appear lopsided. Without makeup she looked older and unhealthy. She wore no jewelry, and without those few customary pieces she looked to have been stripped of her insignia. Without her earrings, the holes in her ears looked like old wounds. The overall effect was that of an ill, elderly, frightened and worried woman waiting for something terrible. Only her upright posture, squared shoulder and uplifted chin gave lie to my impression of her.

What must she be thinking on the brink of such an outrageous prospect as brain surgery? My God! Could a person's brain even permit itself to think about the process it was about to undergo? I needed to be more clear-headed than she was through all of this and yet I could barely cope with what was going to happen.

"Shearlean Duke," someone called from the doorway.

We both stood up as a woman in scrubs greeted us. She chatted pleasantly as she led us toward double swinging doors and ushered us into the organized mayhem of surgical preparation. I followed Shearlean as we were passed between escort after escort who led us through the maze of cubicles, doors, curtained stalls, wheelchairs, and both occupied and empty gurneys.

Slowly, throughout the morning, Shearlean was transformed. She would disappear and reappear, altered by some new medical attachment, a different color wristband, a swatch of gauze and tape on her arm, and a fresh new folder on her growing stack of folders. More than 15 doctors, nurses and technicians arrived to introduce themselves to us.

I tried to write down everyone's name, but some appeared and disappeared so quickly I never learned who they were. Since Shearlean would be awake during her surgery and would be working with the surgical team as they operated, they didn't want her to be confronted by any strangers. She recognized several of the people because she had already trained with them for some of her procedures.

Still positive to the core, she tried to give each person a little pep talk. "Things are going to be great," she would say, expressing how much confidence she had in each of them. She was able to find a big smile for each greeter and repeat back to them each person's name.

I was with her during the entire pre-op process. We had a few last minutes of privacy behind a curtain until it was swept aside by two cheerful orderlies who said in unison, "Time to go." I squeezed her hand as I fought back tears and tried not to think about how this could be the last time I might see her or the last time she would be the Shearlean I had loved for most of my life.

> SURGICAL TEAM NAMES
>
> Nurse Katy
> Nurse Kelly
> Nurse Pinky
> Kathleen
> Therapist Sandy
> Grace
> Mimi
> Adrian
> Jacob
> Stephanie
> Dr. Li
> Dr. Crouse
> Dr. Dannels
> Nurse Cynthia
> Dr. Steinberg
> And others

Janet and Jeff were in the surgery lounge (something of an oxymoron, I thought, since no one looked relaxed or at ease), which was full of puzzles, magazines, coffee and water, telephones and had a concierge with a computer who could relay occasional updates on patients' progress and status. There were small rooms with doors for privacy where doctors could meet with families. Based on what I supposed transpired there, these rooms seemed sinister and forbidding.

Shearlean's surgery was to take about four hours. She went in at 7:30 a.m., so we expected in our minds that everything would be over by 11:30 a.m. My emotional buildup became excruciating as 11:30 a.m. came and went. Just before noon the concierge called my name and I stepped up to her desk. In her practiced hushed tone she told me the start of surgery had been delayed. It was nothing unusual, but it would probably be about 1:30 p.m. before we would hear anything.

I told Janet and Jeff, and we hunkered down for more waiting. But we couldn't do it. It was too much. We decided to take a long walk and get some lunch and try not to return to the waiting room for a while. That didn't help. We found ourselves back in the lounge in just 45 minutes because we were worried we might miss something. Finally, at 2 p.m., Dr. Steinberg appeared. His face gave nothing away as he motioned us toward the nearest private room and closed the door. I paid no attention to Janet or Jeff, but locked eyes on Dr. Steinberg and felt certain things had gone well. Somehow, I had never thought otherwise. Though the words skeptic and pessimist fit me perfectly, I was certain Shearlean would come through surgery with flying colors. I think her confidence had infected me and the first syllable from the surgeon had an unmistakable ring of success. If success hadn't been the outcome, I don't think I would have been capable of comprehending it.

Shearlean was fine, no complications. Though surgery went well, Dr. Steinberg wasn't sure if he'd been able to remove as much of the tumor as he'd hoped. He'd wanted to take out at least 98 percent of it but was unsure whether he achieved his goal. He would know more later with a post-op MRI. He didn't talk about the implications of his not getting the whole tumor, and I didn't ask. I just wanted to see her. Shearlean was now in recovery and we could go see her immediately. If all continued to go well, she would be moved to intensive care later that day and we could visit her there as much as she and we desired. We were told that she was talking (what a relief) but that it would take a long time to evaluate the full consequences of the surgery on her verbal ability. He added with an admiring smile that Shearlean had encouraged him throughout the surgery to stick with it, get it all and not worry about her.

Our first and biggest hurdle had been cleared.

~

Walking into Shearlean's recovery room, I felt very high and very low simultaneously. Just that she was alive filled me with joy, but she looked so beat up, bandaged and pathetic that I grieved for her. She recognized us right away and managed a wan smile, and then she closed her eyes and nodded off. I was glad she was asleep again rather than having to be conscious of what she had just been through. The turban-like bandage on her head was skewed to the left, nearly covering her left eye. The left side of her face was swollen and discolored. The nurse, hovering in the background, told us enthusiastically about how well Shearlean had done and how her vital signs were good.

Exhausted from the tension of long hours of waiting, but feeling secure and confident about Shearlean and her condition, we realized we needed some recovery time ourselves. We headed back to the hotel for some much needed rest. We agreed to meet in my room at 6 p.m. and go to dinner. We chose a raucous sports bar near the hotel because we thought the noisy crowd and wall-to-wall TVs would be a welcome distraction. Jeff and I drank too many beers and Janet indulged in a couple of forbidden appetizers before we walked back to the hotel. We were completely drained, mentally and physically, and desperate for the oblivion of sleep to heal our traumatized souls. Our last duty before retiring was to agree that we would each visit Shearlean tomorrow separately, to not overwhelm her. We would work out a more comprehensive schedule after we each had an opportunity to evaluate her for ourselves.

The day after surgery, Janet was up early and visiting Shearlean when Dr. Steinberg's resident made morning rounds. He told Shearlean and Janet that they had in fact removed *all* of the tumor they'd hoped to; there was no sign of tumor on the post-surgery MRI. However, the pre-operation MRI showed that the tumor had grown to twice the size it had been when diagnosed. Between August 21 and September 10, 20 days, the tumor had doubled its size. This made it clear why glioblastoma was characterized as an extremely aggressive form of cancer and why speedy surgery was urgent. Quantifying the tumor in terms of its size and speed of growth brought home the devouring and uncontrollable nature of this monster. No time could be lost in attacking this cancer and pursuing treatment. Time was critical.

When I visited Shearlean later that morning, she was unable to find the necessary words to tell me exactly what the doctor had said, but she confirmed she understood the doctor's findings when I repeated what Janet told me. Shearlean had a huge smile on her face and was already looking better than yesterday. But I was exhausted and devastated by the doctor's news—and fighting back tears. I had to leave her room and pace the hall until I settled down.

What a virulent tumor this was to grow so fast!

I studied Shearlean when I returned to her, wondering how she could take the news so calmly. Growth of the tumor was terrible. I was panicked. Was she so determined to be positive that she refused to recognize bad news when it was presented to her? Did she not comprehend the weight of this news? And Dr. Steinberg's resident: Did he think he had communicated how profound this finding was?

I wanted to hear from the doctor for myself and be able to ask him questions. Neither Dr. Steinberg nor his resident was available that day, but tomorrow's rounds were scheduled for 6 to 8 a.m. and I was determined to be on hand.

Janet, Jeff and I met Dr. Steinberg's resident the next morning in Shearlean's room and listened as he repeated yesterday's news. He was unperturbed and emphasized that virtually 100 percent of the tumor had been removed. Again, Shearlean was beaming, and I didn't have the heart to ask any challenging questions in front of her. Everyone else in the room seemed pleased with what the doctor had to say or, at least, was not inclined to question him. Instead of questioning the doctor I was silently questioning myself, examining my motives in wanting more information. The doctor was emphasizing the good news—they had gotten the entire tumor. That's what Shearlean had heard. That's what Janet and Jeff had heard. I realized that the stunning news about the growth of her tumor had exposed my denial of her condition. Measuring her tumor revealed its power to ravage her brain, and transformed it from a meaningless shape to a devouring killer, which I had not had to face squarely until the resident explained its size and growth.

We told Shearlean we would be back to visit individually throughout the day, so as not to tire her. I was again on the verge of tears. Aware of my state, Janet and Jeff were silent as we took the back stairs down to the park-like hospital grounds bordering Portage Bay. A winding path paralleled the water with widely separated benches set under trees and nestled among groomed shrubbery. Solemn individuals and prayerful couples sat hunched in intense stillness, seemingly listening to an internal voice or waiting patiently for a dreaded summons.

We found a bench at the edge of the water to view the passing yachts, their throaty diesel engines murmuring over the humming street traffic that circled the medical center.

I was highly agitated by my self-revelation and the wild swing of my emotions. I thought we made quite a trio. We were obviously together but were behaving like strangers, neither separating nor approaching each other, each tentative. We had never shared anything like this before.

I couldn't hold back my tears any longer and buried my face in my hands, trying to just let them flow. Between waves of sobbing I poured out my despair at the rapid growth of the tumor. Janet scooted across the bench up against me, draped her arm over my neck and recited a list of Shearlean's and my strengths, and her confidence in our ability to deal with this. Then Janet shuddered and sagged, as she could no longer restrain her own tears. Jeff stood, agitated, his face twisted with confusion about his role in all of this as he watched us, looking for a clue. I moved away from Janet and said to Jeff, "Here. Sit down here, your mother needs you."

Eventually, I was beginning to breathe normally and the tears ceased flowing. I felt better and saw that Janet and Jeff were at ease. We three looked around the park and at each other as though we had gone somewhere without noticing and had now returned to real life where everything was tidy and normal, just as we had left it.

A handsome yacht moved through sparkling water partially screened by trees in full bloom, viciously oblivious to our recent agony. I watched it, wishing for a similar oblivion.

It wasn't even 9 a.m. and we still had to face the whole day.

Janet suggested that we walk back to the hotel, just 20 minutes away, and then meet for lunch at the shopping center across from the hotel. As we walked, we worked out a schedule for visiting Shearlean. If she slept through a visit we would leave a note for her on her room's marker board. We agreed to reconvene for dinner and exchange our impressions from our visits then.

During our visits in the next couple of days we were each able to receive firsthand nursing reports and to participate in Shearlean's care. We shared meals with her, walked her up and down the hall for exercise, assisted her to and from the bathroom, and adjusted her bed and bedding.

Shearlean progressed quickly into rehabilitation: eating, using the toilet and showing no adverse symptoms. By day three she could walk the halls with an escort and a safety harness around her waist, pushing her IV stand garlanded with a drip tube and bag.

Her speech was limited to an occasional word, so mainly she communicated with facial expressions and body language, and expressive exclamations. All the signs indicated she understood speech and could read postings on the marker board on the wall opposite her bed. It was all incredibly encouraging to her and to us. I had decided not to share with her my reaction to the growth of the tumor; I feared the effect it might have on her spirit.

There were hints she might be discharged on Monday, September 14. That morning, at rounds, she was told she was going home the next day. I was as eager to take her home as she was to go.

All of the familiar staff faces suddenly disappeared; perhaps reassigned to other patients or departments. As soon as her discharge was set, Shearlean became yesterday's news at the hospital. I was frustrated because the new cadre of nurses and aides was brusque and quick to disappear if consulted about anything. Now nobody knew anything, and when they said they would find out something for us, they never reappeared. The marker board on the wall that had listed the names of staff, their shifts, and words of encouragement was wiped clean. She was already no longer a patient here, so she rated minimum attention.

Case In Point

IT WOULD TAKE a long time for me to fully comprehend the formal definition and role of caregiver, but I quickly got a practical lesson in the need for a dedicated caregiver to protect a patient's interests in the context of the behemoth healthcare system that consumed us.

In one mere four-day period we soared to the heights of the best American healthcare has to offer and lows of everyday care available to most of us. What was most impressive was that state-of-the-art surgery existed side-by-side with indifferent "general care," and one shifted so fast to the other that you could miss it if you blinked. When Shearlean was surgery's patient, care verged on spectacular, but when surgery approved her for discharge, general care took over and the level of care plummeted.

It was easy to see why the epithet "brain surgery" is often used to distinguish the highest achievement in science and technical difficulty. With Shearlean's brain surgery we experienced the epitome of American medicine. It was everything I had ever been led to think it could be. I couldn't even believe it was available to such ordinary people as us. It seemed to be everything you could ask it to be: efficient, courteous, personal, caring, thorough, seemingly expert at every stage and level. It was a far cry from the ordinary care most of us see most of the time. I was to learn (more than once) that at its apex, technically and scientifically advanced healthcare in America is a marvel verging on miraculous. But like the top of a pyramid, the apex is but a point with no space for more than a rare few to practice or be treated. From the apex it is all downhill (with the exception of a few rare individuals and, rarer still, institutions).

As you move through the system from "brain surgery" to recovery room, intensive care and then to general care, the health system deteriorates rapidly. Packed into just four days, from surgery to discharge from general care, the decline in care and providers was alarming. By the time Shearlean was scheduled for discharge, I was about ready to kidnap her from University Medical center.

By then, the nurses on the floor didn't know the names of the doctors on the floor. When I told a nurse that I wanted to see Dr. X she hurried off and shortly a doctor appeared, but not whom I asked for. I thought there was no point talking to him since he didn't know me and probably knew nothing about Shearlean. I went into the nursing station (off limits) and asked the nurse why she sent me the doctor she did. She confessed she didn't know Dr. X nor did she know the doctor she sent to me.

Why wouldn't she just say so in the first place?

Regardless of the difficulties and dangers of my unskilled care for her at home, just four days after a craniotomy, we would both be better off than if she remained under current conditions. These conditions powerfully brought home to me the benefit a dedicated caregiver can bring to patient care regardless of his lack of knowledge and skill. Any doubts I had about myself vaporized and I knew I was ready.

For discharge I received a slip of paper and was directed to the hospital pharmacy where I was given a bag of medications and asked to sign for the $160 cost. I balked. I had no idea who was paying or what deductible applied or even if the prescriptions were covered by insurance.

I asked, "What if I don't want them?"

With a puzzled expression, the pharmacist said, "Your wife's doctor ordered them. They are precautionary."

I caved. I was willing to pay $160 exit fee just to get Shearlean and me out of there.

It turned out all of these meds were for nausea or constipation. She had no need for them and eventually I threw them out.

Shearlean and I had been swept up by the shock of diagnosis, the urgency of immediate treatment, and the drama and terror of surgery. We had to surrender ourselves to the system in exchange for the promise of surviving long enough to receive other treatments that could extend Shearlean's life. We were breathless from the pace.

Now, though, we were preparing for the long haul of surviving the rigors of continual treatment and living with this monster that had invaded our lives and was holding us hostage to its implacable consequence.

Jeff had to leave to return to his job, but Janet was staying to help care for Shearlean at home. I got the car from the underground parking garage. When I pulled along the curb at the hospital's exit, I saw a heavily bandaged and pale elderly stranger slumped in a wheelchair. The attendant had turned over control of the wheelchair to Janet at the hospital exit. We loaded Shearlean into the passenger seat and Janet got in the backseat for the drive home.

From diagnosis to surgery we had been overwhelmed by a tsunami of terror, urgency, numbing fear and desperation. We'd survived by clinging to any debris of hope or promise that came within our grasp. Now, as suddenly as we had been swept away, we were thrown upon a devastated shore, surrounded with the wreckage of our former lives and facing the challenge of surviving from what we could salvage.

Our rescuers had done all they could. Now it would be up to us—up to me in particular—to use the resources at our disposal to construct a new and worthwhile life. Shearlean was alive and apparently intact. She had already proved herself a heroic patient. But now the question was if I would be up to providing the care she needed and meeting the unknowable challenges that lay ahead.

What was expected of me? What would Shearlean be capable of? Did she have the strength to keep going? Did I? Was there enough money? Whom could we count on? Where could we turn for help when we needed it? Could we ever get beyond the question of, "Why us?" What would we have to endure in the months to come?

CHAPTER SIX

Rise of the Caregiver

"I am so lucky. My surgery went so well and 98 percent of my tumor was removed by my wonderful doctor."

OF COURSE I wanted Shearlean out of the hospital and at home. She came home on a Tuesday, September 14, just four days after surgery. It was the day before the start of the university's fall quarter, annually a pivotal day in our "normal" calendar. As if to accent the urgency of her care, I was already mulling over the fact that tomorrow we must make another 180-mile round trip to Seattle to start chemo and radiation therapy.

Having her in the house wasn't as familiar and comfortable as I had anticipated it would be. Even with Janet there, I felt alone, isolated. Shearlean was so drugged and exhausted she hardly knew where she was. She just wanted to go to bed and before I even had the covers arranged over her, she was asleep.

I sat on the edge of the bed listening to her steady, rhythmic breathing, wondering what I was dealing with in terms of her physical and mental needs. In many ways she might be a stranger, potentially saying and doing aberrant things. She might have physical, even fatal problems I would be unable to deal with. I was afraid and apprehensive, yet overwhelmed with a desire to care for her and to make every minute of her remaining life the best possible. I could only hope I was up to the task—whatever it may be.

I swiveled around and prepared to rise from the bed when I was knocked back by the realization that from this instant forward I was totally committed to Shearlean's care. The bed sagged under my weight; I slumped from the burden I was now carrying. It was what I wanted ... wasn't it? In the dimness, I paused to sort through the responsibilities I had so eagerly accepted.

I'd decided to be Shearlean's caregiver the moment she was diagnosed. At that instant, caregiving only meant to me that she would remain at home throughout the course of her illness and would die at home in her own bed with me beside her when it was time. Beyond this goal, I knew nothing about caregiving in the full sense of caring for or treating a terminally ill person.

I had no training or prior experience or even prior knowledge of caregiving. Time to learn what I needed to know was limited and critical; the learning curve would be nearly vertical, beginning with something as big as caring for her after brain surgery.

What was "care"? Being a literal learner, I'd decided to look up the word before Shearlean came home. According to the dictionary, to be a legitimate caregiver I would have to pay serious attention, to do things correctly, and to avoid damage or risk to my patient. Further, it would be up to me to provide what was necessary for Shearlean's health, welfare, maintenance and protection.

Well, I had vowed to do that when we married—along with the third definition of care: Looking after and providing for the needs of someone.

I could do that. I had 40 years of practice.

The Next Step in Care Web site provided a more specific health-care-oriented definition. It said I was a caregiver if I took care of someone who had a chronic illness or disease.

Now we were getting down to brass tacks, although Shearlean's disease was acute.

As a caregiver I would be responsible for managing medications and talking to doctors and nurses on Shearlean's behalf. I would help bathe or dress her when she was too frail or disabled to do it herself. I'd done that for her once long ago when she'd had a hysterectomy at age 32. I knew I could pull it off. Lastly, I would do housework or, in the Web site's terms, "take care of household chores" like meals or bills when she could not do these things alone.

I knew there was more to it than my simplified goal to keep

her comfortable and to live up to these basic definitions. We had to go from a standing start to full speed to transform ourselves into capable patient and competent caregiver. When the patient wakes up dying there can be no gradual buildup for learning caregiving.

At least I was no stranger to generic caring. Long before it was politically correct—referring to the politics of modern marriage—I did my share of cooking, cleaning, shopping and household chores. Since I'd retired years earlier and Shearlean had continued to work (principally for health insurance), I had become a full-fledged househusband and was quite content in the role. But caregiving for a terminally ill cancer patient, I intuited, would be a far cry from mere house husbanding. It would probably be a blend of practical nursing, life-and-death decision-making, hospice management, and daily negotiating with a vast and indifferent bureaucracy. I had no idea what other staggering obstacles I would face.

I was resolved, however, that the quality of caregiving I would provide would define the value of my life better than anything that came before or that could come afterward. This was all or nothing. I would hold nothing back. There was no tomorrow.

The sound of water running in the kitchen sink, closing cupboard doors, and clinking pans on the stove dissipated the fog of reflection I was lost in. I sprang off the bed, glanced at Shearlean, and hurried to see what I could do to help Janet.

~

I believed that approaching caregiving like any of the large technical writing and publishing projects I had managed or participated in might serve me well. I had served as a documentation consultant for organizations such as NASA and Fortune 500 corporations. Our situation now had all of the earmarks of such projects. I would be dealing with multiple people (doctors, family, etc.) all with different interests.

Writing technical reports and manuals involved researching huge volumes of engineering and technical data to distill information needed by managers, supervisors and technicians so they could operate and maintain complex and dangerous equipment ranging from weapons systems to space vehicles to scientific computer systems. The key to doing this as a technical writer or journalist (who was *not* also an engineer, scientist, astronaut or technician) was to persuade people to share their knowledge with me so I could perfect my materials for the ultimate user. Consequently, I saw doctors, nurses and the whole host of healthcare providers—from insurers to lab technicians to administrators—as sources to be interviewed and consulted in order to construct a working knowledge of Shearlean's treatment and care.

Through my long career, I learned project management techniques that were responsible for the success of the projects I worked on. From what I had seen of the healthcare system up to this point, it was every bit as complex as any technical or business system I had ever seen; it spoke its own arcane language and was populated with smart, highly educated (but not necessarily well-rounded), and knowledgeable people.

I knew how to start out knowing little and how to proceed to learn a lot. I knew what techniques and methods to employ to acquire, organize and use large quantities of data. I knew what pitfalls and obstacles to avoid. And I knew what kind of records to keep and how to move forward against organizational resistance.

I needed, I felt, to define my objective and come up with a concise mission statement. Don't laugh; it's actually useful to create a goal for caregiving. My objective boiled down to this: *Remove every obstacle in caring for Shearlean to ensure that she receives the best treatment with the least hassle, and experiences the greatest comfort and convenience attainable in order for her remaining time to be of the highest quality and free of pain.*

By electing palliative care, Shearlean had decided to forfeit longer life for a better quality of her remaining life. This decision represented a big sacrifice on her part and was something I would not let anyone tamper with. It was a sincere bargain struck solemnly between Shearlean and her elected primary doctor at the very outset of treatment, but there was no way to inform everyone else who would become involved in her care over the next months. I needed to protect Shearlean from worries and problems that might disrupt or destroy the comfort and convenience that would contribute to her dearly purchased quality of life. Besides her doctor with whom she had made her bargain, I was the other key person who could guarantee that she would have the best possible remaining time. I could do this by protecting her from non-treatment related demands on her time, energy, strength and emotions. I would be her moat and wall, and deal with everything she wouldn't have energy for.

My next task was creating a streamlined mission statement. I was taught that the best mission statements were as brief and elementary as possible. The epitome of this was reputed to be the mission statement of the old AT&T conventional telephone monopoly (once known as Ma Bell) whose rock-bottom mission statement was: *Provide a dial tone.*

My mission statement for the responsibility I carried was a question: *Who pays?*

I was retired on Social Security and covered by Medicare. Shearlean had continued to work for her own health insurance because she was too young for Medicare. Neither of us qualified for pensions, and so our retirement depended on Social Security and savings. Several times we had discussed her retiring and relying on private insurance to cover a medical disaster. We were thankful now that we hadn't chosen that route.

More than cancer, we feared the financial ruin the American healthcare system is notorious in causing for the underinsured. If we could preserve personal financial stability, I felt certain we could achieve our care objective. Without money we would be lost. I believed we had few allies and were facing an overwhelming army of indifferent healthcare apparatchik. In other words, I was paranoid and, therefore, in the best frame of mind for the class struggle to come: patient versus healthcare system. I had an inkling I would have to approach it as an adversarial situation.

I had little idea, however, of how or where to start, so I began with a list of questions beginning with: *Who pays?* And from there the list grew.

~

With my caregiver role taking shape and a plan developing regarding all I would have to navigate, I was shocked to realize I was actually enthused about the prospect of taking care of Shearlean. For more than a year I had been adrift, seeking some new direction for my life that was appropriate for my age and diminishing physical abilities. I was 71 years old and though my health was excellent, my strength and agility were declining. My right leg was weak and I sometimes suffered crippling back pain. If I were not careful and made no adjustments to accommodate my limitations, I could seriously injure myself and maybe ruin the rest of my life. Last year I had resigned my beloved seasonal job crewing aboard a Southeast Alaska charter boat.

Every summer the skipper, the cook and I had cared for six charter guests. It could get very physical with long hours. I moved around on the heaving, rolling boat, going up and down ladders and along slippery decks. Hauling on heavy lines to pull the boat close to the dock against strong winds required all my strength. I thought I should quit while I could still do the job. The skipper and guests relied on me and I didn't want to let them down in a crisis.

MY LIST OF ORIGINAL QUESTIONS

- Would our existing health insurance cover everything?
- How could we avoid bankruptcy from surgery, ongoing care or long-term nursing?
- What if Shearlean were to be so disabled that I could not provide all of her care?
- Were our current legal documents adequate to our needs or should they be modified?
- What was it safe to tell her employer?
- What recourse might we have against her employer if it were not supportive?
- What help might be available from city, county and state? What's required to qualify? How to start the process?
- What computer disability aids were available to help her work, such as voice recognition software for typing?
- How should we negotiate with the university and state bureaucracy to obtain a desirable employment status with maximum benefits?
- Should we consult an attorney?
- What should we guard against in dealing with her employer and others?
- What should we watch for in dealing with insurance companies?
- Can Shearlean qualify for Medicaid?
- Should we make any statement or declaration about sound mind before brain surgery?

I had already gone the "just one more season" route and decided I was past due for finding something new and more appropriate for my energies. But after I quit, I felt lost.

And now here was something urgent and important right in front of me. What could be more worthwhile than being Shearlean's caregiver? I had few qualifications, but I certainly had the desire. I had the love and tenderness my patient needed and envisioned my project management and administrative skills being utilized to deal with the healthcare system for her.

I was stunned when I first realized that this was benefiting me, that I was viewing her tragedy as a boon to me, her illness a new project—a new direction—for *my* life. But I didn't wallow in guilt about this. I knew I could guarantee she would have the best of

- What should we look for in documents we are asked to sign?
- Are there steps we should take to protect assets?
- Should we involve our CPA and what would that cost?
- What assets are immune to lien or seizure?
- Is bankruptcy an option?
- How was university retirement affected by Social Security benefits?
- How would we know whether some medical procedures were elective or not, or covered by insurance or not, so we could choose?
- How would we know whether our treatment choices would interfere with the medical protocols of University Medical?

What if Shearlean:

- Retired?
- Elected disability status?
- Took early Social Security?
- Qualified for Social Security disability?
- Took medical leave?
- Took a professional leave of absence?
- Worked part time?
- Remained department chair because teaching in a classroom was impossible?

care. She would be free from worrying about what would happen to her, be able to remain at home, and be allowed to die in her own bed. It was something we knew we each wanted for the other, and I would be able to give it to her as my last and greatest gift.

My moment of shame gave way to joy at being so unexpectedly blessed with a noble calling so late in life. Listing my questions had been helpful to get me started in my new role. It focused my thinking, but what I really needed were answers.

While Janet busied herself with unpacking and looking for dinner ingredients, I undertook my first caregiver's task. I studied the "Patient Discharge Instructions for Duke, Shearlean, U2749393, Neurosurgery." *(See Illustrations Exhibit 4.)*

Under the heading Clinic Appointment I saw I was to call Dr. Steinberg's office to schedule a post-op follow-up on Wednesday,

UNSTRUCTURED MEDICATIONS LIST

Scheduled

- **citalopram** 5 mg Oral Daily. *An antidepressant.*
- **dexamethasone** 2 mg Oral Twice Daily. *A potent synthetic member of the* glucocorticoid *class of* steroid *drugs. It acts as an* anti-inflammatory *and* immunosuppressant *and is 6.6 times more potent than* prednisone.
- **docusate** 200 mg Oral Twice Daily. *A common ingredient in consumer products, especially laxatives of the* stool softener *type.*
- **omeprazole** 20 mg Oral Daily. *A Prilosec generic* proton pump inhibitor *used in the treatment of* dyspepsia, peptic ulcer disease, gastro esophageal reflux disease, laryngopharyngeal reflux *and* Zollinger–Ellison syndrome.
- **pantoprazole** 40 mg Oral Daily. *A* proton pump inhibitor *drug that inhibits* gastric acid *secretion.*
- **scopolamine** 1.5 mg Transdermal Every 72 Hours. *A* tropane alkaloid *drug with* muscarinic antagonist *effects for the treatment of* motion sickness *by use of a* transdermal patch.
- **senna** 2 tab Oral Daily Bedtime. *Laxative.*
- **levetiracetam** 500 mg Oral Daily 12 Hours. *An* anticonvulsant *medication used to treat* epilepsy *and marketed under the trade name Keppra.*

September 16, just two days from now. So I called and set it up for 11:15 a.m. that day.

Next, I went through the "Wound Instructions": Keep head incision clean and dry, no scrubbing, no soaking, no gels, no lotions, wear crani cap (medical speak for a shower cap) at all times. Great. I understood all of that.

But last, I had to turn to the daunting and cryptic "SCHEDULED MEDICATIONS" and "MEDICATIONS TO BE TAKEN ONLY AS NEEDED" lists. What a mess!

The list was overwhelming and unusable as is. How could I make a quick reference to make sure Shearlean was getting what she needed when she needed it? I put down the list, got out a pen and some paper, and re-listed, dividing it into daily divisions of doses so I could manage and administer the medication accurately:

- **levofloxacin** 500 mg Oral Daily Bedtime. *A synthetic* chemotherapeutic antibiotic *of the* fluoroquinolone *drug class that is used to treat severe or life-threatening bacterial infections or bacterial infections that have failed to respond to other antibiotic classes.*
- **cholecalciferol** 2000 units Oral Daily. *A form of* vitamin D, *also called vitamin D3. It is structurally similar to* steroids *such as* testosterone, cholesterol, *and* cortisol.
- **estradiol** .25 mg Oral Daily. *A* sex hormone *that is about 10 times as potent as estrone and about 80 times as potent as estriol in its estrogenic effect.*
- **multivitamin with Minerals** 1 Tab Daily.
- **niacin** 500 mg Oral Twice Daily. *Also known as vitamin B3, niacin is an* organic compound *and, depending on the definition used, one of the 40 to 80* essential human nutrients.

As Needed

- **fluticasone** Nasal 1 Spray Each Nostril Daily.
- **oxycodone** 10-15 mg Oral Every 3 Hours for Pain.
- **loratadine** 10 mg Oral Daily.

MORNING

dexamethasone 2 mg.

docusate 200 mg.

omeprazole 20 mg.

senna 1 tab.

multivitamin with minerals 1 tab.

niacin 500 mg.

MIDDAY

cholecalciferol 2000.

estradiol .25 mg.

citalopram 5 mg.

pantprazole 40 mg.

BED

levofloxacin 500 mg.

levetiracetam 500 mg.

senna 1 tab.

dexamethasone 2 mg.

docusate 200 mg.

niacin 500 mg.

EVERY 3 DAYS

scopolamine 1.5 mg transdermal.

I recognized this list of medications was a combination of new drugs for her surgery and tumor, and drugs and supplements she was taking routinely before surgery. The combined list, 17 in all, included all the drugs and supplements that were safely compatible for her to take.

For the new drugs, I read the prescription labels and fact sheets, and looked them up on the Internet to learn more about them, especially side effects. This was a demanding task that would have to be done continually throughout her illness (sometimes daily) as medications changed, dosages were altered, and drugs restarted while others were withdrawn. To help manage Shearlean's drugs, I would be keeping notes on changes in symptoms and side effects so I could answer doctors' questions accurately.

What was her mood or physical or mental condition? Did she have a rash or agitation? To what degree did she feel relief or experience diminished pain?

Every doctor and nurse would want to know exactly what she was taking, in what dosage, how long had she taken it, and for how long it was to continue. I would have to keep a continually updated list. (If we didn't have such a list the doctors would read a list from Shearlean's chart and ask for comments on each medication—I wanted to save us from this tedious and error prone process.)

While I dealt with meds, Janet put a light dinner on the table consisting of a chicken breast and a small portion of mashed potatoes and steamed broccoli. Shearlean was right-handed and her tumor affected the right side of her body. She had difficulty picking up and gripping her fork that first day. She dropped it a couple of times and finally used her left hand to put the fork correctly into her right hand. She stared at the chicken breast not knowing what to do, so Janet leaned across and cut it into small pieces for her. But Shearlean immediately dropped her fork into her lap and couldn't pick it up again, so Janet took it from her lap and set it on her plate. I watched as she struggled again to grip it and it came up upside down. Using her left hand she turned it right side up.

> **PRESCRIPTION MANAGEMENT APPS**
>
> For those with time to prepare for managing prescriptions, there is an app for that. There are apps not only for scheduling medication but also for referencing drug information. To name just two iOS medication management apps for iPhone, there are Pillboxie and MedCoach. For drug information there is Drugs.com's Medication Guide for iOS and Android.

She pulled her fork across her plate, through her food and came up empty, but continued with the empty fork toward her mouth. She missed the opening by a bit and repeated this twice until I finally told her she had no food on her fork. She looked at me blankly. She switched the fork to her left hand but this was more awkward in its own way than her dysfunctional right hand was. But at least this way she could capture a bit of food and move it to her mouth.

As the meal progressed, Shearlean struggled to chew and swallow food, and sometimes choked and spit food back onto her plate. Clearly, she was growing agitated with her difficulty and was tiring from the effort. Leaving most of her food on her plate, she drank all of her ginger ale. Later we learned she was suffering temporary partial facial paralysis that affected chewing and swallowing. In our conversation that night, Shearlean spoke in short halting sentences but with some familiar words distorted by difficulty articulating. She could understand us better than she could speak. Occasionally she would be stymied for a word and lapse into silence and not finish the thought, but we could communicate adequately. At one point, she surprised us with bizarre words with no obvious context whatsoever. We were discussing James Bond movies and Shearlean seemingly in the conversation with us said, "Layer cake." Janet and I looked at each other puzzled, while Shearlean's expression at our reaction said, "What?!" Janet started naming actors who had played James Bond and when she got to the most recent incarnation and named Daniel Craig, Shearlean shouted triumphantly, "*Layer Cake*!" She smiled broadly at our comprehension while Janet and I tried to choke back our laughter.

The more we talked through the evening the more this happened, and our conversation turned into a game of 20 Questions, trying to figure out what she meant. Shearlean was certain she was saying the correct word and so repeated the meaningless word more emphatically. Somehow, Janet had a gift for interpreting Shearlean's meaning and could guess what she was asking for. With Janet's help I would learn in the days to come that "bake" was "ice cream," "whed bed" was "want fed," and "bag" was any type of container—glass, cup, bowl, plate, etc.

My inability to translate her words terrified and frustrated me. I strained to make sense of what she said while she shouted the word repeatedly and clearly: "Bag, bag, bag. BAG!"

Before the brain tumor we could finish each other's sentences and would often simultaneously come up with the same word or phrase. When I left the room one night early after bringing her home, Janet told me later that Shearlean whispered to her, "What's wrong with him?"

When I returned I had a small paper bag in one hand and cereal bowl in the other. I stooped in front of her and thrust out the bag and said, "This is a bag." I withdrew the bag and thrust the bowl in front of her face and said, "This is a bowl. A bowl is not a bag and a bag is not a bowl."

Indignant, Shearlean sat up straight and said, "Bag," looking very satisfied with herself. I moved the bowl forward and she said, "Bag." I put the bag on top of the bowl and she said, "Bag. Bag, bag, bag."

I finally crumpled to the floor laughing as Shearlean broke into a big smile, but refused to laugh out loud. As time went on we shared many big laughs over her choice of words and my confusion. We soon learned that her speech fluctuated with how rested she was.

Fortunately this particular communication problem lasted less than two weeks and never reappeared. But before Janet, her interpreter, went home, Shearlean pleaded with me to make a set of flash cards with the names of everyday items printed on them. We could run through them to help her identify a key word she was seeking, but I never got to it because of her daily improvement.

Soon, after a full night's sleep, Shearlean could speak almost normally for three or four hours before she needed her noon nap. After a nap her speech was good for up to an hour before it started to deteriorate. She had to nap about one hour out of every four and still found it easy to sleep through the night.

The situation with her handwriting was similar to her speech. I asked her to write her name on her third day home while I sat beside her on the couch with a tablet and pen. She began, confident that she could produce her signature, but was shocked to discover she couldn't. Her first attempt was pretty good but she couldn't complete it. She got as far as *Shear...* She started again with the large looping S, but it quickly dribbled into a meaningless scrawl and devolved into a string of figure eights. Handwriting would continue to be an on-and-off function with improvement on par with speech, but like speech, it was impossible to sustain for long. These fluctuations in writing and speech proved to be proportional to fluctuations of edema in her brain.

EDEMA

In all of Shearlean's postoperative MRIs, differing amounts of edema were visible as a cloudy gray area in the vicinity of her surgical site. Dexamethasone and prednisone, powerful steroids, were used to control edema, but their side effects limited their use. It became obvious that fluctuations in brain symptoms were in direct proportion to the extent of edema, which was proportional to the dosage of dexamethasone or prednisone. That's why there were many fluctuations in dexamethasone dosages as Shearlean's symptoms waxed and waned.

MRIs clearly showed a void—an excavated pit—in Shearlean's brain where her glioblastoma tumor had been removed by surgery. The growth of the tumor had put pressure on the surrounding brain tissue, causing seizures and affecting functions controlled by that brain area. While removing the tumor relieved its effects on the brain, surgery itself traumatized a wider area, producing temporary malfunctions in the body. Because of the void created by surgery and trauma to the tissues, edema resulted. Edema is an accumulation of fluid in a body cavity. In this case it is the cavity created by removing the tumor. Within the confines of the skull, accumulating fluid applies pressure to the enclosed brain tissue and interferes with brain functions.

Typing was a little better because when spelling errors crept in I could easily decipher the correct word from the context and make corrections for her. Understanding speech was never her problem. Even right up until the end she understood spoken words.

~

Rather quickly, much to my relief, Shearlean's condition improved steadily throughout September and depending on the time of day, she could appear to be symptom-free to the point that people began to believe I was the patient, not her. I had to wonder what that said about my appearance, but I decided it was just ageism at work because I was an elderly male already past my three score and ten.

~

I was pleased that our September 16 post-op appointment with Dr. Steinberg was before noon, while Shearlean was alert and speaking well. Just the 90-mile drive to Seattle was tiring and our apprehension at being back at the scene of our recent trauma felt tangible. Considering what we had been through over the past week, we thought we should be calmer for a simple appointment, but instead we were on edge.

Many staff recognized us and greeted us warmly when we walked into the office. They told Shearlean how wonderful she looked. When we entered the examination room Dr. Steinberg's resident was waiting for us. He beamed at Shearlean like he was eying a prize specimen (which Shearlean was) and stepped right over to her to begin removing the bandage from her head. A nurse entered with a towel-covered sanitary tray and set it on the stainless steel table beside the doctor. With a few words of approval and encouragement, he donned gloves, uncovered the tray, picked up an implement and began removing the surgical staples that held Shearlean's scalp in place. He blotted the blood that oozed out and finished up quickly—and mercifully. Shearlean was obviously a bit shocked, but it had not hurt.

The resident stepped back, continuing his smooth congenial patter interspersed with occasional admiring remarks about Dr. Steinberg's work. He pushed the tray away and asked Shearlean details about her condition and then launched into a review of coming radiation and chemical therapy. He explained that Dr. Majorski would be in charge of chemotherapy and would be in shortly to talk to us. His speech was brisk but not brusque, efficient and friendly, but he left us rather breathless. The bottom

PLASTIC BRAIN

Science has proven the brain is a highly plastic organ. That is, it is highly adaptable. It readily converts underutilized areas to new functions and adapts other areas to take up functions lost to disease, injury or stroke. Given time, functions lost or destroyed are restored by the brain's self-healing adaptability. An example of this amazing capability was well documented in Jill Bolte Taylor's book "My Stroke of Insight: A Brain Scientist's Personal Journal." The book is her autobiographical account of her recovery from a stroke that was a demonstration of the brain's ability to modify itself, a convincing example of its plasticity.

line was that everything was healing well, and Shearlean's condition was perfect.

We never saw Dr. Steinberg on this visit or afterward. He had done what he did best and his special skills were of no use outside the operating room. Shearlean, I'm certain, would have liked to see him again outside of surgery and when she was fully conscious, but he had moved on to the 250 more patients waiting for him in the next 12 months.

Shortly after the resident left, Dr. Majorski entered. It was our first time meeting him. He was stocky and exuded a certain European reserve and manner that was inconsistent with the extroverted staff we had become accustomed to at the clinic. Dr. Majorski's job was to prescribe Shearlean's Temodar chemo dosage and to monitor her blood chemistry for the duration of radiation therapy. As he began speaking, I instantly got negative vibrations from him because he was so tentative and distracted. Shearlean, however, immediately turned on her charm to recruit a new advocate to her cause. I tried to put my intuition on hold and let her do what she did best—make friends.

Dr. Majorski told us about Temodar, the primary chemotherapy drug. It was a pill to be taken in combination with radiation and then continued at intervals after radiation was completed. I watched Shearlean's reaction as he told us about Dr. Hinton, the Bellingham radiologist with whom his nurse already had made an appointment for us. He described potential radiation and chemo side effects, and explained that he would be monitoring Shearlean's condition and the effects of Temodar in conjunction with the radiologist.

It seemed that nausea was the most profound side effect of Temodar, but that it could be managed with medication. He would write a prescription for both the Temodar and the anti-nausea medications, and see Shearlean again at the end of her radiation treatment in six weeks. Six weeks without seeing the oncologist seemed like a long time to me, but what did I know? Dr. Majorski, the radiologist (Dr. Hinton), and the testing laboratories would share information with each other to continually monitor her condition. I made a mental note to figure out how to track and communicate with all of these different parties. It seemed to me like something could easily slip through the cracks if I didn't stay on top of things.

Learning what lay before us was a lot to take in. Shearlean

was attentive and asked obvious questions while I listened closely and took notes. To me, driving to Seattle two hours each way for *monitoring*, even every few weeks could be a hardship, but I didn't want to be the one to break up Shearlean's team. Nevertheless, Dr. Majorski's manner and tone reminded me of deadbeat corporate executives I had encountered who said all the right things, but the bottom line was that they never performed. I found I just didn't trust him. Some people were sycophants whose primary skill was avoiding being dismissed. I hoped he wasn't such a person.

When we checked out of the department, we scheduled our next appointment with Dr. Majorski and asked about the Temodar

---

TO MAKE THE BEST OF THE HEALTHCARE SYSTEM

My advice regarding how to make the best of the healthcare system is:

- Be alert for problems at every step of care and treatment. No one cares as much as you do about yourself and your loved one.
- Some providers are better than others so don't be afraid to change if you are dissatisfied.
- Support reform that will replace the existing system with one that everyone can understand and use, and that minimizes profit as the purpose of dealing with disease and death.
- Prepare for the end of your life, or else. Or else the state or a stranger will make end-of-life decisions for you because you are unable to.
- Acknowledge that acute disease requires different care than chronic disease.
- Know your healthcare system before you must use it.
- Don't rely on your provider to understand how to use your healthcare system for your benefit, because there are too many systems that change too often for providers to keep up with. And not all existing systems are equal. Some are easier to use and provide better care than others. Choose wisely.
- Monitor the functioning of your healthcare system and the care you receive as it occurs.
- Know what you want in the way of care and treatment, and define the results you hope to achieve.
- Demand the most you can get from the system you are in and do not accept less than you want and deserve.

---

prescription. Dr. Majorski's nurse appeared and said the prescription would be sent to us by mail later, after the doctor computed the correct dose. It was past noon now and we both felt spent and were eager to get back home to rest, so I didn't think to ask more about the prescription process. If all we did in one day was have a medical appointment, we were exhausted. I think it was because of the tension that started when we awoke and mounted until the appointment was over. Shearlean was also affected by how she felt from medication and symptoms. With me, I think the exhaustion was from a combination of being on high alert for problems and feeling empathy for Shearlean. Since at least I wasn't sick, I never suffered as much as Shearlean did, but she could crash when we got home after an appointment and I couldn't because I had so much to do.

By the time we left our appointment that day, it was clear to both of us that Shearlean was no longer a patient of University Medical or of Dr. Steinberg. The surgeons were done with us. She was barely even a patient of Dr. Majorski. I could see and hear the letdown she felt about not really being under anyone's direct observation, but we both understood that we needed to move on, and so did her surgical team. Surgery was over and treatment would now be in other hands. Still, we both felt a pang of loss and disappointment.

With surgery clearly behind us, Shearlean's biggest hurdle was passed and we could expect recovery. The signs of her getting better became abundant, as the early growth of spring overwhelms the bleakness of winter. By two weeks after surgery, Shearlean's problems with swallowing, chewing, using utensils and finding correct words faded away. They might surge back if she were especially tired, but they became rare enough that we could ignore them or work around them with scheduled rest and other coping methods. She would remain substantially free of post-op symptoms for nearly the length of her illness, until two months preceding her death.

II

Caregiving and the Healthcare System

CHAPTER SEVEN

Communicating With the World

"I thank the universe and I thank all the people who have prayed for me. I am so grateful and I do believe I am healed."

BEFORE THE SURGERY, we had told only Shearlean's sister and nephew and my sister about our situation. It was now time to fully inform other family, friends and colleagues—to tell the world—about Shearlean's condition now that surgery had succeeded and she was recovering at home, preparing to proceed with long-term treatment.

Is there a perfect way to break such news? Probably not, but every effort should be made to be thorough and accurate, and not raise more questions than are answered.

Both being journalists, we agreed to tell a straightforward, matter-of-fact and upbeat story such as we might write about someone else for a general audience. It was news now that she was through the surgery, not pending drama. We wanted the facts to speak for themselves and not impose our feelings on others. So when we returned from our post-op appointment I sat down and wrote the first of many emails about Shearlean's condition and treatment:

Dear Family, Friends and Colleagues

September 16, 2009

While in Kenya, Africa, this past summer, Shearlean had what later proved to be convulsions or seizures caused by a glioblastoma brain tumor. This was her second year in Kenya as part of a Western Washington University (WWU) faculty group that took students to Africa to help work with high school girls orphaned by AIDS.

It began at a Maasai Mara safari camp with one seizure. The pain from that first episode subsided quickly and Shearlean felt normal enough for us to carry on with our sight-seeing, but before long, she began having repeated attacks until she had as many as 15 within 10 hours.

As soon as we returned home, an MRI showed a brain tumor, probably a glioblastoma, a very aggressive tumor unique to the brain. She was told she might survive one to two years.

We immediately applied to the tumor board of the neurosurgery department of University Medical Center. Surgery was scheduled for September 10.

On the day of the surgery, I was able to stay with her right up until they took her into the operating room. She was in surgery for more than four hours while they mapped her brain to identify the functions of areas of the brain around the tumor. Because her tumor was located deep in the left side of her brain in the area that controls movement, sensations and speech, a mistake in the movement area could paralyze her right side (left brain controls right body), a mistake in the sensation area (our five senses) could result in bizarre convulsions, or in the speech area, she could lose her ability to speak, understand and write words. Since a glioma tumor grows integrally with the brain, removing the tumor removes a portion of the brain.

The good news from the surgery was that they were able to remove 98 percent of the tumor (none remained visible on the post-op MRI) and Shearlean lost only a little verbal ability, seizures are minor and there are small difficulties using her right hand. The bad news was that the tumor had doubled in size in the three weeks between the diagnostic MRI on August 21 and surgery on September 10.

Shearlean was discharged from the hospital on Monday, September 14 just five days after open brain surgery.

The post-operative tests have confirmed the tumor to be a glioblastoma stage IV, the worst of the worst. Shearlean has been told she might have 12 months to live if she chooses to follow surgery with six weeks of radiation therapy combined with ongoing chemotherapy. That said, the doctors remind us that she is unique and so is her tumor (there has never been anyone like her or a tumor like hers) and so she might do a lot better than the 12 months average. Shearlean is very determined to beat the odds and I know she is very strong and capable of overcoming even the greatest obstacles.

By choosing surgery immediately and following up with radiation combined with ongoing chemotherapy, Shearlean and I can look forward to some very good times together and being able to get the most and the best out of however much time is available. We have been together since 1968 and have shared a terrific life. We plan to go on sharing every minute of every remaining day.

We are still laughing, having fun and making plans for new adventures and good times. We both say cancer is just another of life's big adventures like so many other adventures we have shared and thrived on.

Here is a word from Shearlean:

Friday, Aug. 21, 2009, when my doctor told me I had a brain tumor, that it was brain cancer, and that I may be dead in a year, I went home, cried for two days, bought books on dying and put my affairs in order.

Sunday I awoke, dry-eyed and with a fierce determination to do everything in my power to prolong my life. I believe a patient is more than a chart, a diagnosis, and an MRI report. I am a unique individual who has overcome great obstacles, beat tremendous odds, and accomplished the impossible.

Shearlean and Bob

~

Life with cancer was complicated. Treatment added layers of complexity and confusion that threatened to overwhelm what remained of ordinary life and everyday routine. It was nearly impossible to adequately communicate to others what we were going through and how we were navigating the healthcare maze with its inundation of information and demands. Patient and caregiver struggled daily just to keep up with what was required merely to stay alive.

Surgery was just the beginning of treatment. Now we were to begin a protocol of outpatient treatment combining radiation and chemotherapy that would evolve into chemotherapy only, with no end date. We were warned that the protocol was urgent because timing and continuity were critical.

While still recovering from surgery, Shearlean was facing a regimen of powerful medications, coping with the effects of radiation and chemotherapy, and trying to piece together a quality of life to make it all worthwhile. I was, as I would be for the months to come, managing medications, diet, medical bills, schedules and a never-ending bureaucracy. I didn't realize it, but my first email informing our circle about the surgery would be my primary link to the world outside of what had to do with Shearlean's treatment and care.

One week after discharge from University Medical, I wrote the first Update on Shearlean's treatment:

UPDATE 1: Cancer Center
September 20, 2009

Hello All

Shearlean is getting ready to start her radiation. Tomorrow she will go to the Cancer Center to have a mask made that she will wear for each radiation treatment. The mask is a tool for making sure each radiation treatment hits the target and is geometrically accurate. Apparently the mask-making process is a claustrophobic experience and she is advised to take Valium before it gets started.

On Tuesday, September 22, she goes to the hospital's main building in Bellingham to a radiation planning session for setting up the parameters for each radiation treatment. Again, this procedure ensures that each radiation treatment will be identical and hits the target every time.

We were advised to get all the flu shots available because Shearlean's treatment will make her vulnerable to every infection and ailment that comes along. Along this line, Shearlean will be avoiding contact with people in general in order to prevent exposure to disease. Unfortunately, going to the hospital five days a week for six weeks for radiation treatments means going to one of the most disease-ridden places in existence, but that's unavoidable. She intends to take what precautions she can, though.

When she starts radiation, on September 28, she also starts chemo, so it will be a double whammy to her immune system and defenses.

We can do radiation here in Bellingham, but will have to do chemo supervised from Seattle. Chemo consists of taking a (self-administered) pill called Temodar. It was developed especially to treat the glioblastoma Shearlean is battling. Consequently, we will have to go to Seattle but only once every four weeks to meet with the doctor there directing her therapy.

Thankfully, after six weeks of intense radiation and chemo, Shearlean gets a four-week break from treatment and then resumes a regimen of self-administered reduced chemo that goes on indefinitely.

Shearlean and I are counting on the reduced chemo period, with its treatment-free intervals of four weeks, to do the things we want without being on a leash for treatment. Shearlean's choice to have surgery immediately after diagnosis was meant to give her the highest quality of life and best functionality for the longest time. Any options that increase survival time at the cost of quality and functionality are options she has decided to reject. We think that the treatment program she has decided to undertake ensures the best use of the time available for continuing to live the same fulfilling life she has always enjoyed.

She remains very positive and optimistic, and is looking forward to all the benefits her chosen treatment promises.

Bob Duke

~

To free me to care for Shearlean, I hired a housekeeper. With daily radiation treatments and dosing with potent chemicals, Shearlean was forced to withdraw into her meditation and self-nurturing and do for herself what no one else could do for her: stay positive and practice alternative healing techniques.

Meanwhile, Tuesday, I got on the phone to secure the chemo drug, Temodar, and confronted my first potentially deadly healthcare behemoth: RxB, a specialty mail-order pharmacy. My frustration level became so intense that I had to speak on the phone out of sight and sound of Shearlean to spare her the agony of hearing about the threat against her life RxB's incompetency proffered.

I wrote about the ordeal in my next note to our circle of friends and family:

UPDATE 2: Radiation and Chemo Day 1

September 28, 2009

Hello All

After I fussed at Shearlean about doing laundry when we had hired someone to do such work for us, she decided she had to refocus (and stay focused) on a plan for getting well.

Here's her plan from the journal she is keeping:

- *Goal: Eradicate cancer*
- *Do radiation*
- *Do chemo*
- *Get a lot of rest*
- *Exercise*
- *Watch nutrition*
- *Do no unnecessary work*
- *Accept help*
- *Take naps*
- *Write journal 2X per day*
- *Practice imagery therapy*
- *Watch comedies and old movies*
- *Do fun things such as bake a pie, eat a scone*
- *De-stress everyday*
- *Stop! (Doing anything I shouldn't)*
- *Decide about my future*

- *Write thank you notes*
- *Call people*
- *Listen to music*
- *Meditate 2X per day*

At 10:50 a.m. this morning Shearlean had her first of 30 radiation treatments with Dr. Hinton at the Cancer Center in Bellingham. The actual radiation treatment takes less than 15 minutes, but the first appointment took nearly two hours, after meetings with other staff to work out details of ongoing treatment. Radiation will be completed in six weeks and no other radiation is anticipated.

Chemotherapy also started today. It was planned and scheduled to coincide with the beginning of radiation. She is taking a capsule called Temodar that was developed especially for treating glioblastoma tumors, the kind Shearlean has. She will take her chemo dose at night before bed. Temodar is powerful, maybe more powerful than the radiation, as far as side effects go. We won't know the full extent of the impact of combined radiation/chemo for several days. Since Shearlean is so healthy and has no allergies to medication, we think she might get by with minimal side effects.

Our only near-setback since surgery was getting the prescription filled for Temodar from her chemo doctor and the pharmacies involved. It was a nightmare, and we had nearly a dozen doctors, nurses and others trying to help us. I spent more than four hours receiving and making phone calls on Friday trying to get Shearlean's prescription filled and delivered in time to take on Monday morning.

The short version of the story is that the chemo doctor, Dr. Majorski, had plenty of time (since September 16) to write the prescription but didn't do it until Tuesday, September 22. The chemo doctor's nurse sent the prescription to "RxW" mail-order pharmacy, which sat on it for three days because it came without instructions and they didn't know what to do with it. On Friday afternoon, (we're now talking about three days ago) RxW sent the prescription to "RxB"—another mail-order pharmacy—which took no action on it because "the prescription lacks sufficient chart notes and lacks sufficient authorization for the quantity ordered." No RxB employee or any other healthcare professional contacted us. We had to take all the initiative (thus, my four hours on the phone). In the end, RxB shipped the medication overnight by FedEx for delivery Saturday afternoon. For this big favor RxB charged us $23.

It certainly is a troubled industry. If the doctors, nurses, pharmacists, and insurers would cooperate for the benefit of the patient, we would have had our medication without all this stress.

I hope I won't have to write another editorial to you during the remainder of Shearlean's recovery.

Bob Duke

During this time, friends became adamant about caring for us, better aware, perhaps, than we were about our needs. I had promised myself to welcome help when I saw the need for it, but we couldn't let people come in the house until we knew how Shearlean's immune system would react to chemo and radiation. Dinners delivered to our doorstep would be a blessing. It all depended on Shearlean, though.

Fortunately, Shearlean settled easily into her radiation and chemo with only mild side effects. We had heard such stories of the hell of radiation and chemo that we dreaded much worse. When we realized Shearlean was adjusting better than expected, we decided we didn't have to be so extra careful to stay away from human contact.

UPDATE 3: Accepting Help
September 30, 2009

Hello All

Long before surgery, Shearlean began avoiding exposure to anything that might make her sick and cause her surgery to be delayed or imperil her recovery. It was September 3 when we started being cautious, and so it will soon be a month of self-imposed isolation. She continued her precautions until she got experience with radiation and chemo.

Today we talked with Shearlean's radiologist here in Bellingham and had the chance to ask some questions, mainly about exposure to germs from people and objects. The good news is that radiation is not a major factor for her immune system and Temodar (the chemo pill) has a good history of minimum immune system impact. We can expect to safely visit with healthy people on an individual basis. Things to continue to avoid are schools, airliners, restaurants, children, students—basically any crowded, confined space.

As backup information about her general health, the radiologist pointed out that weekly blood tests (required for chemo therapy) will reveal whether Shearlean's immune system is being adversely affected by chemo because it will show whether her white blood cell count is dropping. If that happens, she will have adequate warning to isolate herself again.

So starting next week we look forward to visiting with friends again. We are relying on our friends to warn us if they think they might have a bug.

We asked our "Meals for Shearlean" captain to pass the word that the Dukes last needed meal will be October 5.

See you soon.
Bob Duke

~

With our self-imposed infection quarantine rescinded we could now be more optimistic about treatment and begin to plan ahead. The prospect of maintaining a somewhat normal life and resuming routine activities over the next year or so now seemed realistic. I was lucky not to know what lay ahead in terms of managing the details of Shearlean's care. Ignorance can give a person moments of freedom and relief, however fleeting they may be.

CHAPTER EIGHT

Help's Many Forms

"People are bringing us food, sending us positive energy and I feel extremely hopeful. Not scared, but ready to eradicate my cancer."

THOUGH INDIVIDUALLY and as a couple, we prided ourselves on being self-sufficient, Shearlean and I were realistic enough to recognize that we needed help. While I could cook and clean with the best of them, and had the prime responsibility for those chores during the last several years, I couldn't manage all of the chores along with Shearlean and her illness, too. Everything had suddenly grown enormously complicated.

We had been renovating our house for the past few years with the plan to sell it when Shearlean retired and was eligible for Medicare at 65 in June 2011. Now, not knowing whether she could ever work again and being unclear about what our income might be that far into the future, I decided we had to sell the house as soon as possible. To put it on the market, though, I had to finish the remaining renovations. I wanted to get the best price possible. I had to repair the fence, replace the deck, make some crawl space drainage repairs, finish interior painting and replace kitchen flooring and living room carpet. I was doing a lot of the work myself, but contracting out what I couldn't do. I had subcontractors to deal with, materials to purchase, jobs to coordinate and money to budget. And on top of it all, we had to also find a replacement home and move.

To help with housework I hired Lisa, a young woman I'd first met when she was cooking on a charter yacht in Southeast Alaska. Prior to looking for more exciting work on a boat, she had been a cook in a Buddhist monastery where she was known by her Buddhist name of Ensan. After cooking for a season on the ocean-kayaking mother ship I also crewed on, she moved to Bellingham for the winter where I ran into her again and learned she was looking for work. I hired her for $15 an hour to come in four hours every week to clean, do laundry, change beds, vacuum and prep meal ingredients for me to cook.

Shearlean wasn't pleased at first to have someone doing so much. This took me a bit by surprise because we'd had housekeepers before, and agreed that we needed to have help now. She chafed at Lisa's pleasantries and the hubbub of vacuuming, moving furniture, and the general clatter of house cleaning. Since Lisa was a tranquilizing influence on me as soon as she walked in the door, I couldn't make sense of Shearlean's reaction to her. Lisa was quiet, competent and serene; qualities that I rightly or wrongly attributed to her long Buddhist training in Japan.

I could easily recognize Shearlean's agitation and each time Lisa arrived, I went to her immediately to soothe her. Not only was Shearlean irritated with someone being in the house, she was annoyed with herself for being irritated in the first place. She knew it was not rational, and she recognized Lisa's quiet demeanor and thoughtful ways, but sometimes just couldn't cope with having another person present. Usually when Lisa arrived, Shearlean disappeared into the bedroom and watched TV to avoid confronting her own annoyance. I explained this to Lisa and she was clearly sympathetic (and since she would be starting registered nurse's training in the spring of 2010, she even had a professional interest in situations such as ours). I asked her not to ask Shearlean any questions about housework (ask me instead) and not to initiate any small talk. Basically, speak with Shearlean only when spoken to. Lisa graciously accepted my request and, over time, Shearlean settled into the routine and grew comfortable with Lisa.

~

While Lisa was one easily managed piece to our "help" puzzle, the meal brigade was made up of several people, most of them individuals Shearlean had worked with for 10 years. When they found out about the tumor, they were as shocked and felt as helpless as we did and felt they had to do something. Although at first I stood in their way, insisting we didn't need their help, I ultimately realized that as Shearlean's colleagues, they had a stake in her welfare too.

We began accepting all offers for meals.

Our friends each had their own take on how best to deliver a meal, but one couple was determined to raise it to an art form. Our fussy friend Herman showed up one night, with his partner Leo, and three bulging plastic shopping bags. They were both practically dancing with excitement in the circle of the bright porch light. "Wait 'til you see what we have," Herman cooed as Leo arranged the three bags on the stoop and deftly lowered each bag like a theatrical curtain to reveal the sparkling containers inside.

Shearlean crept out of our living room and farther down the short entry hall for a better look at what was now partially hidden by the doorsill. Herman was ready with a list of ingredients and instructions that he insisted on reciting so we would know what we were in for. He read from his list as Leo squatted on the stoop and waved his hand over the appropriate bag and container that corresponded with the narration.

As prelude to his elaborate presentation, Herman proudly pointed out that nothing from *his* dinner had to be washed or returned, it was all throw-away.

It was clear that Herman and Leo had raided the salad bar and deli counter of our local gourmet market for luxury plastic and paper containers, plates, utensils, napkins and plastic glasses which they now proudly offered us. I hoped they wouldn't get in trouble on our account.

As a final flourish, Leo swung a shoulder bag from his back, unzipped the insulated bag and handed me a chilled bottle of Shearlean's favorite white wine. I gathered up the three bags by their handles, while Herman and Leo backed down the sidewalk, still talking as they went. I half expected them to bow, but they did a smart about-face and got into Herman's car and waved as it pulled away from the curb.

Each of the half-dozen couples bringing us meals had developed its individual shtick, but none so elaborate or amusing as Herman's and Leo's.

At first I was grateful for visits such as this, but, as well intentioned and practical as the meals were, I became swamped with trying to coordinate and schedule the generous platoon of well-wishers. Managing donated meals took more time and energy than cooking and cleaning up would have. Now that I had accepted, though, there seemed to be no turning back.

Once the *Meals for Shearlean* captain, a colleague of Shearlean's from another department at the university, realized how I was struggling to manage, she created a spreadsheet schedule online where all meal donors could access and post their meal dates a week or a month in advance. Donors could see what dates were available, and I could see who was delivering what and on which day. This way the meal donors could manage themselves. I would know which days I might have to cook, and I could see what time a donated meal would be delivered. By knowing who was coming next, I could have food containers ready to return to the right person. This smoothed out the process for me considerably.

Delicious and lovingly prepared food was delivered now with little hassle at the convenience of both the provider and the recipient. Everything proceeded smoothly after that, and when we were well recovered from the worst effects of chemotherapy, it was easy to wind down the project.

From this first encounter with accepting help I learned two important lessons in caregiving: First, a caregiver should accept help as soon as it is offered because it may be too late by the time he realizes he needs it. And second, even as he is accepting it, he should be cautious, because help is not help if it increases the caregiver's burden.

Many anonymous things turned up on our doorstep during the meal delivery time. Occasionally there were bags of marijuana, flowers, houseplants, books, CDs and newspapers. Instead of food, one faculty member who lived nearby delivered the journalism department's copies of The New York Times and The Wall Street Journal.

It seemed to be a nearly universal perception that marijuana eases the effects of radiation and chemotherapy, and improves the appetite, but in Shearlean's case it had a negative effect. Because she had a brain tumor, she was nervous about any unusual brain activity (or inactivity) for fear it might signal some sort of symptom or malfunction having to do with the effects of the tumor. Though she tried it, Shearlean found that marijuana made her paranoid about how her brain was doing. So we spread the word about the cannabis—thanks, but no thanks.

I smugly decided that now that I had given in to accepting help and was dealing with it constructively, I had mastered the role of caregiver. To my ultimate chagrin and near devastation I learned the hard way that accepting help that was offered to me was not the same as proactively seeking help. My hubris was thinking that the help was for me and failed to recognize what help and encouragement Shearlean might need apart from me.

For example, I was frankly amazed at the powerful effect cards, notes, email and flowers had on how Shearlean felt. At times the effect was greater than the most powerful medicine. Cards and flowers came not only from friends, relatives and colleagues with whom Shearlean had routine contact, but from alumni and current students, and distant relatives she hadn't seen in 30 years. From their school in Kenya where Shearlean taught summers, a couple of African girls sent long letters of sympathy written in block letters with pencil. Refrigerator magnet slogans, enclosed with cards, offered upbeat and life-affirming sayings and quotations. Boxes arrived containing self-help books and meditation CDs, an American Cancer Society Relay for Life medal, and once, a glass block etched with "Learn from Yesterday, Live for Today and Hope for Tomorrow."

As she opened each card and letter Shearlean intently studied its message, often repeating the ritual two or three times before putting the card aside. Frequently, she returned to the card a few hours or a few days later, handling it again as happily as the first time. She set the cards on the edge of tables, shelves, the mantle in the living room and on the dining room sideboard. Eventually, we ran out of space, so I ran strings around the office walls near the ceiling and hung the cards by their spines for easy viewing.

When it came time to move to our new home, I put all of the cards and memorabilia into a large attractive wooden box to take with us. Periodically, Shearlean rummaged through the box, looking at items and rereading messages.

"This is my first aid kit," she told me once. When she was feeling down she could get it out and remind herself of all the thoughtful people who cared enough to send their wishes and prayers for her recovery.

~

Help and encouragement from friends and hired help weren't all we needed. We had some needs, both of us, which only professionals could satisfy. As part of her goal to be the perfect patient, and thereby reap all the benefits of the best of care, Shearlean saw a speech therapist on October 14, 2009, about a month after surgery. She was motivated by a desire to get an evaluation of her functionality and to learn what therapy might be available to help her heal.

Aphasia was a general term for the consequence of her cancer and surgery on the language center of her left brain. It was the loss of ability to understand or express speech due to brain damage, and included loss of skills in reading, writing, speaking, typing and listening. As a journalist and teacher, Shearlean relied heavily on these abilities, and her employment, hence her insurance coverage, depended on whether she could perform the duties of chair of the Journalism Department.

Shearlean was excited about the prospect of a therapy that might improve her condition, but like so much else the news she got was mixed. When she got home in mid-afternoon from her speech therapy appointment, she flopped down on the sofa looking tired and disappointed.

"There's nothing the speech therapist can do," she said. Then she added, "She told me that any kind of excitement—anger, sadness, emotions, fatigue, frustration, pressure, stress and anxiety—could make my aphasia worse. She told me to avoid groups because they could be more challenging than one-on-one interaction."

The therapist said that because of Shearlean's advanced education and career, she had an exceptionally large vocabulary, and she could easily find substitute words when trying to speak. She was already doing all the right things to manage and improve her condition.

Then brightening, and with a bit of the verbal swagger she showed whenever she was praised, she said, "The therapist stated that anyone suffering from serious aphasia could not take notes and converse simultaneously as I was doing with her." Settling into the sofa and letting her weariness show, she added, "She said I would probably improve with time and did not need therapy."

She seemed rather glum, considering no treatment was recommended, and yet I was pleased that she was in such relatively good condition.

In retrospect, I can see that the therapist's prognosis proved accurate. Over the entire course of her illness, Shearlean's language abilities remained good, though highly dependent on her overall emotional condition and physical strength. Though she almost ceased speaking during the last two months of her life, her muteness was the result of painful swelling of her tongue and throat, not brain disease.

In addition to the speech therapist, a friend of Shearlean's referred her to a colleague who specialized in psychotherapy for terminally ill patients. Shearlean saw this therapist regularly for months and was pleased to talk to someone in whom she had confidence. I offered to attend meetings, but was never invited. I had no idea what Shearlean and her counselor talked about because I never asked and was never told. I knew that if she ever wanted to talk about it she would, but I also knew Shearlean had a private side she didn't share with anyone, and I respected that.

We always had an intimate and trusting relationship, but there were always the three of us: me, her, and us. Her? As a child Shearlean was the little adult in a dysfunctional Appalachian miner's family. College and a profession were her means of escaping poverty and an ordinary southern rural woman's life. She took herself and her profession seriously, and so I'd better take it seriously too.

Me? I was from a small river valley mill town south of Pittsburgh, Pennsylvania, where boys were advised to leave town when they turned 18 because there was no future for them there. I was bent on seeing the world and finding adventure. Nothing should prevent me from taking off for a week or two for some place I had never been to do something new and exciting. Conventional family life, such as I had grown up in, was not for me.

Us? We were a couple who believed in each other's dreams

and saw no reason why we each could not have what we wanted. We supported each other's goals and recognized the other as an interesting person with whom to spend time and share things. Time apart was never a problem and time together was always the best. We joked that what we both needed was a homemaker to take care of our home and us while we are off doing things.

A few years before Shearlean was diagnosed with cancer, my middle-aged primary care doctor lost his wife at age 49 to kidney cancer, leaving behind two preteen children. Because I knew he spoke from personal experience, I needed no persuasion myself to accept his advice about maintaining my own mental and emotional health. The caregiver is prone to depression and illness, too. My doctor put me on generic Prozac and recommended I stay on it for the duration of Shearlean's illness. He also referred me to a psychotherapist I saw three times over the months. We talked mainly about books, authors and philosophy, and a little about Shearlean's situation. The meetings helped me to verbalize many otherwise unspoken thoughts about life and death, sadness and optimism, and feelings. After three visits I felt we were already retracing earlier discussions and I knew he had already made a positive report to my doctor, so I said I would make a fourth appointment if I needed one, but I never did. Still, I was learning how to take care of myself along with taking care of my patient.

CHAPTER NINE

Struggling Through the Healthcare Maze

"Bob! He is patient, hopeful, loving, good, kind and I love him so much."

WHILE I WAS LEARNING to care and be cared for, Shearlean was proceeding through her treatment. Besides being the author of our Temodar prescription fiasco, our assigned University Medical chemo doctor, Dr. Majorski, never answered a phone, returned voice mail messages or responded to faxes. I took these issues as signs of more problems to come. Though I hated the prospect of disrupting Shearlean's care and severing her connection to University Medical, I foresaw worse if I didn't find a new doctor. With Shearlean's approval I wrote a letter canceling our upcoming appointment in preparation for breaking ties with him altogether. While my letter was in the mail, a letter from him arrived telling us he would not be available on our

COPING STRATEGY

I had resolved at the outset of Shearlean's illness to instantly challenge any problem. I believed that if I deferred dealing with a problem, I would never be able to get back to it. I didn't want anything to build or accumulate and to get out of control. That was why I started out and remained aggressive and confrontational the entire time. I think it was the right choice and would do so again. Nothing snowballed into an avalanche of disaster, but there were close calls, such as RxB.

appointment day because he would be at a conference. This was my confirmation that firing him was the right thing.

UPDATE 4: Obstacles to Care
October 19, 2009

Hello All

As you know, it's been two months since Shearlean's diagnosis. She continues doing very well with radiation and chemo with little or no side effects.

Unfortunately the biggest obstacle to her treatment has been one doctor who seems to be unable to write a fillable prescription. It is not all his fault because he has an ally in the mail-order pharmacy we are required to use, which also seems incapable of keeping anything straight. What makes this especially critical is that her chemo and radiation are done simultaneously and unless both are in sync neither can be done properly. So having chemo prescription problems not only affects chemo treatment, it also affects radiation.

Because of the importance of the timing of her treatment, we made a big decision to change chemo doctors. We felt that starting over again with a new doctor (one not part of the original surgical and treatment team) was less risky than sticking with the marginally performing Dr. Majorski who was assigned to her a month ago.

We told our radiation doctor about our decision, and he referred us to a local oncologist and even made the appointment for us. We will see the new doctor October 21—the same day we would have seen the troublesome doctor. A major bonus is that this new doctor is in Bellingham while the one we dismissed was two hours away in Seattle.

On another front, friends organized "Meals on Wheels for the Dukes" and so we have had the wonderful and interesting experience of having dinners delivered to our doorstep for the past month. What a terrific variety of food we were able to experience. It was very impressive to see how innovative people were in packaging meals for us with containers that didn't need to be washed or returned to their owners. We had food of every description, some of it dishes we had never heard of and sometimes we weren't sure how they should be served. Some people provided elaborate instructions for combining ingredients (thankfully) and explanations of the origin of some ingredients.

During this period our refrigerator was overflowing. We requested that meals be large enough so that we would have leftovers for future meals.

Originally, we were getting dinners every day, but it proved to be too much so we asked for meals only on Monday, Wednesday and Friday.

The meals really helped out because they saved us a lot of energy and ensured that we had well-balanced meals. While people delivering meals couldn't come in the house because we worried about Shearlean picking up germs, we nevertheless got to see a lot of people and Shearlean could wave to them through the window.

One of the volunteers offered to coordinate the meals among all the providers so we wouldn't get too many meals at one time or get nothing sometimes. Her efforts at organizing things kept us from being buried in salad greens and enabled us to request an occasional dessert. Many times dinners included a bottle of wine.

We asked that the meal delivery be stopped by the end of October because we felt we were able to do for ourselves, since treatment had become routine and we had recovered our strength.

Another wonderful thing about the meals was that they enabled us to get to know another side of friends and associates that we would have never been able to learn any other way. There is something special about the kind of care you experience from people cooking meals for you when you can't do for yourself.

On November 6 Shearlean will be done with radiation and chemo, but will start chemo on a monthly basis after a four-week hiatus. Thank you for your continued thoughts and prayers.

Bob Duke

~

Radiation was cumulative and insidious. Shearlean would still be suffering from its fluctuating effects in ways impossible to anticipate up to a year after her radiation treatment ended. For example, edema—excess fluid in body tissue or cavities—resulted from the radiation that killed cancer cells. This fluid caused pressure on the surrounding brain, which produced seizure-like symptoms similar to the effects of cancer. Edema is treated with a powerful steroid, dexamethasone, but it has the undesirable side effect of suppressing the body's immune system and so exposing the patient to other potential dangers.

Steroids were powerful and insidious too. The good and bad effects were profound; Shearlean might be without pain, have a good appetite and be free of tumor symptoms, or she might be unable to eat, be fighting severe pain with narcotic meds, and experiencing fear that her tumor had returned because of recurring symptoms. Using steroids was a delicate balancing act between immediate benefits and ultimate ruin of the body's own anti-inflammatory mechanism. Taking dexamethasone for a long time may suppress natural hormone production of the adrenal gland, resulting in a life-long dependence on artificial hormones, but with a terminal prognosis, life-long is a short time. The decision to continue taking dexamethasone was an easy one for Shearlean because she had already elected palliative care for quality of life and that outweighed the negative effects of dexamethasone.

Our palliative care goals helped deal with such tradeoffs by enabling Shearlean to decide what treatment risks and rewards she would tolerate.

UPDATE 5: Body in Turmoil

October 24, 2009

Hello All

Surprises and paradoxes continue to visit us. Occasional setbacks have to be expected of course, but Shearlean has been getting praise from all of her healthcare providers. A radiation technician treating her but not familiar with her case asked at the end of treatment whether she was going back to her office when treatment was over, as though she had just come from work and had a minor condition. When she told him of her recent surgery he was awed.

Some of the people Shearlean works with have the impression she will be back as department chair after one quarter off because she seems so normal—so herself. Radiation and chemo oncologists have also remarked on her lack of side effect symptoms and how well she is tolerating post-surgery treatment. She is driving to her own appointments, whereas others with her same condition seldom drive again.

Shearlean loves praise, thrives on encouragement, and likes

setting high standards, so all of this positive feedback and odds-beating performance just gets her pumped up and determined to do even better. Beating the odds and being a model patient are foremost among Shearlean's goals, so all of this success has been a huge and beneficial motivator.

As good as all of that sounds (sounds good to me, too), it doesn't tell the whole story. Everyone evolves differently through this kind of illness and treatment. During the past week or so she has been losing the hair that had been growing back on her head. She is more tired and needs more naps to keep up her energy. She is achy and feels kind of dull. There are persistent headaches and nighttime sleep isn't as easy. Nausea has crept in and become chronic. She has little desire to eat and even the smell of food is unpleasant.

She has seen a nutritionist and is finding a variety of palatable things she can tolerate—ice cream, sherbet, saltines, juices, bananas, rice and other mild foods. All of those dinner meals so many friends brought to our doorstep that Shearlean relished and looked forward to would be dreaded now if they were still coming. She wouldn't be able to eat them and the savory odors would drive her to the back of the house to avoid them.

While radiation is still quick and painless, it now has a price and she will be glad when it ends November 6. Chemo hadn't previously affected her appetite, and so she had no use for anti-nausea meds, but now she is taking them daily. She was doing brisk walks of up to a mile and huffing and puffing her way up a nearby hill, but now walks are daunting.

Keeping her body in turmoil is her doctor's desire to get her off of the steroids that control brain edema. She cut back from four tablets per day to half of one tablet to none a few days ago but paid the price of flu-like symptoms (whole body ache, headache) and was forced back onto the steroid.

I want to let everyone know this so they will understand she is still in the midst of treatment and has a long road to travel. Things can change quickly and are not as rosy as earlier reports indicated. The way she may sound on the phone for a few minutes is not a true measure of how she is doing over 24 hours.

Shearlean is still in the top one percentile of patients who have gone through this disease and treatment, but now she is more like the mere mortals with whom she keeps company. Overall, I can't say things have gotten worse. Rather they have gotten tougher, more demanding and less predictable.

I'll stay in touch and you please do the same.

Bob Duke

UPDATE 6: Settling Into Routine Treatment

November 4, 2009

Hello All

Thank you everyone for your continuing care for Shearlean. Your cards, emails, phone calls, visits and interest have a tangible and positive effect on her mood and sense of wellbeing. There is still a long and twisted path ahead, and your companionship along the way makes the journey easier because it is shared.

Shearlean is back on top again. Her relapse seems to have been caused by going off dexamethasone, a steroid that controls the brain swelling that results from radiation. She needs to be weaned off of it eventually, but the first attempt was premature. A nurse recognized the combination of symptoms as typical to premature cessation and immediately put her back on the steroid. She still has little taste, so food is unappealing, but she continues to eat enough to maintain her weight. She's lost just three pounds. Here's a typical day's food: a banana and yogurt smoothie, chocolate Ensure, chocolate protein drink, half of a baked potato with butter, vegetable or chicken noodle soup with saltines, fruit-flavored yogurt, rice pudding and vanilla ice cream. When she is hungry (and not nauseous) she might eat all of that in one day. When she is nauseous, she forces herself to eat small portions of the same things.

Thanksgiving and Christmas dinner may be of little interest to her, but that could change because she will be done with radiation and will have been recovering from surgery for close to three months.

In about a month Shearlean will have her first MRI post-surgery, and we will learn how successful surgery, radiation and chemo have been. Then she will have an MRI every month for four months. If the results are good, she will continue on monthly doses of Temodar chemo treatment indefinitely, and life will consist of routine periodic MRI's, blood tests and doctor visits.

Shearlean, on her doctor's advice, has elected to take a second academic quarter of leave (winter quarter) from her job. We estimate that if she tried to work now she might be good for about 30 minutes and then would crash. She would be exhausted and any stress would wreck her language abilities.

The biggest obstacle in trying to work again would be dealing with groups of people. One on one she seems perfectly "normal," and so people tend to think she is recovered, but for now even little things can be too much. We were out for a walk the other day and her hand got cold so she wanted to put it in her jacket pocket. A zipper and a Velcro flap closed the jacket pocket. Trying to simultaneously walk and fumble with the pocket closure became maddeningly difficult and caused extreme frustration. I had to open the pocket for her, and then she became abjectly apologetic for not being able to do something so simple for herself and for getting upset. So you can see she is continually walking a recovery tightrope on which she must struggle to maintain a precarious balance. Every day there is a little improvement, but also an episode that cruelly reminds her where she has been and where she must go.

Please send out your good thoughts, encouragement and prayers that her MRI will be tumor-free just as she is envisioning it.

On the medical insurance front, things continue to be as binary as Shearlean's recovery. We've both been amazed and disappointed simultaneously, grateful and damning in the same breath, getting good news and bad news at the same time over insurance issues.

Good news: The bills for tens of thousands of dollars for Shearlean's treatment have finally been submitted to the insurance company, and we have received many of the statements. *(See Exhibit 6.)* Our health insurance is through Shearlean's employer, Western Washington University, and ultimately the state of Washington. We are with Uniform Medical Plan, which it seems insures the majority of healthcare professionals we have been dealing with. Everyone has told us it provides excellent coverage and our doctors and nurses told us they were familiar with its coverage, but not sure how it works.

When we were told that Shearlean's surgery and treatment would cost nothing, we frankly didn't believe it or supposed it was a well-intentioned exaggeration. Well, it has proven to be no exaggeration. In most cases the benefits statements say that the "Patient Responsibility" amount is zero dollars. We paid a $600 co-pay the morning Shearlean checked in for surgery and have paid zero since for surgery and related procedures that would ultimately total more than $80,000.

Most of our out-of-pocket co-payments have been (so far) for prescriptions, imaging, labs and other such peripheral services and supplies. To a degree, we can manage these costs, though over time they will mount up to thousands of dollars.

This is where the bad news comes in: The biggest cost cannot be measured in dollars and cents, but in inefficiency, confusion, delay and, if we are not careful, jeopardy to Shearlean's successful treatment. In particular, the difficulty of getting prescriptions filled is nothing short of disgraceful.

The insurance companies, such as Uniform Medical Plan, have the pharmacies by the throat, and they control every move to the point of depriving the patient of lifesaving medication. Basically, as I understand it from talking to nearly a dozen mail-order pharmacy employees, the pharmacies have no common sense discretion about how they fill prescriptions; every move they make must have prior approval from the insurer. When time is critical for a patient, the pharmacy nevertheless refuses to act unless the insurance company approves. As a result, prescriptions sit unfilled and unshipped while the patient panics about timely treatment. In Shearlean's case, a doctor wrote her chemo prescription late and did not include adequate documentation or authority for it to be processed as written.

Every step with the pharmacies has been a nightmare. After nearly eight weeks of effort, we hope the problems are finally resolved, but I am afraid to let down my guard. Everything I've learned so far is something I needed to know before we even started treatment, but I have not yet discovered who in the system could have helped me at the outset. God help the patient who would have to do this herself.

Friends, beware of this shotgun wedding between health insurance companies and pharmacies if you face a life-or-death situation. If you get sick, come talk to me.

Bob Duke

BIG P.S. Yesterday was Shearlean's best day since surgery. She got through the whole day without a nap, remained energetic until bed at 9 p.m., and spoke well the entire day.

CHAPTER TEN

Anxiety and Fluctuating Symptoms

"Since I finished radiation and chemo and cut back on steroids, I have had the following:

1. *Horrible lower backache.*
2. *10+ pain on right side of back.*
3. *Pain in left calf so intense keeps me awake.*
4. *Last night awake with a start at midnight in intense pain with nausea.*

By late November of 2009, Shearlean was scheduled for imaging every 30 days or so. As each MRI date approached, our shared anxiety increased. Like everything else about treatment, we viewed the MRIs with both dread and eagerness. It was like having your fortune read and nearly as open to interpretation.

What would the test reveal? Progress or relapse? Source of pain? Effectiveness of treatment or impending doom? Would it tell us any more than I could decipher daily by observation? As miraculous as looking inside someone's skull at a living cancer could be, it could not answer everyday questions.

UPDATE 7: Spying on Patient

November 22, 2009

Hello All

A necessary part of caring for someone with a serious condition involves watching closely to try to detect how she is doing. I couldn't rely on verbal reports from the patient. (In Shearlean's case she is so determined to be positive I can't trust what she tells me.)

A while ago Shearlean was napping in the darkened bedroom. After I thought she was asleep I went in the room and sat in a chair listening to see whether she was still or restless or asleep. It always seemed a little like spying and I regretted it, but whether I wanted to or not I often found myself "watching" her constantly for signs of progress or decline.

Watching was something I'd talked to my counselor about a few times. I guess it made me somehow feel sneaky and when I wrote notes about what I was seeing it made me feel disloyal. But I didn't know what else to do to stay in tune and in touch with her nonverbal cues about how she was coping.

I realized I had to keep doing it, but didn't think I'd ever be comfortable with it.

Another phenomenon of caregiving is how intangible progress and improvement turn out to be. Objectively, things are better because there are always at least small improvements. Subjectively things seem worse because progress is often slow, small and sometimes unsatisfying, and there are always hints that there might be something sinister behind some nearly intangible sign.

Shearlean has developed serious pain in her lower left leg. Then it moved up to her lower back and then it was her whole left leg. It was frightening because the first sign of her brain tumor was similar pain in her right leg.

Worst case, the pain could be caused by brain swelling, the same cause as her original right leg pain. So, does she need a bigger dose of steroid to reduce swelling? Is the leg pain coincidentally caused by a common lower back problem?

We have a good supply of strong pain medications but they haven't done much good. Sometimes the pain moderates, but never goes away entirely. Lying in bed seems to make the pain worse so Shearlean has been sleeping on the living room floor in front of the fireplace, or in the recliner at night. I get up to be with her, but there isn't anything I can do.

Shearlean's right hand has become increasingly numb making it difficult to type and to hold objects. She is exercising it more but hasn't seen any improvement. She has had more energy and gained some additional endurance. She started yoga classes and spent two hours at her first session. Amazing. An improvement? Maybe.

Every time Shearlean can do more she does a lot more and

gets tired. When she gets tired her speech suffers and the condition tarnishes the shine of improved energy. How much better or worse is she? I don't know.

Because the brain is involved, absolutely anything is possible for better and for worse. The brain can do everything. No part of the body is safe from its effect. This makes treatment and recovery more of a guessing game.

We have visits scheduled with the radiology and chemo doctors on December 2 and December 4. Nurses from both doctors' offices have called frequently and been helpful. They are staying on top of her situation, but are unable to do much without knowing the cause.

The next MRI, which is still more than two weeks off, may provide some clarification or not.

Meanwhile, all we can do is to keep on keep'n on.

Bob Duke

When the nurse called to ask about her medications, Shearlean told her, "On a scale from 1 to 10, the leg pain is 20. It is excruciating and frightening."

The nurse was sympathetic, but didn't know what it could be. She suggested Shearlean contact her doctors, but no one could figure it out. Finally one doctor ordered an ultrasound of her leg. I took Shearlean to the hospital at 8:15 a.m. on a Friday morning for the ultrasound to see if there was a blood clot or circulation problem that might have been caused by radiation treatment. The test was negative, but everyone saw her pain as a source of concern nevertheless. I was helpless to do anything besides help her manage her symptom.

Through it all, terminal cancer—a death sentence—should have obliterated any semblance of normal life. There were days when this was true—like when Shearlean had great pain, but mostly it wasn't. A balm to our souls was how ordinary life remained. I was still me. Shearlean was still Shearlean. We still had the same ticks and quirks. I tried to convey this to friends in my updates so they would know that, although things were hard, confusing and frustrating, we were also okay in many respects.

UPDATE 8: Fun With Cancer
December 1, 2009

Hello All

Does cancer kill fun? Not in our experience. We are amazed how much fun we still have and how often we are able to laugh. There is nothing "funny" about cancer. It is terrible, painful and often deadly. But until you have a personal encounter with it, the notion of cancer seems too horrible and grim to imagine that cancer and fun can coexist.

At first, after Shearlean was diagnosed with her brain tumor, I was embarrassed and uncomfortable to find myself amused over anything. It was like laughing in church—out of place under such solemn circumstances. There should have been no more fun or laughter in the world under these new conditions.

While there can be little argument that cancer changes everything, there is the paradox that on the other hand, nothing changes. Fundamentals seem to be unaffected by cancer. For example, Shearlean has told everyone, including her surgeons (even as surgery was being performed) and doctors, that her brain surgery was the most interesting and adventurous experience she has ever had. This is saying a lot coming from someone who has led such an adventurous life. It is her fundamental life outlook to see the adventure in everything she does. At the very least, this viewpoint seems a good coping mechanism that continues to transform negative events into positive experiences.

Over our years together, Shearlean and I have learned the art of making lemonade from the lemons. We still try to do that.

Yesterday, when we were playing cards with a slippery new deck, I told her she better not try to shuffle the deck because with her numb and hard-to-manage right hand, she might send cards flying all over the room. We laughed at imagining cards flying and the mess we'd have to pick up.

Here's another lemons-to-lemonade example: When you have radiation treatment for a brain tumor, they make a plastic mask of your face that you wear during treatments so the radiation is delivered accurately. The mask has a sturdy frame around the perimeter that allows the technicians to clamp your head to the table during treatment to immobilize it. Given Shearlean's penchant for not following instructions well, it was a good thing the procedure had the means built into it to tame her independent streak and ensure her safe treatment. More than once we thought bolting her to the treatment table was pretty funny. We have her mask at home, and I've threatened to use it to bolt her head to the floor if she doesn't follow her doctor's instructions conscientiously.

Reader's Digest used to have a feature titled "Laughter is the Best Medicine," and that is Shearlean's philosophy too. It works, and we're always looking for more fun. Our experience indicates that cancer isn't the end of the road. Rather it is a fork in the road and those traveling this new direction are much the same people they were before they reached this point in their journey.

Bob Duke

~

Santa arrived at the Dukes' home at 10:30 a.m. December 9, 2009. This is the day we heard Shearlean's December 4 MRI results. The images showed dead tissue in the area where the tumor had been. The job of the radiation was to kill cells (good and bad) in that area in an attempt to kill any cancer that may have been left behind after surgery. There was no proof Shearlean was cancer-free, but there was also no sign of renewed cancer or any indication that radiation/chemo had not been successful so far.

As our replacement Bellingham oncologist, Dr. Kozlowski cautioned, however, we wouldn't know anything conclusive until more time passed and more MRIs were administered. Shearlean's current treatment would proceed for six more months with monthly (Temodar) chemo and periodic MRIs to monitor progress.

Shearlean had been very busy the week before we learned the good news. She'd spent several days in visits to doctors attempting to get a diagnosis for the severe pain in her left leg.

Just days before her last MRI, Dr. Kozlowski told us he thought her left leg pain might be caused by the anti-seizure medication she'd been taking since August. He ordered her to stop taking it.

Medication

NOT EVERY DOCTOR agrees with every other doctor about medication, and so changes need to be negotiated. A cavalier doctor might replace one drug with another without alerting the patient; merely saying it is an anti-nausea medication but omitting that it is not the familiar one the patient was used to.

In our case, one doctor blamed non-tumor symptoms on a particular medication and recommended stopping or changing it without consulting the original prescribing doctor. I always checked with the prescribing doctor before I accepted the change, which did nothing to endear me to the doctor seeking the change. On more than one occasion, changing or stopping a vital medication was vetoed by a key doctor's superior knowledge of the medication in question. Later, when acute symptoms arose, I had to make several medication changes in just a few days.

I think I have lived my life in a practical and self-sufficient way, making well-reasoned decisions and meticulous plans. But if I get sick, suddenly my qualities or competencies evaporate in the ablative healthcare atmosphere. I am instantly reduced to the lowest common denominator and forced to follow practices I would have thought previously were appropriate for fools. Suddenly, I know nothing; I am unreliable, ignorant and untrustworthy. Though I am seen regularly, I am treated at each successive visit like someone who's never been seen before.

If I am sick I am presumed to be stupid, disorganized and incompetent, unless it serves the healthcare provider's purpose to treat me like a fully functioning and capable adult unaffected by treatment, disease or medication. It is infuriating.

Doctors were either pushing drugs on Shearlean that we didn't want or refusing drugs that she desperately needed. Cost seemed to be the deciding factor. The drugs were usually presented by nurses and pharmacists as precautionary, but seemed aimed at forestalling a patient's eventual request for such medications. Dispensing preventative medications is a legitimate cost strategy, but it cut only one way, in the direction of the providers.

One of a patient's most important tasks is managing her medication and taking it properly. Providers cite patient failure to properly manage and take prescriptions as a major problem in providing care. Yet the most daunting task I had as a caregiver was managing prescriptions and medications with the doctors, pharmacies and insurance agencies. The system provided plenty of cost control, benefit management and controlled substance regulation, but very little support or help in delivering the medication to the patient.

Because I routinely harped at her about following instructions, Shearlean started out defensively questioning this latest order. I surprised her when I cut her off by saying, "I don't think he knows what he's talking about." Keppra (her anti-seizure medication) was a basic first-line medication prescribed by her surgeon, who regularly treated this condition. She seemed relieved that I had read her mind, and answered, "I'm afraid to stop. I'm going to call Dr. Steinberg's nurse to ask what he thinks." Before her next dose of Keppra was due, Dr. Steinberg's nurse returned Shearlean's call and said emphatically not to miss a dose and not to stop taking Keppra under any circumstances.

For us both, this was just another strike against Dr. Kozlowski and his growing tendency to offer knee-jerk reactions. For our mutual peace of mind, I once again reviewed the online literature about Keppra and its side effects. Yes, limb pain occurred sometimes, but symptoms that Keppra controlled were far more detrimental than even severe leg pain.

Eventually her left leg pain ceased, but we didn't know any more about why it stopped than we did about why it started.

The next step would be to see a neurologist. One more doctor for me to manage! I hoped it wouldn't come to that.

CHAPTER ELEVEN

Conflicts and Charisma

"I need to achieve better changes, not big changes, and they will add up to key changes."

THE ONE GOOD THING that came from our association with University Medical's Dr. Majorski was his referral to Dr. Hinton as our radiologist. Dr. Hinton's influence on Shearlean's long-term care proved to be a blessing. He was Shearlean's elixir for depression and low moods, and for me he was the one doctor I could count on to quantify each aspect of treatment. He illustrated his discussions of Shearlean's tumor with thorough analysis of the MRI images upon which so much hinged.

Dr. Hinton's appearance was rather bland; he was slender, under six feet tall, wore glasses, was casually but neatly dressed, and he was relaxed and at ease. What made him stand out was that he was alert and engaged when he was conversing, and obviously listening when you were speaking with him. He never seemed to be on his way somewhere else or to have wandered off mentally. He was with you when he was with you, but when he moved on to his next appointment or task it was useless to try to retrieve his attention.

For Shearlean meeting Dr. Hinton was love at first sight. Movies have been made and books written about the relationship between women and their doctors. Shearlean was smitten and I was happy for her. Dr. Hinton was a more effective medication for Shearlean than any prescription drug and the beneficial side effects for me were welcome. An appointment with Dr. Hinton was one we both looked forward to.

Something that set Dr. Hinton apart, which eventually proved important, was his willingness to accept and respond to emails. He even answered his own telephone. Dr. Hinton provided close support by phone and email while we were in Palm Desert in 2010 when Shearlean's condition was worsening rapidly.

Dr. Hinton's office was at the Cancer Center in Bellingham, a small building on the hospital campus. As buildings go it was nothing special, but at least it was pleasant and easily accessible even by wheelchair. What set it apart, for me, was the staff. It was mainly a group of older women who paid close attention to their work and like Dr. Hinton, were actually involved moment to moment with the patients. They had a clear understanding of what patients were dealing with. Each woman greeted Shearlean by name and demonstrated that she knew what condition she was being treated for and where she was in the treatment process. They knew which doctor was responsible for treating Shearlean and whether he was on time or running late, and reported this information to us accordingly. If there was a supply of new wigs, hats or books in the lounge since Shearlean's last visit, they invited her to help herself to whatever caught her fancy. When Shearlean left me in the public waiting room to go to the private patient's waiting room near the treatment room, no one from reception pursued her with "just one more question (or one more form), please."

This is the way more medical personnel should operate! Reception and administration should be limited, efficient, personal, knowledgeable and considerate. They should never preempt the patient's tranquility, equilibrium, peace of mind or personhood.

As good as Dr. Hinton was personally, and as well-run as the Cancer Center was, the office had its share of healthcare system bumps just like every place we'd encountered. Once, Trudy, who was a nurse and the chief administrator of the Cancer Center, had a hissy fit with me over the phone when Ed, the technician, asked her on my behalf whether Shearlean's MRI CDs had arrived from the imaging center. I explained (over her protests) why I needed to know and how it came about that Ed was asking for me. It wasn't a big deal. I'd merely made an aside to Ed. Such a question was routine for me. She said she was not in the habit of calling patients to report receipt of items. I understood this, but explained to her that as Shearlean's caregiver, I followed up on everything all the time—everything. Healthcare system bureaucracy was apparently so pervasive it was impossible to avoid even in Dr. Hinton's office, but because Shearlean loved Dr. Hinton, and because the center was largely an oasis of sympathetic care and comfort to so many desperately ill patients, I bent over backward to be civil, polite and appreciative of the staff.

Still, as far as I was concerned, no one's turf was off-limits to me or my job of managing Shearlean Duke's care.

Trudy and I had a few other minor run-ins, one in which she followed me out to the parking lot exchanging words about a confusion at the reception counter. I was waiting there for a prescription that never arrived while Shearlean sat in the car waiting to go home to rest after a radiation treatment. Trudy challenged me with the remark, "We have other patients." A remark I'd heard from others.

I mustered up all the authority of my role as Shearlean's partner and as the one caring for her day and night, and stared at Trudy long and hard before saying, "I have only one patient. There are no other patients." There is no compromise or alternative when there is no tomorrow and yet you are forced to compete for resources. Desperation is justified.

Though I could never let down my guard completely, I did eventually learn to be more trusting of the functioning of the Cancer Center than any place outside of University Medical's Neurosurgery. Dr. Hinton's handling of radiation had everything to do with that.

Radiation was considered the second most effective treatment for glioblastoma cancer, behind surgery and ahead of chemo. The protocol at the time of Shearlean's treatment was to combine radiation and chemo initially, and to then continue with chemo thereafter. The reality of radiation treatment in Shearlean's case was far different from its general reputation. Radiation is portrayed in fiction and rumored to be terrible. Shearlean's mild reaction to it may have had a lot to do with the location of her tumor; we never learned explicitly why this was the case with her.

Radiation is effective because it is powerful. And because it is powerful it must be delivered precisely to the site of treatment and in carefully controlled doses to avoid complications and potential damage to healthy tissue. In Shearlean's case her optic nerve was in the immediate vicinity of the treatment area, and without extreme care it could be damaged, resulting in blindness.

To guarantee accurate treatment she wore the custom facemask that made us laugh sometimes. This allowed her head to be clamped firmly to the treatment table during radiation. The treatment table and the source of X-rays could each be maneuvered in three axes to radiate the treatment area from all sides without jeopardizing healthy tissue. Shearlean suffered a few mild side effects from radiation. The only surprise radiation treatment sprung on us was how long-lasting its effects were. Yes, the side effects were mild, even subtle, but they lasted nearly to the time of her death 14 months after the end of radiation treatment. Radiation came up time and again through the duration of treatment as the probable cause of new or ongoing conditions or the need to alter medications and dosages. The effect of radiation never fully dissipated as we mistakenly thought it would, but we were grateful it was never a major problem.

In fact, radiation treatment was so pleasant—compared with every aspect of chemo—we almost yearned for more of it. But it was too potent and its efficacy so well understood that the patient received every bit she could tolerate and benefit from, and no more.

The environment at radiation treatment was like a cool breeze on a sultry day. From reception to treatment it was pleasant and reassuring, and the way it was conducted made us wonder why other forms of treatment couldn't follow the radiation model. From the private patient waiting room, a smiling, calm escort led Shearlean down a short, deserted hallway to the treatment room where two casually dressed young men whisked her inside. Normally that was the last I saw of her until about 15 minutes later when she reappeared, looking substantially the same and none the worse for the experience.

Then at one treatment appointment, coming almost as an afterthought, her escort asked if I would like to observe a treatment from the control room. "Of course," I said.

He led me up three steps and through a door conspicuously marked NO ADMITTANCE. It was jammed with equipment with no room for the three men and two women jostling each other for access to controls and monitors. There was just one chair in front of an array of equipment where the chief controller sat looking through a large window at the nearly empty room beyond.

The treatment room was not so empty as it first appeared. There was Shearlean being assisted onto the platform beneath the looming arm of the radiation machine. Her two host technicians positioned her in preparation for applying the special facemask that would lock her head immovably to the platform. Because the platform and radiation source had to move, roll, pitch and yaw to irradiate all sides of the tumor, the perimeter of the treatment room as well as the ceiling were empty. Momentarily I saw myself as a vengeful inquisitor witnessing the breaking of a heretic on the rack in a very clean and well-lighted dungeon. *No, no Bob, turn off your imagination, this is modern medical treatment for something worse than heresy.*

"See here," the chief technician said, pointing to a small black-and-white TV monitor directly in front of her. It provided a close-up of the two technicians, wrenches in hand, snugging down the clamps on Shearlean's head-immobilizing mask. "Those red and blue lines you see drawn on the left side of Shearlean's mask are targets for the radiation source to follow to aim precisely at the area of the tumor. See the X in the center of the blue square?" The chief then touched a switch and a duplicate of the lines on Shearlean's mask appeared on the TV monitor. "When the lines on the screen exactly overlay the lines on the mask, Shearlean's tumor will be zapped with a dose of radiation."

All of this takes longer to tell than to do. Meanwhile in the control room, home-baked cookies (a gift from the last radiation patient) were being passed around. As they partook, the crew commented on what a good patient Shearlean was and how well she was responding to treatment. They asked about me, too. What did I do? Where was I from? And how long had I lived in Bellingham?

As I enjoyed my second cookie, I gazed through the window at the incredible ballet around the platform Shearlean was attached to. The giant arm of the radiation source soundlessly and effortlessly moved around the room, paused, moved again and at last came to rest where it had started.

When it was over, the two technicians reentered the treatment room, unlocked Shearlean and helped her off the treatment platform as I watched her exit the room on the TV monitor. A moment later, she entered the control space and thanked everyone for her care.

At a later treatment, when Shearlean's sister, Janet, was there, she watched a treatment from the control room and was equally impressed.

Exhibits

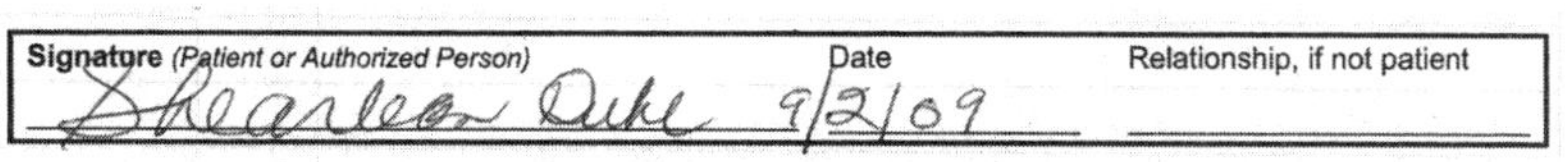
Signature (Patient or Authorized Person) Date Relationship, if not patient

Thank you for your responses. Please return this form to the Medical Assistant or Front Desk.
This form is to be placed in the medical record.

EXHIBIT 1 *(above)*
Shearlean's Signature a Week Before Surgery.

The quality of Shearlean's signature varied hour to hour and day to day throughout her illness.

EXHIBIT 2 *(left)*
Shearlean's Signature After Surgery – Tired.

EXHIBIT 3 *(below)*
Shearlean's Signature After Surgery – Rested.

Shearlean's post-surgery signature frequently degenerated into an unrecognizable scrawl that was little more than a pen stroke sliding across a sheet of paper. Other times she was unable to will her hand to perform the task her brain clearly wanted.

Discharge Medication Instructions
SCHEDULED MEDICATIONS

citalopram 5 mg Oral Daily
dexamethasone 2 mg Oral Twice daily
docusate 200 mg Oral Twice daily
omeprazole 20mg Oral Daily
pantprazole 40mg oral daily
scopolamine 1.5 mg Transdermal Every 72 hours
senna 2 tab Oral Daily, at bedtime
levetiracetam 500 mg Oral Every 12 hours
levofloxacin 500 mg Oral Daily, at bedtime
Cholecalciferol 2000 units oral daily
Estradiol .25mg oral daily
multivitamin with minerals 1 tab daily
niacin 500mg oral twice daily
MEDICATIONS TO TAKE ONLY AS NEEDED

fluticasone nasal 1 spray(s) Each Nostril Daily as needed daily)
oxycodone 10-15 mg Oral Every 3 hours as needed for Pain
claritin 10 mg oral daily as needed

MORNING
- dexamethasone 2 mg.
- docusate 200 mg.
- omeprazole 20 mg.
- senna 1 tab.
- multivitamin with minerals 1 tab.
- niacin 500 mg.

MIDDAY
- cholecalciferol 2000.
- estradiol .25 mg.
- citalopram 5 mg.
- pantprazole 40 mg.

BED
- levofloxacin 500 mg.
- levetiracetam 500 mg.
- senna 1 tab.
- dexamethasone 2 mg.
- docusate 200 mg.
- niacin 500 mg.

EVERY 3 DAYS
- scopolamine 1.5 mg transdermal.

EXHIBIT 4
Patient Discharge Medication Instructions and Revised Lists.

Hospital's disorganized medication list was confusing and difficult to use. Considerable effort was required to organize it into useful form. The risk of making a mistake was great.

STATEMENT DATE
THRU TRANSACTION DATE : 09-14-09 09-19-09

Bill Number	Description	Transaction Amount	Amount Due
·4001	OUTPATIENT SERVICES FOR 09-09-09		
	09-09-09 PHARMACY	64.37	
	09-09-09 STERILE SUPPLY	1,064.62	
	09-09-09 LABORATORY	.00	
	09-09-09 LAB/HEMATOLOGY	33.93	
	09-09-09 DX X-RAY/ARTER	10,569.25	
	09-09-09 OR/MINOR	4,965.30	
	09-09-09 ANESTHESIA	261.63	
	09-09-09 DRUGS/DETAIL CODE	232.00	
	09-09-09 EEG	1,213.90	

	PRIMARY INSURANCE WILL BE BILLED.	18,405.00	

See Reverse Side for Additional Information

Total Amount Due $.00

EXHIBIT 5
Bill for Testing Was Typical of What We Worried About.

Though amount due was zero, the bill had to still be submitted to insurance and we feared the outcome. When this was received we still had no clue what we were responsible for paying or the extent of our insurance coverage.

PAGE 1

Bill Number: 5004 Date: 09-25-09

Summary Of Charges

ADMITTED 09-10-09 DISCHARGED 09-14-09

SUMMARY OF CHARGES

DAILY SERVICE: 3 DAYS@ 1,442.00	4,326.00
DAILY SERVICE: 1 DAY @ 3,787.00	3,787.00
PHARMACY	4,984.29
MED-SURG SUPPLIES	707.00
STERILE SUPPLY	2,247.00
SUPPLY/IMPLANTS	6,176.00
LABORATORY	717.00
LAB/CHEMISTRY	550.00
LAB/IMMUNOLOGY	312.00
LAB/HEMATOLOGY	230.00
LAB/UROLOGY	19.00
PATHOLOGY LAB	786.00
CT SCAN/HEAD	1,090.00
OR SERVICES	15,615.00
ANESTHESIA	3,495.00
PHYSICAL THERP	421.00
PHYS THERP/EVAL	229.00
OCCUPATION THERP	544.00
OCCUP THERP/EVAL	231.00
SPEECH PATHOL	722.00
CLINIC	.00
MRI - BRAIN	5,289.00
DRUGS/DETAIL CODE	679.72
DRUGS/SELF ADMIN	270.70
RECOVERY ROOM	1,236.00
EEG	3,228.00
OTHER DX SVS-ELECTROMYOGR	600.00
TOTAL CHARGES	58,491.71
YOUR INSURANCE WILL BE BILLED	

EXHIBIT 6

Bill for Brain Surgery and Hospitalization.

As with the testing bill, this bill was being submitted to insurance and we had no idea how much, if any of it, was covered. While insurance paid this bill in full, less the $600 demanded at surgery check-in, many other smaller bills followed with insurance coverage still undetermined. Eventually we paid several thousand dollars out of pocket, but insurance covered most of the cost.

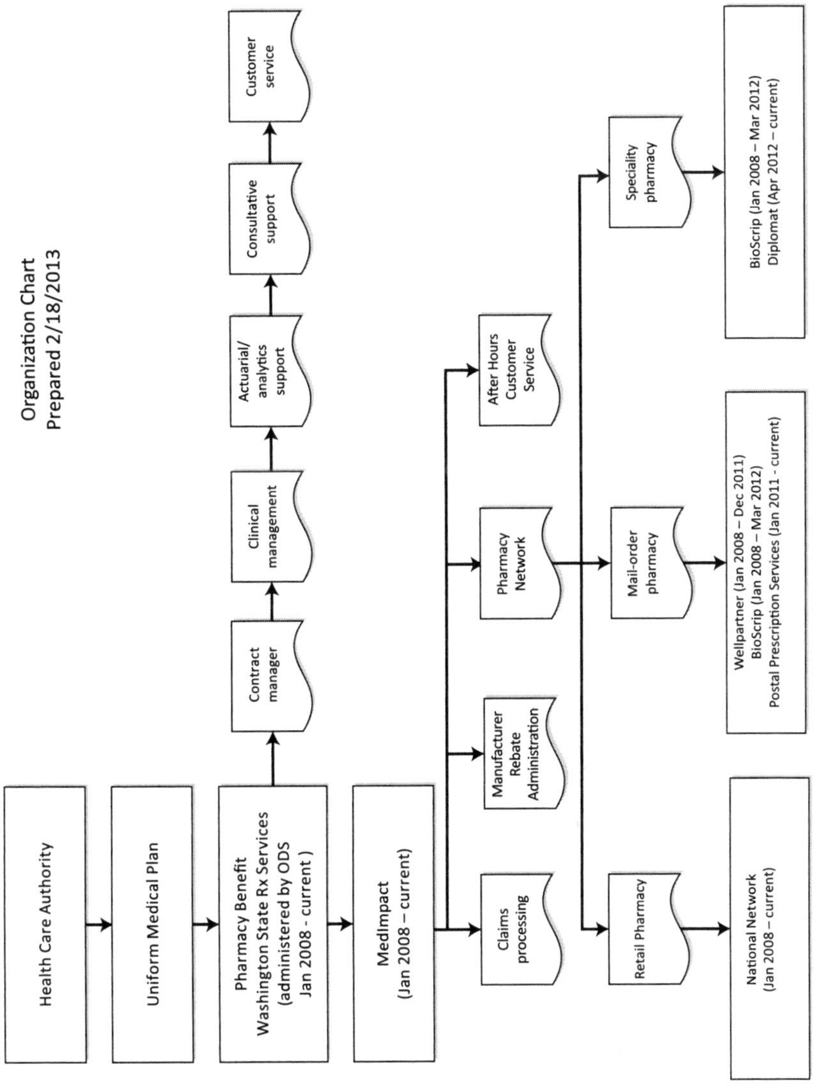

EXHIBIT 7
Health Care Authority Organization Chart Provided by ODS.

You can see from the date of this chart (2/18/2013) how long it took to get an overall description of the Health Care Authority's pharmacy benefits portion of our health insurance coverage. During treatment and care we had access to nothing that described or defined the components of this benefit.

MRI BRAIN, PRE AND POST CONTRAST

Clinical: Right sided pain, paresis. .

Comparison: None

Procedure: A dose of 15 cc of OptiMARK was injected without apparent complications. Creatinine blood test performed. SE T1 Sagittal, FLAIR Axial, Post contrast TSE T2 Axial F.S., EPI Diffusion Axial, T1 SE F.S. Axial, T1 SE F.S. Coronal.

Findings: There is a 1.9 x 2.2 cm heterogeneously enhancing mass within the left inferior parietal lobule. There is a mild amount of surrounding edema extending to the atrium of the left lateral ventricle. No additional enhancing lesions are present throughout the brain parenchyma. There is no obstructing hydrocephalous or midline shift. There are no additional abnormal signal intensities throughout the brain parenchyma. There is curvilinear restriction of diffusion along the medial margin of the lesion.

There is a retention cyst or polyp along the floor of the right maxillary sinus. The visualized vascular flow voids and the flow related enhancement are normal.

Impressions:
1. Solitary inhomogeneously enhancing 2 cm mass within the left inferior parietal lobule. Findings are suspicious for a primary brain tumor such as a and high-grade astrocytoma or glioblastoma multiforme. Suggest further evaluation with MR spectroscopy.

*** ALERT: Follow-up is recommended***

EXHIBIT 8 *(opposite)*
Radiologist's Report of the Discovery of Shearlean's Brain Tumor.

This report is based on an MRI image processed August 20, 2009. The report was sent to Shearlean's primary care physician who ordered the examination. She ordered a second MRI for the following day, August 21, and presented the findings to Shearlean at 1 p.m., August 21, at her office in Bellingham.

EXHIBIT 9
MRI Image of Brain Tumor.

The white circular mass at the right of the skull, viewed from the top, is the tumor described in the radiologist's report in Exhibit 8. Surgery found the tumor had grown to plum-size within three weeks. Though pictured on the right, the tumor was physically located in the left brain

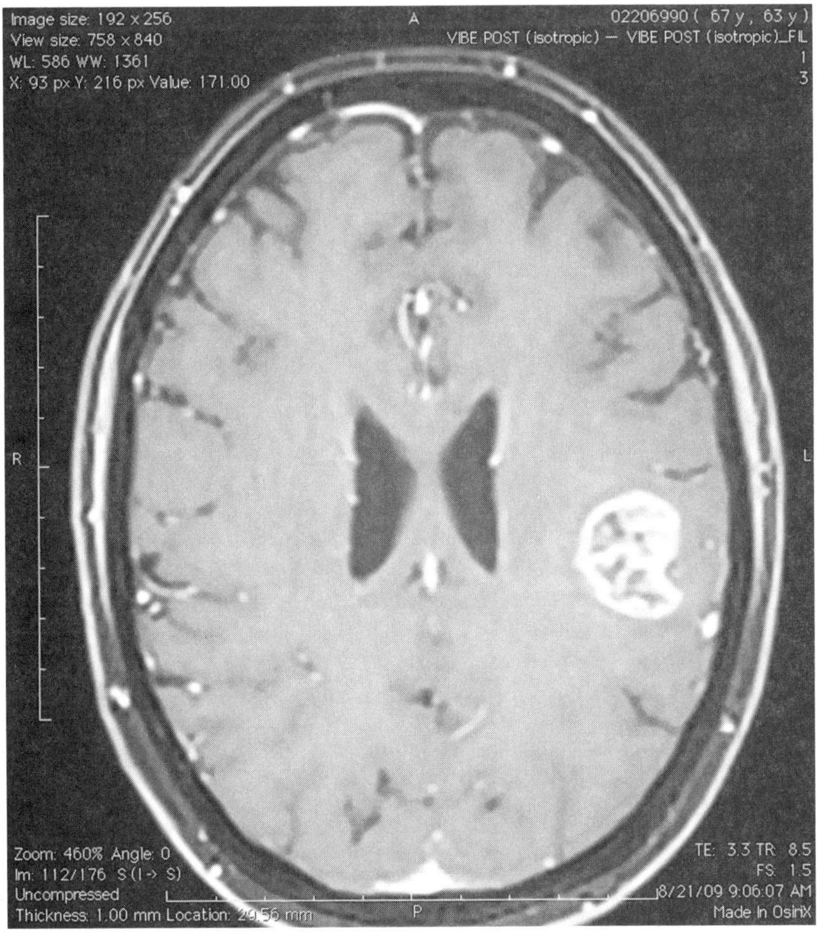

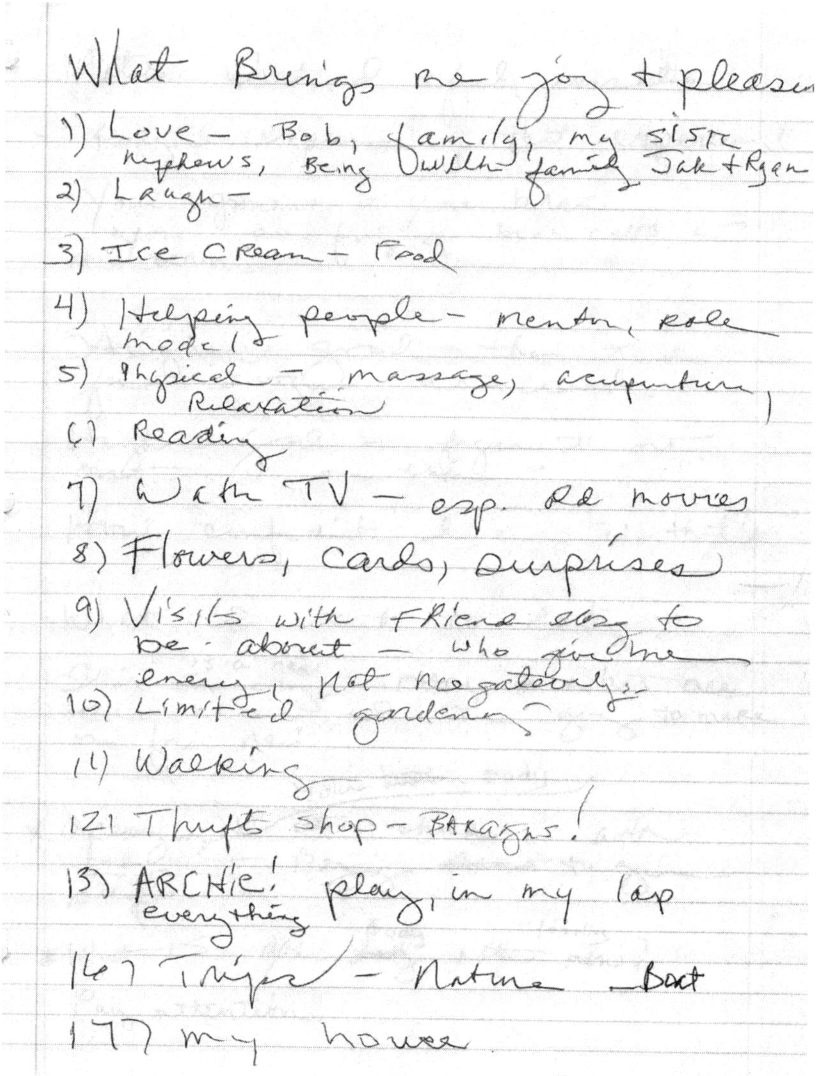

What Brings me joy + pleasu

1) Love – Bob, family, my sister nephews, Being with family Jake + Ryan

2) Laugh –

3) Ice Cream – Food

4) Helping people – mentor, role models

5) Physical – massage, acupuncture, Relaxation

6) Reading

7) Watch TV – esp. old movies

8) Flowers, cards, surprises

9) Visits with Friends easy to be about – who give me energy, not negatively.

10) Limited gardening

11) Walking

12) Thrift shop – Bargains!

13) ARCHIE! everything play, in my lap

14) Trips – Nature Boat

17) my house

EXHIBIT 10

Page From Shearlean's Journal Circa Early November 2009.

Here she gave herself a pep talk by reminding herself what brought her joy and pleasure regardless of the presence of cancer.

Photographs

PHOTO 1
Kenya's Ombogo Girls' Academy Students and Shearlean.

PHOTO 2
Shearlean With Maasai Host During 2009 Kenya Safari.

PHOTO 3
Shearlean Relaxing in Safari Tent.

This carefree moment was before snakebite scare.

PHOTO 4
Home Five Days After Brain Surgery.

PHOTO 5
Shearlean and Sister Janet Soon After Surgery.

PHOTO 6
Archie the Silver Tabby Cat.

Important source of comfort and therapy.

PHOTO 7
Cancer Box Contents.

Cards and encouraging mementos were emotional first aid.

PHOTO 8
Bob and Shearlean Thanksgiving 2010.

First signs of final decline appeared.

CHAPTER TWELVE

Bad Medicine and *Under*whelming Care

"I had a breakdown yesterday. I watched a doctor saying glioblastoma was the most feared and deadly brain tumor, fatal, most die in one year. Really depressed me and I cried for the first time in a long time."

WE HAD DISMISSED University Medical's Dr. Majorski before he even treated Shearlean because he was inaccessible and negligent in handling her chemo prescription. To replace him in time to start chemotherapy promptly we'd asked our radiologist, Dr. Hinton, to recommend someone in Bellingham. Dr. Hinton had recommended Dr. Kozlowski, a hematology oncologist, with whom he had worked. Dr. Kozlowski was proving to be more of a burden than an asset, but at least he was nearby and would actually see patients himself—in his fashion. He was as bohemian and detached as Dr. Hinton was engaged and polished.

When we first met Dr. Kozlowski, Shearlean and I were struck speechless and continually exchanged meaningful glances with each other as he proceeded with his consultation. We'd grown used to younger doctors years long ago, but Kozlowski's grooming, dress, awkward demeanor and adolescent slouching was a startling new low in professional decorum. I had once been treated by a French doctor in a Tahiti clinic naked except for his Speedo and the stethoscope draped around his shoulders. The Tahiti doctor was appropriately dressed for his surrounding, but Dr. Kozlowski seemed out of place and made us both uncomfortable. I worried about how else he might be unconventional.

Dr. Kozlowski looked like Central Casting's epitome of the starving artist or the object of a romance novel heroine's girlish crush. He had shoulder-length black hair with a slight wave, a pouty expression and arresting dark eyes lined with thick lashes. When Shearlean's sister Janet met him and I asked her what she thought, her one-word reply summed him up: "Pretty."

His clothing was generally threadbare with the cord worn off the corduroy trousers at the knees. Threads dangled from his cuffless pant legs. Shoes of unusual construction, with odd-colored decorative stitched panels adorned his feet. His shirts were unconventional too: collarless, sometimes with epaulets, or snaps instead of buttons, and of a gauzy material with one or two buttons undone. What message was he directing at patients by adopting such an unconventional appearance? I thought that if he wanted to make a statement, he could do it on his own time and not inflict it upon nervous and insecure patients. What had become of neutral white coats?

Whenever he sat, he collapsed into a chair and sprawled until he was on the verge of sliding off onto the floor. He assumed an expression of a sullen and bored adolescent, not to be bothered by anything that was not about himself.

Though he was a generation removed from Dr. Majorski, Dr. Kozlowski exuded a similar eastern European appearance and manner that had me wondering whether hematology attracted a certain type of unconventional person. The effect they both had on me was that they were impersonating doctors rather than *being* doctors.

We didn't have the time or energy to keep searching for a different doctor, and so we tried not to be sidetracked by Dr. Kozlowski's appearance. Dr. Hinton vouched for him, after all.

It was Dr. Kozlowski's job to prescribe and authorize chemotherapy in the form of Temodar taken orally, and that would eventually include Avastin administered by infusion. He monitored Shearlean's condition through frequent blood tests and occasional MRIs, and shared this information with Dr. Hinton. Our reliance on Dr. Kozlowski was to last for the duration of Shearlean's treatment.

After signing up with Dr. Kozlowski, we were disappointed to learn that he worked just three days a week: Monday, Tuesday and Wednesday. A part-time doctor would not have been our first choice, but on the other hand we had to see him only one day in a week. However, his three-day week quickly became a torment. Since he elected to schedule Shearlean's MRIs for Wednesdays, she had to wait until the following Monday to see him for the results. Every MRI was nerve-wracking, with us wondering what it would reveal. Waiting was difficult. We persuaded him to schedule her MRIs on Monday so we could get the results on Wednesdays (though his reaction was that we were asking for special treatment). Rescheduling helped somewhat, but another flaw in his makeup detracted from the timely reporting of results. Dr. Kozlowski proved unable (maybe unwilling) to manipulate the MRI images on his computer in order to fully display, compare and report on the imaging results.

Since Dr. Kozlowski was in charge of chemo, he got the results of blood tests and imaging first, so we had to meet with him for initial news. The first time we sat down for such news, we crowded in on Dr. Kozlowski for a close view of the MRI to be displayed on his office computer. Nothing happened. I looked at Shearlean who raised an eyebrow at me.

"Everything okay, doctor?" she asked.

He ignored us both as he pressed keys and pushed the mouse around its pad. Black-and-white images raced across the screen, stopped, changed direction and quickly jumped up and down on the screen. It soon became a maelstrom of flashing images. Kozlowski muttered to himself as he tried to impose some order on the chaos, but admitted defeat and turned off the monitor.

I had to hold my breath to stop myself from calling him an idiot. As if she could read my mind, Shearlean gave me a warning look.

"Well, I read the radiologist's report this morning and it was negative, so there wasn't anything to look at anyway," he said before whirling around in his swivel chair, nearly knocking over Shearlean and me before we could scoot out of the way. He stood, fumbling with folders and papers as he stepped toward the door where he turned and looked us each in the eye to see whether we had anything more to say. When we didn't speak, he was out the door in a flash. Feeling discouraged because we felt deprived of what was vital information to us, we solemnly gathered our things and left.

On our drive home we each expressed our theories about Dr. Kozlowski's behavior and we agreed there wasn't anything we could do to fix him, but we could go around him if Dr. Hinton were amenable.

Up to this point, to get a full and coherent interpretation of

Shearlean's tumor images we had been relying on Dr. Hinton. I was impressed with Dr. Hinton's competence displaying and discussing computer images. He could walk us through each diagnostic report while relating the text to pertinent elements of the images. He could bring up all of the images onto one screen and find the same view from each scan so that we could compare the changes in the tumor and see a stop-action sequence of the tumor receding. With Dr. Hinton's help we could closely examine the site of the tumor and surgery. We could look at the void in Shearlean's brain where tumor and brain matter had been removed and see the ebb and flow, over time, of edema as it was affected by doses of dexamethasone.

Since Shearlean was relying heavily on imaging for meditating and visualizing a cure, Dr. Hinton's proficiency with MRI results was critical to her sense of well-being. We had decided after our last go around with Dr. Kozlowski that we should formalize an agreement with Dr. Hinton to become Shearlean's primary doctor—even after radiation was complete. I sent him a letter:

> Dear Dr. Hinton
>
> Shearlean and I hope that you will agree to help us take the next step in her care. We are impressed with your thoroughness and ability to relate to us. We are comfortable with and confident in your treatment and handling of her case, and want to continue a professional relationship with you during her ongoing treatment.
>
> We do not feel that Dr. Brockman (Shearlean's primary care physician) or Dr. Kozlowski (who practices part-time) is a good candidate for our needs.
>
> What we think we need is a lead doctor to see Shearlean through future palliative care, using whatever resources are available in Bellingham.
>
> We've been told from the beginning that since glioblastoma is incurable, all care can only be palliative. From surgery to the present, palliative treatment has been our choice and we choose to continue on that path.
>
> This choice means that all care decisions must meet the palliative criteria and we would refuse treatment

that would not meet the criteria. If you have issues with this choice or otherwise feel you could not support us in this endeavor, we need to know now, before a new decision point is reached.

Shearlean completed all of the recommended initial treatment and remains cancer-free. However, every doctor we have consulted speaks of "when the cancer returns" not *if* it returns. That being the case, we must be prepared for that eventuality no matter how remote it may be.

The best preparation, we feel, is having a knowledgeable and sympathetic local oncologist at our side when the need arises. We would like that to be you.

If you are willing to consider our request, we would like to meet with you to discuss this further and determine its mutual acceptability. We want to reach an understanding regarding both palliative and hospice care. We want to develop a strategy that will avoid hospitalization or ER visits. We want to maximize home care and ensure that required written agreements are in place before a crisis develops.

If you cannot accommodate us, we ask that you offer us three referrals from which we might choose a palliative care physician as well suited to us as we believe you are.

Sincerely,
Bob and Shearlean Duke

Happily, Dr. Hinton accepted our plea and much to Shearlean's relief, he remained her primary care physician until her death. More than once this arrangement proved convenient and beneficial to her peace of mind and quality of care.

When we'd signed on with Dr. Kozlowski, we'd explained the drug situation with University Medical's Dr. Majorski, and Dr. Kozlowski had clearly been put off by being dragged into someone else's problem. But again, Dr. Hinton's influence (because he fully understood the circumstances) smoothed things over and Dr. Kozlowski had agreed to accept Shearlean as his patient in the end.

Unraveling the Prescription Snafus

Because she was a Washington state university professor, Shearlean and I were in the state's Uniform Medical Plan, one of seven programs under the state's Health Care Authority in 2009. This was the same system in which many of the healthcare professionals caring for us were enrolled, so they told us.

We had dismissed our original appointed Temodar-prescribing doctor because he demonstrated that neither he nor his nurse knew how to write or process a prescription acceptable to our state's insurer.

Worse, however, was that the state insurer's mandated pharmacy, RxB, was both unwilling and unable to fill the prescription that was urgently required to treat an acute terminal illness. Instead, RxB was focused on managing benefit costs for its client, Washington state, rather than its patient, Shearlean Duke. RxB's Web site statement exemplified this: "Our (RxB's) goal is to recognize, understand and exceed our partners' expectations and provide pharmaceutical healthcare solutions that are effective and affordable."

Let me assure the reader of this: *Patients are* not *the partners referred to in this statement.*

Further searching showed that the Web site's oncology page had not been updated since 2005, a sign of neglect for oncology patients. And as was the case with so much else in healthcare, the patient was seen as the problem. RxB's Web site pointed out: "The No. 1 problem in treating illness is patient failure to take medications correctly, according to the National Council on Patient Education."

From my experience, the number one problem was getting *the medication.*

Though we finally got the cancer medication just hours

before it was needed, we were nevertheless devastated. Temodar's manufacturer's published protocol for treating glioblastoma patients was ignored by RxB. The protocol dictated that Temodar be taken for 42 consecutive days simultaneously with 42 days of radiation treatment. Because of an inflexible benefits management rule, RxB would supply only 28 days of Temodar (though the prescription was written for 42 days).

Full of anxiety about getting the withheld quantity of Temodar for this fatal illness, I began immediately pursuing refilling the prescription for the remaining 14 days of Temodar. Though a supplemental prescription for the remaining initial quantity was faxed to RxB on October 6, it did not fill the prescription until October 12. We received it on October 14, just *two* days before it was required on October 16.

Becoming desperate to obtain medication and having received it barely in time for treatment, I wrote an anxious letter to our insurer's case manager on October 11, 2009. I told her that her mandated insurer was jeopardizing a terminally ill patient's life-sustaining treatment. I said RxB was ignoring legitimate prescriptions and published protocols, and was unresponsive to patient needs. The pharmacy was inflicting danger and stress on the patient, and its actions were heartless and self-serving. I asked her to help resolve these problems.

She acknowledged receipt of my letter, but no specific answers or assistance was provided.

Still seeking assistance from healthcare providers and an explanation of how to work with the system in which we were embedded, I made a formal complaint to the hospital against the prescribing doctor and his nurse. An inquiry was made and the offending doctor sent me a letter stating that his actions or lack thereof had met established standards.

Before you think that these Temodar prescription troubles were just an anomaly read on.

The original prescription for Temodar, written September 22, 2009, included a second medication called ondansetron, an anti-nausea pill to be taken with Temodar. RxB filled the ondansetron prescription in two parts, but never filled the whole prescription as written by the prescribing doctor. It sent 10 pills in one shipment and 50 in a second shipment. The ondansetron prescription was written for 80 pills, but RxB *never* delivered 80 pills—only 60.

We had no way of knowing about the missing 20 pills at first because we never saw a copy of the prescription. *(Hereafter, throughout Shearlean's care, we asked for a copy of every prescription, but even this precaution created problems.)*

Consequently, I wrote a letter to RxB in Shearlean's name, which said: "Please provide a copy of all prescriptions written for me (Shearlean Duke) for Temodar and ondansetron since September 1, 2009." I had Shearlean sign the letter because I had learned that communications from caregivers were often ignored.

After about a week I received an undated and unsigned document from RxB titled "Patient's Rx List." It had no cover letter and was anonymous. The mysterious Patient's Rx List showed that two shipments of ondansetron had in fact been billed at $1,831.49 each. I called RxB and asked whether this document indicated it was double-billing for ondansetron. Instead of a yes or no answer, it was explained to me that before any prescription is filled and shipped, the insurer (Uniform Medical Plan) must approve charges, so all charges were legitimate, approved charges. *(Apparently, anything that is **approved** is beyond question and requires no thought or explanation.)* I sent a copy of the Patient's Rx List to our case manager at Uniform along with a letter saying I thought it was a double-billed mistake.

In a note scribbled on a copy of my letter and returned to me, the case manager said she (the insurer) had no authority over the pharmacies or prescriptions *(contrary to what the pharmacy had said)*.

Our local retail pharmacy estimated I could buy 30 ondansetron 8 mg pills for $20. So we could buy the same 60 odansetron pills at retail for under $40, but our insurance or the state of Washington was billed $3,662.98 for two shipments of 60 pills (or double-billed for a single shipment). *On March*

22, 2010, RxB said it was refunding to the state of Washington the original ondansetron charge of $1,831.94 and would instead bill the state at the local retail pharmacy's price for a single shipment of 60 pills. The state eventually paid $0.58 per pill for a total cost of $34.80.

Prescription Defies Professional Help

WHEN SHEARLEAN became his patient, Dr. Kozlowski immediately sent us to Nurse Howard, who handled pharmacy prescriptions. While we had obtained enough Temodar to start treatment on schedule (back in September 2009), we had not received enough to finish the prescribed initial treatment.

Learning that things seldom worked as I was told to expect them to, I decided to reinforce my conversation with Nurse Howard with a letter explaining the Temodar situation in black and white. The basic problem, I reminded her, was getting a sufficient quantity of Temodar for the duration of treatment. For example, Shearlean had been ordered to take Temodar for 42 consecutive days, but the pharmacy had provided only a 28-day supply because of insufficient authorization for more than a 30-day supply. Getting the remaining quantity had been difficult and I didn't want to go through that again.

I asked Howard to authorize Shearlean's next Temador prescription for a quantity sufficient to complete the prescribed treatment in one shipment. If she encountered any roadblocks, I offered to assist her in whatever way I could.

"Roadblock" proved to be a grossly inadequate term for what happened next; reliving a nightmare was more apropos. At Shearlean's next appointment with Dr. Kozlowski, we sat down with Howard to discuss the status of our Temodar prescription, thinking that everything was now under control—with everyone on the same page. They weren't! "I faxed a copy of the Temodar prescription to the pharmacy," Howard told us. "I assumed you'd already received it," she said, her expression bored—or contemptuous, I couldn't tell which.

"I did not receive it," I said simply. But my blood started boiling.

Howard reared back in her chair, her mouth wide for a moment before a loud, long "What!?" emerged. She rocked forward and onto her feet and said she would be back in a few minutes and left her office. When she returned, she told us she had been on the phone with RxB. First, she said, they told her that RxB had been unable to contact us to arrange delivery. Next, an RxB supervisor said it had no record of her (Howard's) faxed prescription. Then an RxB manager said she would arrange for delivery on Friday, December 4, 2009.

I pointed out that this was a virtual replay of what transpired with the first Temodar prescription.

Shearlean had been scheduled for a month to start Temodar again on or about December 7, 2009. RxB had a month's notice and here we were going to receive it (if it arrived) on the Friday (last business day) before she was scheduled to start it on the morning of Monday, December 7, 2009.

CHAPTER THIRTEEN

Christmas Joy and Optimism

"I have so much to be thankful for:

- *Tomorrow is the three-month anniversary of my miracle surgery that saved my life.*
- *I can speak, read and write.*
- *I am stronger every day and can work, use my right hand and* EVEN DRIVE!
- *I live moment to moment."*

BECAUSE CHRISTMAS 2009 could be her last, Shearlean wanted to spend it with her sister and nephew's families, so we rented a condo where we could all gather for the holiday. Wonderfully, it was easy to forget she was dying. We were even talking about her going back to work at the beginning of March for the spring 2010 quarter. She had dealt with her symptoms long enough now that they were just a routine part of her daily life and took little away from her joy of living.

UPDATE 10: Occasional Seizures

December 30, 2009

Hello All

For the first time since starting chemotherapy on September 28, 2009, Shearlean's chemo drugs were delivered on time with minimum hassle from the RxB mail-order pharmacy. The shipment was delivered to our door at our rental condo in Palm Desert, California.

Since recovering from the first round of double-dose chemo (Temodar), Shearlean has been feeling terrific. She has had a big appetite (partly thanks to a steroid she continues taking) and has been able to eat everything. This morning we went out for breakfast and she cleaned her plate: Belgian waffle, bacon, scrambled eggs and coffee.

She still has an occasional seizure of the same sort she had when originally diagnosed with a brain tumor. The seizures come on suddenly and last less than one minute. It doesn't happen every day, nor does it often happen more than once a day. The seizures continue because brain swelling remains a symptom due to radiation and the residual trauma of surgery. We will have to get a better explanation about the effects of chemo because over time we lose track of what we were told weeks or months ago.

We are vacationing in a rented three-bedroom condo in Palm Desert now— at the fourth tee of a par 3, 150-yard hole at the Monterey Country Club. This is some kind of gigantic development built mostly in the early 1970s. We don't play golf, but the course makes for a beautiful setting. There is snow on the crystal-clear surrounding mountains. Days are in the 70s and nights in low 40s. Later, some warmer days are predicted. We had seven family members (all Shearlean's) here for the day after Christmas.

We're doing what we usually do at home, reading and a little writing, and too much TV.

Shearlean will start her next round of chemo on January 4, 2010. We expect to have less severe side effects because we revised our plan for taking it. The last time, she started it without also taking anti-nausea medication, and she took the chemo in the morning so that side effects wouldn't keep her from sleeping, but that didn't work so well. This time she will take anti-nausea meds first and will take chemo before going to bed in the hope she can sleep through the side effects and awaken feeling better. Temodar has to be taken on an empty stomach to guarantee it will all be absorbed quickly. Taking it at night means she will have to eat her last food of the day before 5 p.m. so her stomach is sufficiently empty by bedtime at 9 p.m.

Shearlean continues to be happy, in high spirits, and very positive about her condition and the expected outcome. She has had so many comments from so many doctors and nurses about how well she is doing and how little she was affected by surgery that we both believe she has already been blessed with one miracle in the surgeon she had. It makes the hope for a second miracle seem more realistic. She is truly exceptional and after 39 years of marriage I know what she is capable of.

We met in 1968 and married in 1970 and will celebrate our 39th wedding anniversary on New Year's Eve.

Happy New Year!
Bob Duke

UPDATE 11: Setbacks
January 26, 2010

Hello All

Shearlean continues to improve but with minor setbacks along the way. Her appetite and spirits have been good, and slowly her energy has improved. The chemo drug has been well tolerated, and she was able to eat small amounts of ordinary food while on her January Temodar. She has been recovering quickly from the effects of chemo and after two or three days she is usually fine. We also believe that the last effects of radiation treatment, which ended November 6, 2009, are now gone.

Setbacks seem to come on without rhyme or reason and disappear without indicating why either. A few days ago, she had a spell of aphasia that lasted four or five hours but was gone the next morning. Another day she burned her finger on the oven's broiler element and didn't know it until she smelled burned flesh. Since surgery she has several times experienced various degrees of numbness in her right hand and on her right side. Sometimes her face and mouth/throat are numb and make it difficult to swallow.

Of course she has her emotional ups and downs, too, wondering about her tumor, her future, and the benefits of treatment. She doesn't talk much (or enough) about her feelings and fears, but she keeps a journal that I'm permitted to read, and so I get some help from it to understand her state of mind.

As happens so often to most of us, when she talks about her cancer diagnosis others tell her about their encounters with cancer. Suddenly (or so it seems), many people we would never have guessed about tell her of their personal or family encounters with the disease. Some days it seems like the world is full of cancer, but the feeling we get from it is that we are far from being alone in dealing with this.

Our trip to Palm Desert, California, was a great success. We had clear skies and bright sun that were a terrific tonic for both of us. Shearlean's family and friends came to visit and stayed for days. I'm sure she got all the visiting she could handle. We went there on December 24 and returned home January 10, 2010.

We are hoping to sell our house this spring if the real estate gods will smile on us. We've got the place nearly ready for the market, and I'm having a hard time keeping Shearlean from getting too involved. We plan to stay here in the Bellingham area. Besides liking it here, this is where all of her care is available and where the insurance is a sure thing rather than a gamble.

Chemo starts again February 1, 2010 and will end February 5. There will be three more courses of chemo, ending in May. After that, we don't know what is ahead in treatment. May will also be the end of all the treatment that was planned to follow up her September surgery.

Keep your fingers crossed and keep sending good, positive thoughts Shearlean's way.

Bob Duke

Though she was doing well, time was against Shearlean. As treatment neared its end, what could be done to prolong her life also came to an end. Talking about the end of treatment was equivalent to talking about the end of life. The longer she lived, the closer she got to dying. Of course that's true for everybody, but it's not as imminent for the rest of us.

I, being the more calculating and analytical one, was constantly weighing the time expired against the time remaining. Every day for me was sand through the hourglass. As part of our initial bargain, I remained committed to the doctors' evaluations of the course of her disease. For her part, Shearlean saw only the bright side of everything, pointing it out to me and verbalizing it to boost her confidence. I remained silent, fearing any misspoken remark might come across as "I told you so." The status quo was what we wanted and what we had, and both of us—I assumed—dreaded tampering with it.

UPDATE 12: Tickled Pink

February 26, 2010

Hello All

We visited Dr. Kozlowski, Shearlean's chemo doctor, February 24, 2010. He was, to quote, "tickled pink" about her condition.

She was recently trying to wean herself off of the steroid dexamethasone that she has been taking ever since surgery. It is a powerful and risky drug to take unnecessarily, so we have been working toward eliminating it. We finally got down to ½ mg once daily. Then she went cold turkey to stop and suffered a lot of discomfort, pain and speech problems and slept for 18 hours one day. After two days of this we thought we might go back on the ½ mg, but take it every other day. This situation coincided with seeing the doctor, so we asked about taking the ½ mg every day without trying any longer to get off of it.

A ½ mg dose being the smallest amount you can take is also, we thought, likely to do the least harm and would take very long to have an adverse effect. Yet, that little ½ mg keeps Shearlean feeling good and functioning at a high level. Since feeling good and functioning well have been the goals of all of our care decisions since this started in August of 2009, we thought it was worth the minimal risk to decide to continue taking it instead of stopping.

Our doctor agreed.

In other news, all of Shearlean's blood work looked good and was normal. She continues to be very healthy overall.

More good news. After her sixth chemo treatment in May that will be the end of it. As long as her MRI scans continue to be normal, there will be no more treatment. If the cancer shows signs of returning, she will start treatment with another anti-cancer drug (taken intravenously, I think) called Avastin.

Meanwhile we're on a roll. Smooth sailing and blue skies ahead. Shearlean will be going back to work March 30 as department chair but will not be in the classroom. Although she dreaded the prospect for a while, she is starting to look forward to it now. Everyone who knows her and her condition is convinced that it will be good for her, and she can do it.

And yet more good news. We sold our house. While we were putting the finishing touches on the house in order to list it April 1, a realtor asked to show it, and the first person to see it bought it. The buyer was a retired couple from Olympia, about our age, who had children in Bellingham. They wanted us to rent back until July 31, which works well for us. We didn't want to rent some place while looking for a new home. Now we expect to find something by July.

Thank you all for continuing to wish her well and your interest in her progress and welfare.

For my part, it is nice to have you all to talk to like this.

Thanks.
Bob Duke

My enthusiasm for the prospect of caring for Shearlean when she was diagnosed had been fully realized now. As ashamed as I was when I thought her tragedy might be a boon to me, I cringed now at the realization that I felt better than I had in years. At age 71 I felt 50 again. I was full of energy and enthusiasm, putting in long days without naps or letdowns. My aches, pains and minor complaints had disappeared.

It didn't seem right or fair. Here was Shearlean at the low point of her life and here I was reborn. On the other hand, I was everything I needed to be and grateful to discover I still had it in me to marshal the resources we desperately needed now. I thought I could detect in Shearlean relief and gratitude that I could carry on. No days were too long no work too hard and no demands too great.

My days were full of dealing with Realtors, homebuyers, lenders, house inspectors, exterminators, landscapers and contractors. Medical bills were flooding in and had to be reconciled with statements and payment checks written. Household goods had to be sorted and packed. Items listed for sale on Craigslist had to be shown to buyers. I had to hire someone to wash all the windows, clean the barbecue, clean the roof gutters, pressure wash the driveway and sidewalk, and spray moss treatment on the roof. I was productive.

And with Shearlean planning to return to work in a few weeks, we had to work out new ways for her to cope: use her secretary as more of a buffer; set stricter office hours; establish a new routine and rearrange management priorities; set fixed rest periods during the day; explain to everyone what her new limitations were; forget the old Shearlean and accept the new Shearlean; avoid conflict and confrontation; go in to the office late and come home early; and take Fridays off.

Managing all of this was only a fraction of what I was doing in addition to caring for Shearlean and accompanying her to all of her treatment appointments. I kept this up right through her death February 2, 2011. It was probably just momentum, but I carried on with the funeral and a celebration of life event into April 2011 before I crashed.

CHAPTER FOURTEEN

Working for Insurance

"HR called to talk about my future options. They were confusing, complicated and left me depressed. I became very emotional and upset, and cried through most of it for two reasons:

1. *Bob talking and arguing.*
2. *My frustration at what I was offered. Nothing good."*

IT WOULD HAVE REASSURED US to know from day one what Shearlean's employer could do to accommodate her needs. As with most bureaucracies, though, it served itself first by never disclosing anything preemptively. The university continually demanded that we choose among benefit and retirement programs without revealing details of what each had to offer. With a straight face we were told that once we made a choice we would be told what benefits our choice would provide. Shearlean sometimes walked out in the midst of Human Resources meetings in tears of frustration. Some of the meetings early in Shearlean's treatment journey resulted only in scheduling another meeting.

Eventually, circumstances played a bigger role in resolving Shearlean's benefits than any decision on our part or any offer from her employer. Shearlean would turn 65 on June 21, 2011 and be eligible for Medicare, and this would take employer health insurance out of the picture and thereby simplify her benefits choices. Meanwhile, she was able to remain employed through a combination of sick leave and intervals of work, which provided income that could sustain us if supplemented by our savings. We weren't certain, but we supposed that with private health insurance replaced by Medicare, savings would see us through to when Shearlean would be eligible for Social Security (because of her birth date, her full Social Security benefit was not available until age 66). Thus we were charting a path for the future that would bypass HR's benefits puzzle and provide us with some much-needed self-determination. This was another of the several advantages that our substantial savings provided. It might be costly, but we need not be at anyone's mercy, and that gave us mental and emotional strength and negotiating leverage.

In the end all of our time spent with Human Resources proved moot, but while it was happening it was a source of great anxiety. When Shearlean died she was still at full salary, fully covered by private state health insurance, and our savings were substantially intact.

Ultimately the state of Washington proved to be compassionate and generous, but its process and procedure were brutal.

HR: OFFICE OF CIRCUMLOCUTION

During editing of this book, the editor made the following comment about text she felt should be deleted from this part: "Bob, I cut this because there is a lot of vague language that doesn't feel helpful to the reader: 'all of our options,' 'best choices,' 'certain prerequisite choices,' 'other choices,' 'discretionary decisions,' etc. One doesn't know specifically what you're referring to here, so it just feels like words without clarity."

Paradoxically, she advised me to delete exactly what I was trying hardest to convey to the reader. Editorially, her evaluation was right on, but this vague and evasive language was precisely what Shearlean and I experienced from Human Resources. I decided to salvage and comment on this bit of discarded writing as the best example of what Dickens meant in his novel, "Little Dorrit," about the Office of Circumlocution. As nonsense, it perfectly describes what we were dealing with.

Job and More Bureaucracy

Work is essential to a person's dignity and sense of identity. Shearlean had worked since she was a teenage drive-in carhop in Copperhill, Tennessee. She had worked continuously for the past 50 years, and much of her identity and self-worth were tied up in what she did for a living. Work was "normal," and she wanted more than anything else to feel normal again. Work also provided the only health insurance we had (though I was on Medicare A), which was our only protection from destitution—real or imagined. For all we knew at the outset of her illness, brain surgery and cancer care were million-dollar expenses; we had no clue about coverage or deductibles. Many, if not most, people who are suddenly struck with a serious illness are grappling with the same lack of knowledge. For us, until we knew how our circumstances were going to be handled by her employer, Western Washington University (aka state of Washington), and how the details of her benefits would actualize, we thought it prudent to insist she *could* work and not to volunteer anything otherwise until we knew the rules of the game we were now required to play.

We were thrilled to learn that medical leave renewed each year. Shearlean took her first medical leave in the fall of 2009 after her surgery and would be eligible again for leave in 2010, so winter quarter (2009/2010) was covered. We'd mistakenly thought she would be forced to retire, take disability or work half time (this is the sort of thing no one would explain to us in advance). But none of those things turned out to be true. We went through a lot of torment and anxiety wondering what to do when the solution would have been simple if we'd been able to get good information.

I went online to research the employee policies and procedures of her employer, but found them impossible to understand on my own. I read and reread the literature I received from HR, but found more questions than answers.

The following is typical of the lists of questions we took to meetings with HR in an effort to learn about Shearlean's benefits. We weren't knowledgeable enough to develop all of these questions at once, rather they developed over time along with the numerous pointless questions we started with. On more than one occasion Shearlean walked out of these meetings, to return only after she had calmed down and regained her composure. Her walking out of these meetings as well as some others was in part my fault because I would keep grilling the person we were meeting with to try to force useful answers to our questions. Had Shearlean been feeling stronger, I'm sure she would have been the intent journalist I knew who would not tolerate obfuscation and circumlocution.

Questions that ultimately yielded information we needed were:

1. When does medical leave renew?
2. What does Shearlean need to do to go back to work in spring quarter?
3. Can we use Consolidated Omnibus Budget Reconciliation Act (COBRA) to buy the same healthcare insurance currently provided as a benefit of WWU?
4. What is Shearlean's employee status after two quarters of leave that finishes at the end of winter quarter 2010?
5. What are an employee's work, leave, benefits, income and other options after two quarters of leave?
6. How do we pay for insurance and other benefits that are currently payroll deductions if there is no payroll check?
7. If an employee goes half time, can she get full benefits?

8. What is the difference between Social Security (SS) disability and straight Social Security? We were going to apply for straight SS, but the application asks if the applicant has been disabled in the past 14 months.
9. How does an employee get reclassified from "disabled" to "able?"
10. Who else should we be talking to about benefits: PEBB, state of Washington, union, other?
11. Is an employee eligible to take over the premiums on benefits (life insurance, for example) if she terminates her job?
12. Is there an advocate or ombudsman to represent an employee's rights and needs?

Over time we found that we could learn what Shearlean's options and benefits were only piecemeal, and had to figure out each next step in small increments as the system ground its way forward. This is the nature of the university system and government bureaucracy. Process is everything. By the time she got sick, Shearlean had 12 years of experience with the university system and she understood and accepted it. I didn't. My outlook was more corporate, which could be boiled down to: identify what obstacles are between you and your goal, develop tactics and strategies to efficiently get what you want, and move on to the next objective. My outlook didn't work well with the university.

I had learned to understand and respect the differences between corporate and academic institutions, but I had not learned yet how to function effectively within the academic system.

As kind and helpful as people at the university were, it was clear that process was more important than an employee's circumstances. It was clear there was nothing malicious nor neglectful nor uncaring in how things were done—many people's care and understanding came through in talking with them—but the process was the process, and nothing was going to change it. Not Shearlean Duke or cancer or terminal illness, and least of all Bob Duke.

We met with HR three times in an effort to make necessary decisions about Shearlean's leave and insurance but came away without sufficient information. We were faced with making end-of-life, end-of-career, end-of-income, end-of-security, end-of-job, end-of-insurance and end-of-everything decisions about what we'd worked for our whole lives with little guidance.

After each meeting we learned a little more about how the system worked and how information was doled out slowly, and so we made *some* progress. (We feared there was no going back once we decided for Shearlean to apply for retirement versus Social Security disability, for example, so we were on hold until we could find out what the consequences of applying would be.) Eventually, though we came to believe we could trust the state, the university and its administration, though it required lengthy frustrating meetings, ultimately it proved moot. Shearlean died before we had to make any life-altering or long-range decisions, or have any forced on us by her condition or circumstances. And this was a worthwhile lesson in itself. That lesson being: Learn all you can about your benefits as soon as you can, but make no decision until you must because matters beyond your control may resolve issues for you and your benefit provider. This was a nerve-wracking game, but there was so much at stake—and our benefits provider was playing the same wait-and-see game—so we dared not make a mistake. It could have been devastating.

It turned out that the system was quite generous, and others should be so lucky as to have the benefits Shearlean had. It took a huge load off both of us when we were finally able to let the system take care of us. I only wish we could have understood how good the benefits were sooner so we could have turned our efforts toward other matters instead of squandering them on something that didn't require our diligence.

UPDATE 13: Gambling on Insurance
March 20, 2010

Hello All

After being on sick leave for two quarters, from October through March, Shearlean is preparing to return to work on March 30, 2010, for the Spring Quarter.

She has her doctor's and her boss' approval and is cautiously optimistic about returning. Her energy and endurance have continued to improve, with few setbacks. While working, though, she will be taking her chemo pill five days out of every 28 days. Her next round of chemo is scheduled to start March 29, 2010. The chemo has little negative effect on her, mainly curbing her appetite and making her a little achy, so we hope it won't impact her work.

Since she is not nor will ever again be exactly the same person as before her illness, she will have to do her job differently than before. She and others are pretty certain that with a little time back on the job she will regain much of her former ability, but she realizes some changes are nevertheless mandatory.

Relatives, doctors, nurses, friends, colleagues and I are unanimous that getting back to work—back to normal—will probably do the most to help Shearlean regain much of what she has lost due to illness. If she can ease herself through the first couple of weeks of the transition into the work environment, she expects to be fully recovered by summer.

Your cards, prayers, good wishes, encouragement, affection and love have already had a miraculous healing effect on Shearlean. She has passed every test with flying colors and her spirit and optimism are at a peak. She is ready for the next challenge and asks all of us for our continued encouragement and support.

I tell her every day she is heroic and fortunate despite being stricken. I think she can do this, and I know your support is vital to meeting her new challenge.

I have attached some photos that show what I call Shearlean's inspiration room. It is the wall of our home office where Shearlean keeps all the cards she's received hung on the walls and has a bulletin board where she posts affirmations, drawings from her nephews, letters from the African girls she taught in Kenya, and treatment calendars. She uses all of this material to inspire herself and as reminders of everyone's support.

Bob

~

So much of Shearlean's identity and self-worth were tied up in her work, I didn't believe she could feel well and normal without it. I was certain that being back at work was the best mental and physical therapy she could have. We had just one car, and I took Shearlean to work and brought her home every day, so there was no need for her to drive. We arranged her treatment appointments for times when I could take her from work to the appointment and then directly home. By adroit scheduling of office hours and meetings, she could usually go in late and come home early, shortening her days without inconveniencing anyone. For meetings she couldn't control, she either simply showed up at the appointed time or sent a delegate to represent the department. She instructed colleagues to try harder to resolve more matters themselves rather than let issues escalate to her involvement. She strictly controlled meeting agendas and scheduled personal meetings for the morning when her verbal skills were strongest. She had a pad and pillow for daily naps on the floor of her office when she locked the door and turned off the light.

Shearlean was worried that all of the concessions she had to make would be objectionable to her colleagues. But I had a thorough discussion with her about the management practices I had seen among executives I had worked for over the years. They all had their idiosyncrasies—time- and annoyance-saving strategies they employed to fit their working styles. I convinced her that none of the things we planned to make her job easier was anything unusual. I told her she wasn't cheating, rather what she was doing was simply smart time and work management; she was still running the department and that's what others wanted of her.

I suggested that if her condition turned ugly one day to just give me a call on my cell phone and I would come directly to her office and take her out of there to spare her any embarrassing breakdown.

Shearlean appeared to accept my perspective and the concessions she would have to make, and I could see she felt safe and comfortable with our plan, so I felt safe and comfortable about her going back to work. Besides, door to door, I was no more than five minutes away from her office. Our ace in the hole was Shearlean's secretary, Carol, who was a pillar of strength and protection on site and someone who could run the department any day Shearlean could not.

~

The Sunday before her first day back at work we went to her office at the university and spent a little time just sitting there. I thought if she sat in her old chair at her familiar desk, surrounded by the artifacts of her career, she would be comforted and would feel like her old self. I hoped this extra time in the office would reduce the awkwardness of the first day back at work.

She plunked herself down in her chair and ran her palms along the edge of her desk. This is where she had shined as an administrator. "You can do this," I said. I had brought with me a printed checklist of the procedures we had worked out and I began reading from it to remind her—in her office setting—of the changes she would make.

She smiled at me and nodded. Shearlean would never say she doubted her decision, but I thought I saw a shadow of anxiety in her expression. You don't know someone as long as I'd known Shearlean without being able to read her face. I got up from the guest side of her desk and walked around to her chair, leaned down and nuzzled her neck, and whispered into her ear, "You can do this."

"I can do this," she said with a wan expression revealing the strain she was feeling.

UPDATE 14: Work Heals

April 21, 2010

Hello All

Shearlean has been back at work for three weeks and has been doing well. In fact, I could say she is thriving under the influence of being there among colleagues and supportive friends. She is not even as fatigued as she was before returning to work. Her naps are fewer and shorter.

She will take her last course of Temodar chemotherapy starting Monday and will receive no further treatment of any kind in the future. When we saw Dr. Kozlowski about an hour ago he congratulated Shearlean on her excellent MRI results from her Friday, April 16 screening. She remains cancer free and her next MRI is not scheduled again for three months, at the end of July.

After waiting anxiously since Friday, we were greatly relieved to hear these results because during the MRI they had taken one additional unplanned picture, and that had scared Shearlean into thinking that one of the other images might have shown something unusual. Not so, though.

It is hard to think of how things could be better unless we were still getting this same news a year from now.

Since we sold our house and are now preparing to move, we've had to take down all the cards and corkboard mementos that have been in the home office these past months. These items were your affirmations and inspirational things Shearlean relied on to keep her spirits up.

From an idea inspired by a friend's cancer blog, we got a large attractive wooden box to put all the cards and other memorabilia into as a symbolic way of saying Shearlean is cured. We call it her "cancer cure box," and everything to do with her cancer is now in that box and put away. Now that we have confirmation that she is cancer free, our timing turned out to be perfect. We are keeping everything, though. If she ever needs it in the future, Shearlean can get everything out and look through it.

We'll write again when there is news.

Bob Duke

UPDATE 15: Selling Our Home
June 21, 2010

Hello All

Shearlean finished working the spring quarter as chair of the Journalism Department at Western Washington University on June 15 and is now off for the summer.

A quarter is 10 weeks, and as you know, this was the first time she has worked since being diagnosed. Last year, she was off for the summer of 2009 when she went to Kenya, Africa. Then, after her diagnosis and surgery, she was off the following fall 2009 and winter 2009/2010 quarters on medical leave. Overall going back to work was a positive experience, one that everyone, including her, thought would be good for her. Work had its drawbacks, though. It took a lot of effort and tested her patience a few times, but her new self-imposed work rules helped. Her rules made sure she rested periodically and avoided confrontations and controversies. Using a kitchen timer on her desk, she took charge of her time as she managed meetings. On the down side, she found that some of her impairments are probably permanent and they become more severe when she tires or is stressed. Since the language area of her brain was most affected by tumor surgery, her typing, writing, reading, listening and speaking are impaired. Of course, impaired is relative. All of her language abilities were highly developed and outstanding in some ways, and now she must exert a lot of effort to be just ordinary. While she can still function acceptably, as she tires or gets stressed and her proficiency declines, she gets discouraged and frustrated.

In cancer-speak, Shearlean's condition continues to be "NED"—No Evidence of Disease. Symptom-wise, she continues to have daily seizures of the same type and degree as she had from the beginning. She often feels like she has the flu and it may last a day or longer. Her medication consists of prednisone, a mild steroid to control edema, and levetiractam, an anti-seizure medication to limit seizure severity.

As you know, we sold the house we've lived in since February 2006 and will move on July 22 to a less expensive home about three miles from where we now live, but still in Bellingham, Washington. Our PO box, email address and telephone are unchanged.

If things continue as well as they have, Shearlean will return to work again in the fall, in mid-September. Then, in the following winter quarter of 2010/2011 she will take a leave to finish the service-learning project she went to Africa to work on in 2008 and 2009.

Our only personal plans are to enjoy our new home and spend our time together doing simple things and sharing life one day at a time.

Bob Duke

P.S. My sister, Jean, is celebrating her 10th anniversary of being free of breast cancer. That's NED too.

During her summer break, in July, Shearlean flew from Bellingham to Palm Springs to stay for a week with Janet. I thought that the stress and strain of moving to our new home would be too much for Shearlean, and I wanted to spare her that ordeal. Frankly, I also wanted her out of my way so I could accomplish the move expeditiously. I had a ruthless approach to getting the job done. Every move we'd ever done was tumultuous because of this. It was a side of me that Shearlean disliked. I convinced her we would both be better off if I did this alone and besides, there was little she was in any condition to help with. Furthermore, she loved the house and neighborhood where we had been living and moving was just another loss to cancer.

I wrote a special update just for her sister to prepare her for Shearlean's visit.

We were all grateful Shearlean could still travel like this, on her own and away from her healthcare system, but I imagined that Janet had to be anxious about caring for Shearlean. For her part, Shearlean was eager and confident about her visit.

UPDATE 16: Traveling Alone
July 11, 2010

Hello All

Here's an update I wrote with Janet as the principal audience.

Janet

I thought I should bring you up to date about how Shearlean is doing.

In many ways she is stable. She has no new symptoms since she was originally diagnosed, but the familiar symptoms get her down, and she has frequent scares when anything new crops up, even if it is unrelated to her tumor. She's on edge a lot and continually wonders whether any new feeling or sensation might signal a recurrence of tumor growth.

She also gets weepy and depressed over having to live with these symptoms as a constant reminder of her condition. It doesn't help either that she is approaching the one-year mark on her diagnosis of "one- to two-years to live" with her cancer.

Though her symptoms are the same and familiar, they can vary in terms of severity and duration. Sometimes she can't use her right hand at all for hours. Seizures come and go.

Some of her symptoms are the result of trying to reduce medication as instructed by her doctor, or because she forgets to take the medication on time. I constantly ask her if she has taken her meds, and once in a while she hasn't. You may want to help her stay on top of this.

While visiting you, she will be trying to reduce steroids. If she starts having symptoms, she is supposed to go back on a higher dose, which she has with her for that purpose.

She doesn't nap every day, but when she must, it is important that she do so for at least an hour. She is also reluctant to be candid about exactly how she is feeling and she can't be relied on to take the best care of herself. She usually goes until it is too late and needs to be told gently (or strongly) to stop or back off or be still for a while.

I want you to know that we talk freely about dying, funerals, funeral ceremonies and things connected with disease and dying. I let her take the lead usually, but sometimes bring up the subject. She is able and willing to deal with this, and it would not be out of place for you to talk to her about it or lead into the subject and see where she might want the conversation to go. I think it could be good to talk with you about it no matter how briefly or superficially.

Her next MRI comes when she returns from visiting you. July 26. Hopefully, nothing will be found, but getting close to her one-year anniversary has us both on edge.

We have chosen Dr. Hinton, her radiation oncologist, as her palliative care physician. Palliative care is all that's available to her since her cancer is incurable. Palliative care is intended to ensure she is comfortable and pain free, that she will not be hospitalized or have to resort to emergency room visits or ambulance rides. If an emergency were to arise while she is visiting, there is really nothing you or anyone could do. She has all the medicines with her that she might need. Dr. Hinton's office is very familiar with her case and desires, and he would be the best person to contact. I would be the second best if it were a health crisis. Generally, her existing meds, along with time and rest are all that can be done to help her feel better.

I expect to have Shearlean cared for at home throughout the duration of her disease. As long as I am healthy and capable, that will be my goal. I recently had a physical and am in great shape. My doctor says he expects to be treating me for 10 more years. Of course, there is always the risk of my dropping dead an instant from now, but for now there is no reason to think that might happen.

I hope this email doesn't cause you any alarm. It shouldn't. Shearlean is doing remarkably well, but has her ups and downs, and there is always the possibility of something new. Because you are her sister and because she visits you often, I feel a special need to keep you up on what's going on with her. Anyway, I think we would all feel better if you were well informed. I don't know what she shares with you but it is probably a lot different than what you hear from me.

If you have any specific questions or concerns please ask me about them. You can also ask Shearlean because she is quite able and willing to talk about all of this, though she needs prompting sometimes to do so.

Bob

CHAPTER FIFTEEN

One-Year Anniversary and the End of Time

"At night when I take my chemo pill
I see a beautiful blue light that surrounds
any remaining cancer cells and evaporates
them from my body."

AS THE ANNIVERSARY of Shearlean's diagnosis neared, that initial prognosis of one year to live was foremost in our thoughts. Ominously, her tumor returned. The initial prescribed treatment had run its course. We must now embark on a new and unknown path. Though never emphasized to us, there was always the underlying understanding that the tumor would return and as with all else about the prognosis, I had accepted it and saw this news as a continuation of our year-old process. I worried more about how Shearlean would respond to this development because she was wholly committed to beating this threat. I had to be careful not to be caught studying her too intently. Shortly, she seemed to shake off any shock she may have experienced with the news and was again embracing the optimism and attitude that had brought her this far. She was convinced that since she was still alive this was a second chance to beat this thing. Shearlean was ready and so was I for the second round of treatment. Originally approved for treatment of colorectal cancer in 2004, Avastin was approved for treatment of previously treated glioblastoma cancer in May 2009. Little was known about its long-term effects on glioblastoma patients, but it was known to keep tumors from growing by inhibiting the tumor's ability to construct blood vessels to nourish its growth.

UPDATE 17: More Chemo, More Risk

August 11, 2010

Hello All

Shearlean had her first MRI in three months on this past Monday, July 26.

We met with her chemo oncologist, Dr. Kozlowski, this afternoon and learned that the MRI indicated Shearlean's tumor has grown back and doubled in size since her last MRI in April 2010. We looked at side-by-side comparisons of April and July images with Dr. Hinton and could see the increased area highlighted by the dye injection Shearlean was given to illuminate the tumor area.

As has been the case since she was first diagnosed on August 21, 2009,Shearlean's symptoms have not increased or gotten worse. They have remained mild all this time, which has enabled her to travel, work and socialize with ease. We felt that with her early diagnosis, successful surgery and lack of serious symptoms, she had already experienced a miracle. Now, after a year of mild symptoms and nearly normal functioning, we are realizing that she and I have experienced a great many miracles, one every day. We feel blessed and grateful and look forward to many more good days as new treatment is undertaken.

While the details are still being worked out, we know that she will resume taking Temodar, a pill specifically for the treatment of glioblastoma, and she will also start infusion chemo with Avastin, a successful drug that is commonly used for treatment of Shearlean's condition. Shearlean has tolerated all chemo (and other treatment) very well and we are expecting that she will have the same good fortune with the new treatment.

The goal of the new treatment is to arrest or slow down the growth of the tumor. Doing so will continue to keep her symptom free and functioning well so that she can continue to enjoy life and be pain free.

Continuing days of miracles are something we've grown used to and can expect more of. So our plan is to keep on keeping on, one miraculous day after another.

When we have the details and Shearlean begins new treatment I will write a more detailed update.

Bob Duke

Our hiatus from disease and treatment was over. Since Shearlean had already exhausted conventional treatment and had realized the benefits it promised, the only thing to do now was to try something relatively new and to also resume the previous treatment with Temodar. We'd always known that Shearlean might eventually do infusion chemo with Avastin, but the idea of restarting Temodar was news to us. Without any forethought on our part, or emphatic warnings from our doctors, we were launching ourselves into the unknown. Twelve months of the treatment Shearlean had already undergone was the primary treatment the medical establishment recommended for glioblastoma. Every treatment from now on was something of an experiment, and the better the experiment worked, the longer it would be used—and the riskier it became—but there was no less risky alternative. There was just the unspoken acknowledgement that continuing treatment with powerful chemicals was damaging and dangerous to the patient's health. The anti-cancer medications and symptom management medications, such as dexamethasone, oxycodone and OxyContin, complicated life and took a toll on Shearlean. Her outstanding health since her diagnosis was a powerful ally in the success of her treatment, but given the assault Shearlean's body was under, it couldn't last.

By now we had grown somewhat used to Dr. Kozlowski and since his role in Shearlean's treatment had been relatively minor until now, he was mostly an occasional irritation. Now however, he was going to take on a major role in her care and do so at a critical juncture—when Shearlean was becoming more vulnerable. Instead of self-administering chemo, by taking Temodar capsules, Shearlean would have to rely on a complex system for delivering her new medication intravenously. This meant infusion on an outpatient basis, requiring frequent visits to a hospital facility. Infusion, the slow injection of a solution into a vein or tissue, is a drug delivery system used to treat conditions and infections that are unresponsive to orally delivered medicine. Dr. Kozlowski would oversee this process.

When I realized that we were going to have to deal with Dr. Kozlowski more regularly, I immediately grew agitated.

Dr. Kozlowski's part-time work week now compounded our anxiety over each impending MRI. In August, he scheduled an MRI on a Wednesday, his last workday. This frustrated me because I knew he wouldn't be back in the office again for four days. MRI results could be turned around in one day, but scheduling on a Wednesday meant we wouldn't know Shearlean's results until the following Monday or Tuesday when he returned to his office. This left us agonizing over Shearlean's condition for too many excruciating days. If he ordered the MRI on a Monday, he would have the results on Tuesday and we would be relieved of our prolonged dread over what might have been found.

I talked to him about this after the first time it happened, but he was unconcerned about our anxiety and scheduled several MRIs on Wednesdays in the future. I wanted to strangle him.

Hospital infusion involved a doctor prescribing and managing the medication, the hospital pharmacy preparing and delivering the solution to the infusion center, and nurses and technicians delivering the solution by inserting a needle into the patient's arm. The infusion center in Bellingham was a large and complex operation, often serving a dozen patients plus their caregivers simultaneously, typically over multiple shift changes. At each visit, the attending team (up to five professionals, including the infusion technician, the shift supervisor and the center manager) could be different. Shearlean and I found this challenging.

Also, although patients receive their infusions in curtained cubicles, the center was noisy and hectic. In each cubical there was a reclining infusion chair and guest chair. Cubicles were arranged in a horseshoe around the room with the nurse's station to one side. Shearlean brought a meditation tape, others brought music—but unfortunately, many brought their cell phones.

Shearlean's first Avastin treatment was on August 2, 2010.

We checked in at reception and were directed to the infusion waiting room. With the start of Avastin infusion, Shearlean was also to start taking Temodar again, for which Dr. Kozlowski was to provide the prescription. His nurse, with whom we had been working, was to send the prescription to our nemesis, RxB, which had *mis*handled our earlier Temodar prescriptions.

In line with my resolution to receive a copy of every prescription (because of the original Temodar prescription fiasco) I made the regrettable mistake of asking for a copy of the new Temodar prescription. Instead of just sitting quietly with Shearlean until she was called for infusion treatment, I went to the reception desk and asked for a copy of it from Dr. Kozlowski (whose office was at the infusion center). I was informed that because of HIPAA privacy requirements, a copy of the patient's prescription could only be given to the patient (an all too familiar refrain.) Instantly exasperated, I reminded the receptionist that the patient and I had just checked in and the patient was in the waiting room. "She needs to come to the desk and request the copy herself," I was told. I looked into the waiting room and saw that Shearlean was gone, obviously called for her infusion.

Privacy Trumps Patient Welfare

In dealing with healthcare providers it became obvious to me that the Health Insurance Portability and Accountability Act (HIPAA) privacy rule was foremost in everyone's mind at pharmacy RxB, as well as every doctor's office we visited throughout our experience. For the pharmacy in particular, HIPAA clearly took precedent over getting medication to patients. I usually introduced myself on the phone with RxB and elsewhere as the patient's spouse and caregiver. Immediately the person I was speaking to said she had to speak to the patient. I then explained that the patient was unavailable and was unable to speak for herself. This resulted in more than one standoff where I insisted the person speak to me and the person insisted that they speak to Shearlean. Eventually, I took to explaining that the patient had a brain tumor, was suffering from aphasia and could not speak and might not understand what was said on the phone. This had no effect on the other person who usually repeated a demand to speak to the patient and warned me of the ramifications of the HIPAA rule as it applied to healthcare providers. Then I would ask for a supervisor or manager and we started the whole HIPAA thing all over again. When I resorted to bargaining with the person, offering to email, fax or snail mail a copy of my durable power of attorney and patient's healthcare directive to be filed with the patient's records (to avoid the HIPAA dilemma in the future), my offer was neither accepted nor rejected, but the person on the line simply reiterated her demand to speak to the patient.

At last, I pleaded with this person to send me a waiver form (if there was such a thing) that the patient could sign to waive the HIPAA rule and appoint me as her spokesman, caregiver, agent or whatever designation was acceptable to the provider's company. She couldn't do that. By this point, typically, I had been on the phone for maybe 20 minutes. I sometimes hung up in exasperation until I could summon the energy to try again.

Another time, Shearlean was the object of an automated phone call from RxB. Unfortunately, she answered the phone when it rang and had to work her way through various prompts and choices until she reached a live customer service representative. By the time the representative answered, Shearlean had become confused and incoherent, and handed me the phone indicating she could not continue.

An absurd conversation then ensued with a caller named Ben. I identified myself as Shearlean's spouse, advocate and caregiver, and asked Ben what he was calling about. He refused to say and said he must talk to Shearlean Duke. I asked again what he was calling about and he said he couldn't say because of privacy requirements. He kept saying he was sorry but he needed to talk to Shearlean, and I said that unless he talked to me he couldn't talk to anybody.

Basically, Ben insisted I *guess* what he was calling about, and unless I could guess he couldn't tell me why he'd called! I said he had to be explicit, and I wasn't willing to play a ridiculous game.

I finally hung up. By then Shearlean was agitated and weeping from overhearing my side of the phone call.

Eventually, I discovered that I could request a form to authorize access to or disclosure of protected health information with some of these providers. Shearlean signed the forms for both RxW and RxB (the two pharmacies we dealt with regularly). Having the forms on file helped but didn't stop calls from representatives who did not know the forms were on file.

Other System Malfunctions

Another privacy issue was that healthcare providers would not leave any form of telephone voicemail or answering machine message. They wouldn't even leave a message saying they called or asking us to call them. By 2014 some providers were finally addressing this issue, but the discussion was only in its initial stages. I was told in 2011 that one reason for my particular problem was that my voicemail greeting didn't satisfy the provider's requirement to verify that it was really my phone they had reached. I hadn't identified myself adequately, they said.

We all know that you can't call a doctor with any expectation of reaching him. You will almost always have to ask for him to call you back. When he calls back, if you don't answer, you won't hear anything from him. Your best bet is to clearly identify yourself on your voicemail greeting message, but even that may not do the trick.

No Universal Privacy Waiver

The biggest impediment to care throughout Shearlean's illness, with every provider, was that we were not always offered a HIPAA privacy waiver, and sometimes it took great effort to get one. At other times we were asked to sign a new form on every visit. We were told releases were good for just 90 days, although sympathetic doctors advised me to write "Lifetime" in the duration space. At the hospital we were told the release was in our computer records, yet few would *(could?)* access it from their computer and accept it.

We neither wanted nor needed privacy but were forced to accept it, which seemed to us to be a bizarre imposition.

At a time when the sick are at their most vulnerable, they are subjected to "business as usual" and "self-serving practices" that add to their misery and frustrate those trying to care for them.

At his February 25, 2010, White House healthcare summit, President Obama described his dying mother's predicament of lying on her deathbed arguing with healthcare providers about coverage and care. He said he sympathized with "the desperation people feel when they're sick."

I now understood what he was talking about.

Plan B. "Could I speak to Amala, Dr. Kozlowski's nurse?" Amala knew me and together we had sorted out the earlier Temador problems. Surely she would give me a copy of the prescription. The receptionist held the phone away from her mouth and asked whether I had an appointment with Dr. Kozlowski. I said no. She said no into the phone and after a moment said, "The nurse can't see you if you don't have an appointment with the doctor." *I mustn't make a scene*, I cautioned myself.

"Maybe Shearlean could ask her infusion nurse to get a copy of the prescription," the receptionist volunteered.

"Thanks," I said in a controlled voice and hustled off to be with Shearlean in infusion.

When I rejoined Shearlean I was disturbed at how the staff seemed disorganized and uncaring. We had never experienced infusion treatment before and thought we would be offered an orientation or introduction to the process. Technician Donna, who was to treat Shearlean, showed up acting distracted, her eyes darting around the room and her movements tentative. She began preparations for treatment without any preliminaries or formalities. Shearlean recoiled from her approach and angrily demanded that she slow down and focus on the task at hand. Donna balked and said that she couldn't treat an uncooperative patient.

In an attempt to break the icy deadlock between Shearlean and Donna, to give them both time to cool off, I asked Donna if she could get Shearlean a copy of her new Temodar prescription from Dr. Kozlowski or his nurse Amala.

At first Donna didn't seem to know what to do to respond to my request. Then, deciding she could use a break, I suppose, she hurried off in the direction of the clinic's reception desk I had just left. She was gone for nearly a half hour.

Meanwhile, Shearlean was on the verge of fainting. She'd become cold and clammy and felt sick. When Donna finally returned to start Shearlean's infusion, I asked where the copy of the prescription was. She didn't realize she had never actually brought me the piece of paper I was trying to get and disappeared again. Shearlean continued to wait.

She was growing irritable about the continuing delay in getting her infusion started. And I was feeling guilty for causing the delay, even though I thought it was necessary. Finally, Donna returned with a piece of paper that she handed to Shearlean and quickly started the Avastin drip. We settled in to wait for the 90-minute infusion bag to be emptied. When it was empty in 75 minutes, we were alarmed. A pharmacist filled the bag—we thought—and apparently the amount was inadequate for the treatment! I wondered not only whether Shearlean had gotten what she needed, but I also wondered how we would be billed: 90 minutes worth or 75 minutes worth of the drug? Even though the drug manufacturer's published protocol said the first infusion should be 90 minutes, the pharmacy didn't deliver 90 minutes, I feared.

We'd been told repeatedly, verbally and in writing, that she was supposed to receive a 90-minute treatment.

When I asked Donna about this, she shrugged and said, "It doesn't matter anyway. It was the ordered amount of Avastin, it just didn't take as long." I looked over at Shearlean to see if she'd heard this comment. Her face was contorted by a combination of anger and disbelief as she repeated Donna's statement as a question, "It doesn't matter?"

Shearlean and I looked at each other incredulously, mouthing the words, "It doesn't matter?"

When we finally left that Monday and walked back out into the warm August air, I knew that if there had been a choice, we wouldn't go back to that infusion place. The attitude of the front desk was that only Shearlean should be able to receive the information I desired, not me, the caregiver. As good as Shearlean was doing, she was not up to handling the administrative stuff. I had to be allowed to do it.

When we met with Dr. Kozlowski again we told him about our concerns regarding what had happened at the infusion center.

"What is the process supposed to look like?" Shearlean asked. I glared at Dr. Kozlowski and dared him to make her cry as he had before.

"Well, I'm not sure. I've never observed the process," he said. He seemed annoyed by our questions. I watched as he tilted his head back, swung it to settle his long hair, and stared at the ceiling as though he just discovered something fascinating there.

It turned out (which I discovered from my own research later) that Avastin was not provided on the basis of a prescription in the familiar sense of the word. Rather, the Avastin that Shearlean was receiving was based on an "order set." This was apparently something written by the doctor to direct the treatment rather than something that went only to a pharmacist. So, when I'd asked for a copy of this prescription, I couldn't get one because, technically, there wasn't one. Why someone couldn't have explained this to me, Shearlean's worried caregiver who waited for her careless technicians to provide treatment, I would never get to know.

There was no prescribed course of new chemo treatment regarding how long treatment would last, either. It was open-ended based on results. Treatment would continue as long as no tumor growth was found through imaging. We were shocked at this. We'd thought she would only be taking the new chemo until December. All of this information would have helped me, if I'd had it earlier. How was it that this doctor had neglected to explain the process to us, though we'd asked for information at least a half-dozen times?

Before we left Dr. Kozlowski on August 30, he said, as if in an aside, "By the way, Shearlean's October 4 MRI appointment has been changed to September 27." Apparently Kozlowski's patients couldn't make their own MRI appointments anymore. Other doctors in the same system gave patients a signed imaging order and let the patient make the appointment when it was convenient for them. Dr. Kozlowski, it seemed, preferred to make patient imaging appointments that were convenient for him. My frustration was barely controllable as we left him, hand in sweaty hand, heading back down the hall, past reception and then into the parking lot.

When we got home, we felt we had to respond to what we saw as carelessness. We sat down and together wrote Dr. Kozlowski a letter about how uninformed we were, though we'd asked for clarification about the process, and what a surprise his comments were about there being no treatment termination date.

At the next appointment I confronted him and asked for his response to our letter. He fidgeted and stuck out his lower lip in a pout. "The level of detail you want is not generally given to patients," he said squirming on the edge of his chair.

I sat in the hard chair next to Shearlean squirming with my own agitation. "We're out of control without information, and we're uncomfortable not knowing what's going on in our own lives," I replied to him, willing him to understand and step up as a compassionate human being. It seemed we would always leave Dr. Kozlowski's office disappointed.

I next notified hospital management about our concerns regarding the disorganization and misinformation we'd received about infusion treatment. They asked me for dates, times, names and so forth so that my complaint could be investigated. But I declined to be specific because I feared retaliation. While I was repeatedly assured there would be no retaliation if I registered a complaint, I never believed it. What if the hospital staff didn't give Shearlean the best care they could because they were irritated with me or became so defensive that we were shunned? I could never forgive myself. Also, I was certain that any competent manager or investigator could determine the facts by simple observation because the problem was so prevalent.

As time went on, the struggle continued to evolve around infusion. Nurses would tell us that Dr. Kozlowski didn't provide the order for the Avastin, and Dr. Kozlowski would tell us the nurses had misplaced the order. Once, he said the nurses had failed to deliver the order to the pharmacy in time for it to be available when Shearlean arrived for treatment. When I told the nurses what Dr. Kozlowski said and told Dr. Kozlowski what the nurses said, each would say the other was mistaken. I wanted to talk to the hospital pharmacy to find out why the drug was delivered late but was informed the pharmacy was off limits to patients. The whole infusion operation was highly territorial. The nurses were as adamant about their role as the doctor and the pharmacy were. There was a lot of conflict, and it was pretty clear that none of the people there were accustomed to dealing with caregivers, at least not assertive ones.

As always there were just too many people to deal with: Dr. Kozlowski, his nurse, three supervising infusion nurses, a half-dozen treatment technicians, the infusion manager, the pharmacy, infusion reception and administration, and a volunteer or two. For any given infusion we dealt with at least five people, and there was always another staffer who could be summoned to *help* (I say, confront) me if I complained or if my stubborn insistence sent a technician running off crying

Once, out of complete frustration I filched a copy of Shearlean's infusion order from Kozlowski's desk and was alarmed at how sloppy and erroneous it was. I wondered how anyone received the right drug or dose. Infusion dosage was determined by the patient's weight. On Shearlean's order, her weight in pounds was entered as 138 kilograms. There are 2.2 pounds per kilogram. If the order were filled as written, she would receive more than double the dose appropriate for her weight.

The turmoil of each infusion appointment and the endless shuffling of staff even after treatment had begun made me tense and I sweated at every visit. Though I would have rather remained with Shearlean during infusion, instead, after seeing treatment begin successfully, I began going to a nearby Costco store until it was time to pick her up. I had as little contact with the infusion staff as I could manage just to keep myself sane.

Though she tried to keep her positive attitude, Shearlean's apprehension about her condition grew with the return of her tumor near the 12-month anniversary of her diagnosis and the start of the new chemotherapy. She began looking for some radical alternative treatment that might prolong her life. I didn't criticize her quest, but I was pessimistic about whether she could qualify for any of the alternatives.

Shearlean befriended a woman named Becca around this time. She was a cardiovascular surgery nurse diagnosed with two simultaneous glioblastoma tumors in the front lobes of her brain just two months after Shearlean's 2009 diagnosis. Becca had no obvious mental impairments from her surgery or treatment and had immediately returned to work in the operating room. She was fully functional and energetic, but with the same fatal prognosis Shearlean had. As a medical professional, Becca had superior knowledge of alternative brain cancer treatments and had opted for evaluation by the University of California San Francisco (UCSF) medical center.

Ultimately Becca was rejected for the trial treatment, and based on Becca's rejection, Shearlean decided not to apply. Many alternative treatments were for dealing with a growing tumor or worsening tumor symptoms, which neither Shearlean nor Becca were experiencing. Other alternatives involved additional surgery or other invasive procedures to harvest tumor material. Still others were open only to patients for whom established treatment methods were not working, which was not the case for Becca or Shearlean. The trials and alternative treatments we were aware of had such specialized criteria for acceptance that there was little chance that the average patient would qualify. From Becca's example, Shearlean decided not to waste any time chasing speculative alternatives to her existing treatment.

Shearlean began to express interest in knowing how her life might end if her glioblastoma proved fatal. I'd wondered this myself for a long time, but Shearlean was only starting to talk about it explicitly. I was glad she was raising the question. It was more pressing now that she had reached her one-year diagnosis anniversary and soon, on September 10, would have her one-year surgery anniversary. She reconnected with her counselor and began talking through matters that she had been able to avoid for a while.

I wrote a letter to Shearlean's sister, Janet to catch her up on our situation—how Shearlean was managing and what future treatment options would (and would not) be.

Dear Janet,

Here's some recent news about treatment alternatives.

Dr. Hinton says:

"UCSF has an excellent neuro-oncology program. I do not know the specifics of the vaccine trial Shearlean discussed with them, but usually additional tumor tissue is required for vaccine generation. The issue of whether additional surgery is possible would be up to the surgeon. In general, reoperation is reserved for symptomatic recurrences while systemic treatments, like Avastin and Temodar, are used in asymptomatic progression. Shearlean should be evaluated by another surgeon if she develops progressive symptoms or demonstrates radiographic progression on Avastin. She could see someone locally, we have good neurosurgeons here, or in Seattle—probably at the Swedish Neuroscience Institute given your previous experience at University Medical. UCSF is also a consideration as they have some of the most aggressive neurosurgeons in the country. Regarding the end of life issue, I will be happy to discuss that further at our appointment on the 13th. I am glad to hear that Shearlean is doing well. "

We wrote Dr. Kozlowski a letter about how uninformed we felt and what a surprise his comments were about there being no definite end to the infusion treatments. When we met, he was troubled at the level of detail we wanted and said it was not generally given to patients. We said we were out of control without information and uncomfortable not knowing much about what was going on.

Janet, one thing that is causing trouble with Dr. Kozlowski is that Shearlean decided to make her radiation oncologist, Dr. Hinton, her primary care physician. Consequently, Dr. Hinton remains involved when Dr. Kozlowski thinks he should butt out. We hadn't told Dr. Kozlowski about Dr. Hinton's ongoing role until recently because we always ran out of time in our meetings with him. I finally filled in Dr. Kozlowski regarding Dr. Hinton's role as primary care. There shouldn't even be a problem, but there has been. Maybe it will go away now.

From all I've read, these kinds of situations between patient and doctor are not uncommon.

Love,
Bob

I was getting used to Shearlean's symptoms and condition oscillating within familiar parameters. And then a bizarre development took me on an emotional roller coaster ride. Of all the possible effects from the cancer, surgery, radiation, chemo and medication, the one that frightened me the most was a radical change in behavior that happened one day. I had always been afraid that if Shearlean's behavior changed drastically, she would no longer be the person I knew and loved but would turn into a stranger that I might be unable to care for in the way I wanted. I might suddenly find myself forced to take care of someone I didn't know. From the beginning, I was afraid I couldn't face that. But I might have to.

The odd symptoms lasted only several hours, but they shook me to my core. While they were happening, I felt afraid and alone and could think of nothing to do but email the one constant ally we had, Dr. Hinton:

Dr. Hinton

Shearlean is suddenly suffering severe mental problems. I call it paranoia, but I am probably clinically mistaken. Here is what she is doing now that has me frightened and confused about what to do.

She says I'm hiding her pneumonia medication from her.

She whispers to me that she doesn't trust the cleaning girl, one of her students that she hired to help us.

She told me that while I was out she heard a man in the house. Only the cleaning girl was here.

She tells me she is afraid that I am mismanaging her medications and she wants control of them.

When I close her bedroom door for her quiet and privacy, she says she is being held prisoner and not allowed out of the room.

When I go out, she fears I am abandoning her and will not return.

She says I purposely misunderstand her to confuse her. If I quote back to her what she said, she says I'm lying.

Last night I woke up hearing her say, "Too much blood! Too much blood!" I asked her what she was talking about and she said she has been reading too many murder mystery books.

She asks me unanswerable questions in all seriousness, for example: "How could you read without water?"

She sometimes looks at me as though I'm a total stranger telling her the wildest story imaginable.

Her surgeon and others had warned us that surgery or cancer could change her behavior and personality. I'm wondering whether this is it. I called her psychotherapist, whom Shearlean has been seeing for quite some time, and she thinks it is too out of character to be a mental problem and is most likely the result of the brain tumor or medication and needs a clinician's attention.

I increased Shearlean's dex from 1 mg to 4 mg twice daily and got stronger oxycodone and OxyContin, but they have had no visible effect.

Physically she is somewhat better from her recent bout of pneumonia, but mentally she is a wreck.

Maybe we need another MRI.

We have an appointment with you 1 p.m. Monday. She is also scheduled for an Avastin infusion at 7:45 a.m. Monday.

A few hours after I pushed the send button, Shearlean's bizarre symptoms began to dissipate, and I began to breathe again. She turned back into the woman I'd always known. I'd lived through my worst fear.

CHAPTER SIXTEEN

Unwelcome Anniversary

*"I have hoped it would be a year from now,
but I do want to be ready."*

UPDATE 18: Double Chemo
September 23, 2010

Hello All

Shearlean has now talked to all of her doctors and has started two forms of prescribed chemotherapy. Her glioblastoma (GBM) brain tumor returned, doubling in size between April and July according to her July 2010 MRI. Shearlean's symptoms, though, remain the same as they have been since she was diagnosed on August 21, 2009. Chemotherapy is just an effort to slow or retard growth of her tumor at this point.

Growth of the tumor is not necessarily a crisis in itself as long as symptoms are not aggravated. On the other hand, edema has also increased since April. Edema, remember, is fluid in the tissue that has resulted from cells damaged and destroyed by the tumor. Increased fluid can cause pressure on the brain, which can bring about harmful symptoms that are the same as or similar to the symptoms the tumor produces. Basically, the body must be relied upon to carry away the fluid; Shearlean is still taking steroids to help decrease the effects of edema.

She is again taking the pill form of Temodar and has also started a new chemotherapy using Avastin, which is given by infusion (intravenously) once every two weeks. Shearlean had her first Avastin treatment on August 2. She tolerated it so well that we went to visit friends in Montana on August 4.

Another MRI is scheduled for early October to see what effects the Temodar and Avastin are having on the tumor. Hopefully, the tumor will either be reduced in size or will not have grown. That MRI will also look at her edema to see whether it is improving. All of this treatment and monitoring will be continued through December of this year.

You may recall past updates that mentioned various prescription and pharmacy problems, and these continue to plague treatment. Our old nemesis, RxB—the specialty mail-order pharmacy we are mandated to use by Washington state under the insurance coverage we have—is still at it. I was foolish enough to think I had solved the problems with obtaining Temodar from RxB, but have learned it is infinitely inventive in finding new ways to create problems. This time RxB delivered too much medication (better than too little, but still demonstrating it is out of control). Shearlean's prescription for Temodar calls for taking one 140 milligram dose daily for 21 days. Naturally, we expected to receive 21 doses. Instead, we received two bottles containing 14 doses each and no information about what to do with the extra seven doses. (Would they send another 14 doses to which we would add our leftover seven for the next round, and who was keeping score?) This shipment came by overnight FedEx from RxB's main pharmacy in Ohio. Two days later, we received another shipment of Temodar by USPS Express Mail from RxB's Seattle pharmacy. This shipment contained exactly 21 doses. We never knew before that there was a Seattle pharmacy! No one from RxB has contacted us yet, making me think they don't know what they did. RxB, though, is demonstrating that it has no control over the distribution of medications that cost hundreds of dollars per dose.

On the hospital pharmacy level things are equally bad. All the published protocols for Avastin state that the first infusion (of an amount determined by patient weight) is 90 minutes. Shearlean's doctors and nurses advised her that her first treatment would be 90 minutes. Being the clock-watchers we are, we timed the treatment several ways and found it was only 75 minutes. When we asked the infusion nurse about it she said, "Don't worry, it doesn't matter."

While infusion is not an exact process, this is a 17 percent error. When I pursued this with the infusion people (on the advice of Shearlean's radiologist) I was tongue-lashed by the nurse in charge as being an untrusting troublemaker who should be ashamed of doubting their practices and standards.

Duh!

Another criticism I get as Shearlean's caregiver and spokesman is that I should consider the fact that doctors and nurses have other patients. My reply is that I have only one patient and, as far as I am concerned, there are no other patients.

Pardon my ranting.

I will send another update in early October after Shearlean's next MRI.

Your notes, encouragement and prayers are uplifting and obviously beneficial. While Shearlean continues to do well physically and is mentally positive, she is sometimes emotionally drained. Please write when time permits—you have the power to help and to heal.

Bob Duke

Surviving the original 12-month prognosis had now brought Shearlean face-to-face with another milestone. Exceeding 15 months survival loomed as an even grimmer date. Kennedy, for all of his wealth and power, could not survive more than 15 months. Now here comes poor, ordinary Shearlean Duke along the same path, so what hope does she have?

Shearlean managed to be more upbeat than ever, while I became more apprehensive. She saw a limitless horizon ahead, and I saw diminishing alternatives and time running out. I wanted to share her optimism but couldn't ignore the doctors' reality.

One day, sitting at my desk sorting medical bills without really being able to focus on anything I was staring at, I just threw the handful of papers back into the in-basket, swiveled around in my chair to stare out the window at the giant cedars that lined the road past our community and reviewed what I knew: The MRI results sounded good, but they were deceptive. That Shearlean had terminal cancer never changed. Cancer would kill her. So if the cancer was under control, death was deferred. But that would only be true if death were to result directly from cancer. It had begun to dawn on me that death could result from other causes such as pneumonia, which claims many elderly patients before they succumb to more dreaded afflictions.

As these realities came home to me, I gave in to the exhaustion that had been dogging me for so long. I always tried to have something in reserve and to never let Shearlean think that she was too much of a burden. I knew she would try to spare me if she detected weakness on my part, and that was the last thing I wanted her to do. I didn't need rest so much as distraction, so I told Shearlean that when she napped I was going to the harbor to check on our boat. Mainly, I intended to find someone to talk to about boats and harbor politics to get my mind off my pessimism.

CHAPTER SEVENTEEN

Working for Her Legacy

*"Feel good! Up at 7:30 a.m.
Energetic. No aches."*

(She went to work and came home
at 1:30 p.m. still feeling good, Bob.)

AS SHE WOULD HAVE normally, Shearlean took the 2010 summer off and it was good that she did. She needed all her strength to deal with the new chemotherapy and to combat the new growth of the tumor. But even now, fortune smiled on her. No new symptoms accompanied the new growth and the chemotherapy was working to reduce the tumor's size and prevent further growth.

With the agreement of her doctors and employer, Shearlean went back to work again in the fall quarter of 2010. I was concerned about this decision, but as before, I knew that her work was essential to Shearlean's state of mind, so I supported it. After her first day of work with her fellow faculty, I was worried about her ability to function at the level she needed to. We had an appointment with Dr. Hinton the next day, so I sent him an email about thoughts regarding Shearlean's functioning to ask for his help.

September 21, 2010.

Good Evening Dr. Hinton

No reply necessary.

Before we meet with you tomorrow I wanted to give you a head's up about Shearlean's condition and symptoms. On

Monday she competently conducted a five-hour meeting with 12 department faculty about the upcoming quarter. On Tuesday, after her MRI, she went to her office for four hours and did administrative work, including phone calls, but was confused about computer passwords and typing.

She is alert, competent and capable, but perhaps as a result of the medication, her speech is slow, labored and coarse, like she has a sore throat. Her walk and posture are slumped, tentative and unsteady. Doddering.

She has regained normal use of her right hand but has had continued difficulty with numbness in her right leg, which makes her gait something of a shambling ramble. If she applies herself, she can stand straight and walk purposefully, and appear normal. But it takes a lot of effort and she can't sustain it. She is easily confused and irritable, but can plod through to the correct conclusion or action.

I've re-read the side effects for dexamethasone, Keppra, lorazepam and Temodar. They all cause cough, raspy throat, and minor tongue and throat swelling. Her other symptoms can also be attributed to medication.

Given her performance and energy level, I suggest her symptoms are the result of medication, barring anything significant on the MRI. She would like to start cutting back on medication and dosage, if you agree, and would like to come away from our meeting with a regimen for doing so. She more often errs on under medicating and is conscientious about dosage and frequency, but it all adds up. If she weren't working I wouldn't be too concerned, but her impression could be adverse in a workplace.

She had been taking the following prescribed medications and dosages:

- one 4 mg dex twice daily.
- one 1 mg lorazepam twice daily.
- one 500 mg Keppra twice daily.
- one 40 mg Temodar once daily.

On Monday and Tuesday she also took, hydrocodone and/or oxycodone, 2 mg of diazepam and sometimes at night 15 mg of temazepam, along with the above meds.

Your recommendations would be appreciated.

See you tomorrow at 9 a.m.
Bob Duke

While she had been on medical leave, Shearlean's position as department chair (a managerial and administrative job usually with limited classroom teaching) was filled on a part time and interim basis by fellow faculty. On returning to work the previous spring she resumed her chair position full time but with no lecturing responsibilities (which she could not have fulfilled anyway because of her mercurial language abilities). By means of my updates and our regular contact with faculty, everyone in the department had stayed well-informed about Shearlean's condition and progress. With some help from me, Shearlean had redefined her job as chair and worked out new practices for holding office hours, conducting and attending meetings, and meeting with students. All of this had served her nicely her first quarter back and continued to work well at the beginning of the next academic year.

Her particular goal in working the fall of 2010 was to get tenure for two faculty members in order to leave the department in good shape after she was gone. This was what she wanted her management legacy to be. She saw completing this task as a worthy end to her career and would be at peace with leaving the university behind if she could get it done.

Obtaining tenure at the university required preparing huge volumes of documentation to support the application. It involved a lot of writing and word processing and an intensive review of an applicant's publishing history, student critiques, performance evaluations, and institutional and community service participation. I could help some with editing, proofreading and word processing, but Shearlean had to originate the content. Over the first weeks of the quarter, I thought she was doing relatively well. Even though the work was strenuous for her; it made her feel relevant and productive, and in control. (In the end, she did achieve tenure for one person but not for the other, who didn't meet the publishing requirements.)

Before she'd gotten sick, Shearlean had already reorganized the department and had it on a good footing. She had been chair for five years and was popular with her colleagues—though not all of them as it turned out. Two incidents during the fall 2010 quarter were the saddest personal events in her 12 years at Western.

The first incident occurred at an off-campus department meeting, at which department assignments, problems and issues were being discussed and resolved before the kickoff of the fall quarter. It was the first department meeting she had chaired in a year. Two allied faculty members tried to hijack the meeting to ram through their version of a festering issue's resolution, even though Shearlean, other department chairs and one of the deans were opposed to the pair's agenda. Because the issue these two faculty were harping on was a *process* problem and because the process in question was not yet complete, no resolution could possibly be adopted. Shearlean understood this and with a lot of effort, managed to defer the decision until later in the quarter when the process under discussion had run its course.

Shearlean saw this attempt to hijack her meeting as an effort to take advantage of her absence and her weakened condition. She imagined the parties responsible for the conflict expected that there was no fight left in her. They were wrong. She had plenty of fight left in her, but she would have preferred to direct it toward her cancer rather than a petty department grievance.

The second incident came later in the quarter when one of the same meeting conspirators confronted her in her office and following a harangue of the disputed issue, blurted out to Shearlean, "You should think of others in the department instead of yourself. Your situation is making it hard on me and others." Unfortunately, the accusation came from an individual with perhaps the most thorough knowledge of Shearlean's condition and treatment. Her words brought Shearlean to tears—at work—in front of this colleague, something she could have never conceived of at any point in her professional life.

When I picked her up from work that day, I could tell Shearlean was distressed and saw that her eyes were still red. She wasn't ready to talk about what had happened, so I didn't ask. When we got home, she went straight into our bedroom, as was her habit, to change into more comfortable clothes and collapsed in the recliner in front of the TV for a dose of "Seinfeld" and "King of Queens" silliness. I ignored the shows because I had seen all the episodes several times and checked my laptop to see how the stock market had closed. The usual laughter these shows evoked was conspicuously missing, so I looked up from my computer to check on her. Shearlean was silently weeping. I slid from my chair to the floor in front of her chair and put my hands over her hands in her lap while the comedy show's laugh track mocked her sorrow. I was angry, but more than that, I felt deeply sad. I knew that the colleague who'd brought her to tears was one rogue, difficult person, but I couldn't take away the sting of her words and convince Shearlean of this. I simply squeezed her hands in mine and let her cry.

~

As I said, however, Shearlean still had fight in her. She was steadfastly positive and resolute with her own values. Later that day Shearlean dealt with her feelings in her journal with the following entry addressed to her tormentor:

> *This entry is dedicated to the woman who said the cruelest words ever said to me since my diagnosis with terminal brain cancer. But I believe we attract what we need in life, and her words were a gift to me. They inspire me to write this. She is right. Everything we do affects others. I give this to you [the co-worker's name went here] with love. And hope that it empowers you.*
>
> *As philosopher Ernest Holmes, author of "Science of Mind" says, "Change your thinking, change your life." I've changed my thinking about those cruel words you said to me. I have practiced this philosophy for 25 years. And that is why I have a wonderful life. The surgeon who saved my life by removing a plum-sized tumor, along with some of my brain, told me on Sept. 14, 2009 that his operation had given me 5 months to live. But I am still here—a survivor, minute by minute, day by day. I still have a wonderful life. You can, too, no matter what your situation.*

Shearlean made her journal and me the only witnesses to how she felt. She never confronted her tormentor or sent her a copy of her journal entry, but if the person reads this book I am sure she will recognize herself.

UPDATE 19: Unwelcome Anniversary

December 1, 2010

Hello All

Shearlean had another MRI Monday, November 22, and the image was precisely the same as the previous MRI—a tiny bright spot on an otherwise black-and-gray picture of her brain. This indicates that the Avastin and Temodar are working, and her tumor is remaining tiny and not growing as it was.

Shearlean's sister was visiting and was able to go with Shearlean and me to visit Dr. Hinton to see and hear the results of the MRI. "Without wasting any time," Dr. Hinton said, "let me tell you there is no change in the image." Janet got to see the last three MRIs and to listen to Dr. Hinton review Shearlean's condition—and to ask her own questions about Shearlean's treatment.

We are approaching unknown territory now in terms of Shearlean's treatment and survival. She is well past the one-year milestone and will soon be at nearly 18 months since she was diagnosed. Anything beyond 18 months verges on miraculous, and no one, including the doctors, can even speculate about what's ahead.

Since Shearlean tolerates the combination of Temodar and Avastin so well, and because they are having a profound effect on reducing and controlling the tumor, she can continue this way indefinitely. It is equally true that if Avastin stops working, the only alternatives are experimental, but there seems to be a new treatment being announced every three months or so.

Shearlean had her fifth Avastin infusion this morning. It was another of a series of bureaucratic snafus, but the 30-minute treatment was finally completed in two-and-a-half hours. This sort of thing gets us both down and makes us very anxious and upset with the system. Following treatment, I took Shearlean to her office at the university to work. I picked her up and brought her home at 2 p.m. She took an hour-and-a-half nap and is feeling fine now that she is over this morning's difficulties.

It is a shame that cancer treatment cannot go more smoothly so that the patient isn't so apprehensive and aggravated by a system that seems to be unaware and uncaring about how it is treating and affecting patients.

Be advised whenever you face our situation for yourselves that it is worth looking closely and critically at who is going to provide your care and how it will be administered. If you are not strong yourself and do not have a strong caregiver, you are in for a rough ride.

Stay healthy!
Bob Duke

The 2010 fall quarter was to end on December 10. Shearlean was tired, and before her last day arrived, she became convinced she could not work again after the term wrapped up—at least for a long while. It wasn't an easy thing to come to terms with (even tempered with the hope that time off might help her "recover") but she knew she had to step away. She'd recently discovered (nearly 16 months after her diagnosis) that she was eligible for a medical leave of absence, and asked me to write a letter for her to Dr. Hinton to help her get the documentation in order. I did so with grief in my heart because it suggested a finality I was unprepared for.

Dear Dr. Hinton

At my request (with your concurrence) I returned to work the spring quarter of 2010 as chair of the journalism department at WWU. I was able to fulfill my job requirements satisfactorily and after summer quarter break, I returned for the fall quarter of 2010, currently underway.

My goal in working was to win tenure for two faculty members whom I hired and who are essential to the ongoing success of the department. I want this to be the capstone of my tenure as chair of the department and this will be completed by the end of the fall quarter.

As my illness progresses and my medication and treatment continues, I believe it will be increasingly difficult to work the winter quarter 2010/2011. As you know, as a result of the location of my brain tumor, my writing, speaking, listening, typing and spelling abilities are impaired. At my best, I can do all of these things with difficulty, but at other times I can hardly do these tasks at all. Besides the effects of disease, these same capabilities suffer as a consequence of medication and treatment for the disease. Physiologically, I am suffering more frequent seizures that affect my balance and cause partial paralysis of my right leg. When my right hand becomes involved, these seizures affect my ability to use a keyboard or accomplish other dexterity functions. I have tried verbal command software but it is no substitute for someone who has always typed.

I feel I need full-time medical leave to permit me to concentrate on recuperating and dealing with effects and requirements of chemotherapy, which I am told will continue indefinitely. I believe that full-time leave, starting with the winter quarter, beginning January 4, 2011, will free me to deal with the effects of my disease and hasten my recovery. Perhaps by spring quarter, April 2011, I will be recuperated sufficiently to return to work full-time.

I am advised by WWU HR that I am eligible for full-time medical leave as I anticipate I will be unable to perform my responsibilities in accordance with my faculty contract, paragraph 9.1 which states:

> *Tenured and tenure-track faculty members' job responsibilities include a combination of teaching, advising, research or creative endeavors, and service to departments, colleges, the university, the professions, and the community.*
>
> *Additional responsibilities include advising students, attending class, participating in university committees, maintaining reasonable posted hours, working collaboratively and productively with colleagues, and participating in accreditation and program reviews.*

With respect to your medical opinion, knowledge

of my condition and symptoms, and agreement with my needs, I ask that you provide the necessary documentation and support for me to apply for the leave I request.

I would be pleased to assist you in whatever way might be required. I have spoken with the WWU HR department and believe it is expecting your recommendation and is also prepared to assist you.

Forms and supporting documentation are included with this letter.

The earlier you can return the completed form, the more time WWU HR will have to process the request before the end of the current quarter in December 2010.

Yours truly,
Shearlean Duke, Professor
Chair, Journalism Department

Enclosed: WWU Family Medical Leave form
FRM-U5410.03B, consisting of 3 pages.

If she survived, Shearlean would be on family medical leave until she could retire on her 65th birthday, only a few months away (June 21, 2011), when she would be qualified for Medicare.

Even though she knew before Thanksgiving that she was going to need medical leave, Shearlean enclosed the following optimistic note (written in the third person) in each of her stack of 2010 Christmas cards:

MORE TO CELEBRATE THAN MOST

Christmas 2010 and our 40th wedding anniversary, on New Year's Eve, are events we thought we might never see together. For those on our Christmas card list who may not know, Shearlean was diagnosed with terminal brain cancer in August 2009 and had every reason to expect last Christmas to be her last Christmas. After September 2009, brain surgery was followed by radiation and chemo. She is currently doing great and has every reason to celebrate (and new therapies are being discovered every day). Despite what has overshadowed our lives, we are both happy and active, and looking forward to every day, especially holidays. As so many people have discovered, cancer can teach you a lot and give you much to be grateful for. Yes, it is life-altering, but not life-denying. For many, including us, it is life-enhancing. So, with genuine joy, we ask you to celebrate with us and share our happiness in achieving 40 years of happiness and partnership.

Bob and Shearlean Duke

CHAPTER EIGHTEEN

On the Road With Cancer, a Difficult Trip

"I am very depressed, angry, frightened. Wept today and feel sad and cheated."

SHEARLEAN'S SYMPTOMS of decline were not tumor-related, but rather she experienced a general physiological decline, heralded by episodes of falling.

In early December 2010 Shearlean fell for the first time. It was the first sign she was losing her ability to walk. Falls became more frequent but she didn't hurt herself, though she sometimes ended up with severe bruises. At least she was falling at home on carpeted floors. At first I was alarmed and ran to her, fearful that she might have collapsed or injured herself, but each time she got up rather easily and made some excuse about how or why she had fallen. As she grew weaker she was unable to get up by herself and fell more frequently. I urged her and then pleaded with her to be more careful, to hold on to something or to call me to take her hand or help her however I might. She never called for me, but continued getting up and moving and falling and dismissing each incident as nothing. Sometimes I was only a step or two away from her and instead of asking for help she would fall with a loud thump.

I lectured her mercilessly about how bad things would be for us both if she broke something. She could end up in the hospital or we would have to hire professional home care. She remained stubbornly silent and would not engage in a discussion with me. I couldn't figure it out. Was she trying to hurt herself? She seemed bent on self-destruction. I wondered whether this was a tumor-based behavioral aberration and worried about what other self-harming behaviors might manifest. Could it lead to attempts at suicide?

One day, she fell twice within a couple minutes within arm's reach of me, and I snapped. We were in the bathroom. I was washing my hands at the bathroom sink as Shearlean stood up from using the toilet. She fell right at my feet while pulling up her underpants.

"Sweetie!" I exclaimed as I bent to help her off her knees and onto her feet.

"I'm okay," she said, steadying herself by leaning against the vanity counter. As I reached for a towel to dry my hands, she stepped away from the vanity and after two steps sprawled face-first across the bathroom threshold on the carpeted floor beside our bed. This was about the fifteenth time she had fallen and not asked for help when all I had to do was turn around to assist her.

She couldn't get up. And in a fit of frustration, I decided I wouldn't help her. I stepped over her and sat down on the floor opposite her with my back against the closet wall and just stared at her. I guessed there would have to be a showdown over this falling business to resolve it. Not only might she severely injure herself, but also I knew that I might suffer a crippling back injury helping her to her feet over and over again. If one of us were incapacitated, we would have a huge problem on our hands. And it was something we could prevent if I could get through to her. It hurt me to see her in such a pathetic situation, struggling on the floor, unable to crawl a couple of feet to the bed to raise herself, but I had to make my point. I tried to keep my voice even and reasonable. I didn't want to shout at her, which is what I felt like doing because I was so exasperated.

"This is it, Shearlean," I told her. "You can either get yourself up or stay on the floor all night. I'm not going to help you up until you swear you will hereafter let me help you stand and move about."

She was certainly hardheaded, but so was I. We stayed on the floor together for nearly an hour in our standoff. We talked sporadically, and then lapsed into long silences. I had to wonder what she was thinking about my behavior and wondered even more what she was thinking about these repeated falls.

I finally said to her, "You have to ask me to help you get up off the floor—*and say please*. And you must swear that you will not let yourself fall again."

She finally acquiesced.

Shortly after this episode, she stopped being able walk much at all without assistance; there was no opportunity to fall anymore because she was never alone. I was now in the position of having to help with all movement: in and out of a chair, on and off the toilet, in and out of bed, in and out of the bathtub. I went to the Bellingham Lions Club, which lends medical equipment to the public, and borrowed a walker, a bedside toilet, a booster seat with handles for the bathroom toilet, and a bench seat for the bathtub. Now she feared falling when I tried to lower her onto the toilet seat, bathtub seat or walker seat, and at the last instant she would lock onto the back of my neck instead of letting go, and wrench my back while I was stooped. With lower back problems a life-long concern, I dreaded that one day I might be paralyzed by pain or totally disabled.

But even with her serious mobility problems, the quality of life that was our goal throughout Shearlean's illness was freedom from pain and freedom to travel. Freedom from pain could be achieved with medication and personal grit, but freedom to travel was more challenging because of the logistics of caring for her in her most recent condition. Taking cancer on the road meant extending our home medical support and establishing supplementary medical care at our destination, while orchestrating the coordination of the two.

On December 20 we left for a two-day drive to Palm Desert with Archie, Shearlean's cat. We originally planned to stay from December 21 through January 17. We were even planning to host visiting southern cousins Shearlean hadn't seen for 30 years, but this was not to be. Shortly after Thanksgiving Shearlean's condition suddenly worsened. She became unable to walk, could not speak above a whisper, and had trouble swallowing. Perhaps we shouldn't have gone on our trip, but she had been looking forward to it so much, and neither of us was willing to give it up. In retrospect, despite the hardship we both endured as result of this trip, I *am* glad she was with loved ones just weeks before her death.

I had sent the following email to Dr. Hinton before departing for Palm Desert:

Shearlean's tongue is no longer furry but still has five ugly ulcers that don't seem to bother her a lot. She is eating and drinking without complaint, but not eating much. In fact I discovered she was hiding food in her tissue when she wiped her nose while eating. She is getting about half the water I would like to see—I estimate 40 ounces daily, if I keep after her. I suspect she is continuing to lose weight.

She fell several more times since we last talked, but after I confronted her she has not fallen because I insist she not move without first consulting me. Basically, I have to stand over her every instant for fear she will attempt to move with disastrous results. She is bruised all over but nothing critical.

Her pneumonia seems under control, but she expectorates heavily in the morning; it diminishes during the day. It is very viscous and voluminous with traces of blood.

She occasionally still complains of pain in her right thorax, but it disappears quickly and is not so severe that she cries out like she was doing. Her speech is poor. She can seldom complete a sentence. Her right arm and leg continue to be very weak, making it difficult for her to use her walker and nearly impossible for her to stand without assistance. I don't think she would qualify as ambulatory.

She is sleeping for 12 to 14 hours nightly.

Bowels and bladder are normal.

Aside from a moderate improvement in her pneumonia and her improved swallowing, I don't think she is much better than when she saw you on Dec. 13.

We are off before dawn for Sacramento and then to Palm Desert. Her sister will meet us and we have an appointment with a hematologist/oncologist at Eisenhower. We are going to see if we can find some personal care help while there—bathing, dressing, grooming.

After trying 1 mg of dex twice daily for three days I switched back to 4 mg twice daily, and there seemed to be a small improvement but not as significant as past dex results.

I will send another report following her Avastin infusion on 12/27/10.

Happy Holidays,
Bob Duke

It was under these circumstances and in this condition that we made our 2010 trip to Palm Desert. We planned to stay longer this time to receive her visiting southern cousins, among her last remaining relatives. Months earlier, the two cousin couples had agreed to fly from Atlanta to Palm Springs for a visit, which had greatly excited Shearlean.

We had a folding seated walker with wheels to move Shearlean around, to and from restrooms and hotel rooms. As we traveled, I scouted out gas station restrooms that could be easily entered from the parking lot if I parked close to the door. I booked motel rooms on the ground floor with parking in front of the room. We got takeout food and ate in the car and never attempted entering a restaurant. From Bellingham to Palm Desert would be an all-day two-day drive (about 1,300 miles) with many stops. The only serious difficulty arose on the second day, when we had to stop at a highway rest area with an unpaved path to the restroom that was too rough for the walker's wheels. I tried to support Shearlean enough to walk her to the women's restroom, but I was too weak to keep her upright and ended up dragging her in an effort to keep her on her feet. We must have been a disturbing sight to anyone watching.

A woman leaning against a trash barrel dropped the cigarette she was smoking and hurried over to us and asked, "Can I help you with your mother?"

My mother! God, I hoped Shearlean hadn't heard her. *Is that how she looks? I'm 72 and someone thinks she looks like my mother!* I could have burst into tears as those thoughts rushed through my mind. A crowd was gathering around us, as our situation looked more like I was trying to help a drunk to her feet than support my sick wife in getting to the restroom. I accepted the woman's help, and between the two of us we got Shearlean into the restroom. I got her into a stall where I had to wrestle her pants off of her while she sat on the toilet to relieve herself. Then, trying to pull her pants back up, I nearly dropped her onto the soiled toilet stall floor. The helpful woman was waiting outside the stall and assisted me with getting Shearlean back into the car. All this time Shearlean made no sound, said nothing.

"Is there anything else I can do for you?" the helpful woman asked.

"No, but thank you so much. Do you work here?"

"Not really. I come here every day to see if I can help out people. Sometimes I get tips," she said. She smiled and started to back away. I thought this was odd, but I was grateful for her help, so I asked her to wait a minute while I fished around in my pocket for my money clip.

I offered her $5, but she refused it and said that under the circumstances she couldn't take anything. I said, "No, please. I really needed your help and you provided it. I want you to take it. You earned it."

After a brief pause, she stepped forward and took the bill from my extended hand.

From this point on, I stopped only at restrooms with smooth walkways in front of them and didn't risk a reprise of the rest area stop.

That first day as we traveled on, I made sure Shearlean followed her medication schedule and drank lots of water to avoid dehydration. When we stopped for the night, Shearlean went right to bed and right to sleep. I put Archie in the wardrobe closet with his food, litter box and water and closed the door. I didn't hear a peep out of him. I set the alarm for 5 a.m. and fell into an exhausted sleep.

We arrived in Palm Desert early the next evening in a downpour that had followed us all the way across the Los Angeles basin. The poor visibility made every freeway interchange a risk for having an accident or getting lost. Shearlean had been silent nearly the whole trip because she could barely speak above a whisper. I could hear what she said only by leaning across the car to listen closely, which wasn't safe in the traffic. On arrival she again went directly to bed and fell asleep instantly and slept 12 hours.

~

Shortly after we arrived in Palm Desert, we went to see the oncologist I'd arranged to give the next infusion of Avastin.

The Eisenhower Medical Center is in Rancho Mirage, California, between Palm Springs and Palm Desert. The clinic's appearance was disappointing. The parking lot pavement was rutted and pot-holed, the landscaping was overgrown, and the building's paint was peeling. Inside matched the outside: threadbare carpet, worn chairs, overcrowded waiting room with no accommodation for wheelchairs or walkers. The manner and appearance of the nurses and aides gave me the impression they had been hired from the local pancake house.

I maneuvered Shearlean's wheelchair (borrowed from the clinic's corral out front) into an opening beside a dying potted plant, and walked back to reception. When someone finally made eye contact with me, I stated why we were there and was told the patient had to check in herself. I said the patient could not walk and pointed to Shearlean beside the wilted plant. This produced a huge phony smile (intended to mask annoyance, I suppose), and the nurse grabbed a file and marched in Shearlean's direction. The nurse talked fast—like a waitress reciting a food order to the short-order cook—but Shearlean paid no attention, not comprehending a word. I explained Shearlean's condition and offered to answer questions and sign forms. This suited the nurse until she got to the Financial Responsibility form. She said to Shearlean, instead of to me, "Honey, your signature on this form is the most important thing you can do today."

"I have Shearlean's durable power of attorney," I said and offered her a copy.

"Only the patient's signature is acceptable on the form," she said.

"Well, the patient cannot read the form and is unable to write her signature," I countered.

"Doesn't matter," she said, avoiding eye contact with me.

I was getting angry. I said Shearlean's signature was illegible and meaningless, but the nurse ignored me and put the clipboard in Shearlean's lap. She put a pen into Shearlean's hand and placed the tip against the paper. Shearlean looked up at me with an expression that said: "What does she want? What should I do?"

"Sign," the nurse commanded.

Shearlean let the tip of the pen slide across the paper leaving a wavy trail of ink behind. The nurse burst into a big smile, turned on her heels, and broke a trail through the small crowd of other patients back to the protection of the reception desk.

I was fuming, but tried to hide it from Shearlean, who had lapsed into a dazed slouch in her wheelchair.

After sitting a while longer, another nurse with an armload of files paused in front of us momentarily to signal us to follow her down the hall. She ushered us into a tawdry examination room and said over her shoulder as she was leaving that Dr. Davis would see us soon.

We sat there for about an hour, while I grew agitated and then enraged. Just as we were on the verge of leaving, Dr. Davis walked in, cheerily introduced himself, and immediately began taking Shearlean's history. *Her history!* Childhood diseases, parents' and siblings' health, surgeries, and on and on. What a waste of (billable) time.

Dr. Davis had Shearlean's chart right in front of him, sent from Bellingham. She was currently in treatment for brain cancer. She was here to arrange for an Avastin infusion already prescribed by her regular chemo-oncologist and this clown wanted to know whether she had measles as a child. She had spent two hours being processed and waiting for him beyond the appointed time, and he wanted to know whether this 64-year-old woman had regular menstrual cycles.

DURABLE POWER OF ATTORNEY

In a nutshell, the power of attorney for healthcare appoints an agent to make healthcare and related decisions for you if and when you cannot. If you are incompetent or incapacitated, and you have appointed no agent, one will be appointed for you—by the state. If you are unwilling to suffer the appointment of a stranger to oversee your care, you must appoint your own agent, which can only be done with an appropriate legal document such as the durable power of attorney.

My main dispute with the durable power of attorney, in caring for Shearlean, was that healthcare providers took it upon themselves to interpret its use and did so very narrowly. I, the caregiver, on the other hand, was too uninformed to know how to appeal the healthcare providers' interpretation to get what Shearlean and I wanted. As a result, I used persistence, belligerence, intimidation and argument to browbeat or coerce providers to do what I wanted. It didn't always work and even when it did, it left everyone angry and upset. My way was a poor way of handling matters, but it would have been worse to be continually taken advantage of for the convenience of the healthcare system.

Overall, with regard to the legalities of our situation, I felt cheated and betrayed as a caregiver. I foolishly believed (because it is what I had been told) that having these documents prepared in advance and in place prepared and empowered me to be a caregiver of the sort I aspired to be—one who could make decisions that supported Shearlean's care.

God help us.

After I interrupted his history-taking a few times by asking for specifics about her infusion treatment and about her current symptoms, he abandoned his pursuit of her history and began to examine her.

He looked at Shearlean's tongue, asked probing questions about her symptoms, and listened to her breathing, then quickly reviewed the salient facts in her chart and recommended stopping Temodar and Avastin. He wrote out symptom management prescriptions and gave us his card with instructions to call for an appointment the following week. We'd now been there more than three hours and had finally accomplished something, but we were utterly exhausted.

I left his office overwhelmed with a sense of urgency about Shearlean's deteriorating condition and my diminishing ability to care for her adequately. Once we got back to the condo, I telephoned Dr. Hinton.

I told him Shearlean appeared to be going through all of the motions of a person dying: not eating, refusing medications, wanting to sleep all the time, unable to get out of bed, too weak to sit up, listless and not talking. And I told him that Dr. Davis had recommended we stop all chemo treatment.

He agreed, but said no more.

Shearlean never received another Avastin treatment or chemo of any other kind, including Temodar. All treatment from here on out focused on her myriad non-tumor symptoms.

~

Christmas this year was perfunctory. Palm Desert was cold, the golf course was flooded, rain was unabated, and we discovered the condo was uncomfortable and not turnkey-ready for guests. 2010 was not going to be like 2009, but here we were. Shearlean's condition smothered any holiday cheer or festivities. We went through the motions and Shearlean tried hard to participate, but the desire to remain in bed trumped her best efforts to celebrate her favorite holiday. Christmas dinner was a test to see who could get her to taste this dish or that in the hope she would eat something. As a consequence, she was disturbed by our concern and disappointment about her lack of appetite. She tried to be enthusiastic and interested in her nephews' new toys and games but couldn't muster the necessary energy.

Perhaps most symbolic of Shearlean's condition during this period were her efforts to play backgammon. We had been playing three games of backgammon daily since 1983. For me, playing had become a nonverbal way for me to gauge Shearlean's condition. Our efforts at backgammon during the last week of December 2010 spoke volumes. Though she was willing to play, it was plain that she no longer had any idea what the game was about. We sat opposite each other at the dining table with the game board between us. I set up my side of the board slowly and purposefully hoping she would start doing the same on her side of the board. After watching me intently, she began to handle her tiles but she couldn't correctly arrange them on the board and didn't know the purpose of the dice. I reached across the board and slid her tiles into position. She looked pleased at all the attention I was giving her but obviously hadn't a clue to what I was asking her to do. Desperately, I explained the principles of arranging the tiles, thinking it might trigger a memory or at least a response. But she just sat quietly, patiently waiting to see what would happen next, a pleasant expression on her face.

In the background, her nephews Jake and Ryan were providing sound effects for a game they were playing with Christmas toys. Martin was intent on a tough game of Angry Birds that he was determined to win.

Janet was at the end of the dining table, checking email. I was hoping she was paying attention so she could judge for herself her sister's condition. I almost succumbed to the temptation to ask her to watch, but resisted because making an example of Shearlean like this would seem cruel. Still, I wished I could be sure Janet was seeing what I saw. I needn't have worried because a later discussion revealed that Janet had subtly taken it all in.

Our game proceeded in fits and starts as Shearlean picked up tiles and threw them as though they were dice. I explained the difference between tiles and dice, and she nodded as she dumped the dice from her cup and I moved her tiles for her. On her next turn, I put the dice in her cup and she threw them across the board as though she suddenly remembered how to play, but she couldn't count the spots on the dice to know how to move her tiles. Next, I watched as she shook an empty dice cup and threw imaginary dice from the cup. I felt tightness in my chest as I held my breath waiting for her to notice her mistake. She didn't.

I persisted, and for our second game, I played both sides of the board and narrated each move, hoping to stimulate her memory. She smiled with delight (and so did I) when she won our last game because the dice rolled in her favor—though I was convinced that she hadn't a clue about what we were doing. She could still enjoy winning a game.

Still, I was uneasy. Even though none of Shearlean's symptoms were associated with her tumor and all of them were treatable, even ordinary, I was very troubled by them. I sensed something inevitable in them. She was not rebounding. Rather, she was stabilizing in poor condition. I had a bad feeling that I couldn't shake. We should be at home now, not 1,300 miles south in Southern California.

The realization that I needed to get us home overwhelmed me with a sense of desperation that made me feel weak and triggered horrible thoughts of Shearlean dying on the road. It could happen, I realized, and I pondered the consequences. What would I do? Would I keep driving with a dead person in the passenger seat like a scene from a black comedy? Would I have to turn over her remains to some law enforcement people or some small-town officials at some Interstate exit? Could I even keep going with her sudden death on my conscience? The scenarios spun out of control as my thoughts collided with my emotions throughout my tired and weakened body.

As much as Shearlean and I had wanted to stay in Palm Desert, especially to see her relatives, I realized we had to leave. We'd only been there 13 days. If we hurried, we could tell the cousins before it was too late for them to cancel their flights. We had to clean out the condo to guarantee return of our substantial deposit and get on the road home. Janet volunteered to come along to help drive and care for Shearlean. I realized I was near the end of my rope and needed her help. I didn't have to think twice about accepting it. Also, help with driving meant we could get home in minimum time. I thought it was important that Shearlean and her sister spend as much time together now because the future was looking so uncertain.

We celebrated our 40th anniversary lying in bed in the condo watching "Lucy" reruns. We watched the Times Square ball descend at 9 p.m. Pacific time so Shearlean could go to sleep satisfied that she achieved her goal of celebrating the New Year and our wedding anniversary. It was now 2011 and she was still alive 17 months after being given a year to live.

CHAPTER NINETEEN

Symptoms Not Tumor-Related

"Hard to use right hand. Not good dexterity.
Hand hot. Numb. Cramp. Sensitive mouth.
Right side also affected: numb and tingles.
Hard to chew. Lips numb. Hard to spell, too."

WE GOT HOME from our Christmas 2010 Palm Desert visit without incident on January 5, 2011, and Shearlean seemed no worse for the travel. Janet made things easier on me, and so I was feeling stronger. But when I finally cleaned out the car after arriving home, I discovered food I thought Shearlean had eaten and pills I thought she had taken wrapped in tissues and stuck in the door pocket and beside the passenger seat. I found other partially dissolved pills on the floor mat apparently coughed up when she choked trying to swallow them. I was going to have to watch her more closely. I realized, too, that I now had no idea what the status of her medication was.

In Palm Desert we'd bought a used seated walker with big wheels, which made it easier to roll across carpeting. I returned the other borrowed unit to the Lions Club and exchanged it for a wheelchair. Shearlean could not propel the walker herself because she would slip forward in the seat and risked falling out. She could no longer support her legs to keep her feet from dragging on the floor or pavement when I transported her.

Moving her about had become arduous because she could no longer assist me. I arranged a washbasin on the nightstand next to her side of our bed. Now I could pull her upright from the edge of the bed, push the walker under her and swivel her around to the nightstand for her to wash her face and brush her teeth.

As a precaution I also asked her to start wearing a diaper, which she agreed to in our conversation but then avoided using it. I could hardly blame her, but she would awaken me to help her to the bathroom, costing me badly needed sleep. I had to lift her upright, sit her down on the walker seat, lift her up off the walker and sit her down on the toilet seat, lift her off the toilet seat onto the walker seat, and then lift her off the walker seat and onto the bed again. It got to the point where I pleaded for her to use the diaper at night so I could get more sleep, but she refused. As a compromise, I put a portable toilet next to the bed so that at night I could just lift and pivot her around to sit on the toilet. With less distance and less effort I found I could get back to sleep. I feared I was wrecking my back, but didn't care. I hoped I could hold out until it wasn't necessary any longer.

The wheelchair was an ominous symbol—the final loss of any other form of mobility and a precursor to being bedridden. I recalled that when my 88-year-old mother was in assisted living, she often expressed her dread of a wheelchair. Her fear of it was so great that the staff caring for her used the threat of putting her in a wheelchair as motivation for her to keep up with her therapy and exercise. The wheelchair is the equivalent of the bogeyman for the elderly and infirm. I didn't like thinking about where things were leading and was as upset by getting the wheelchair as Shearlean was.

At first I thought I was strong enough to heft the wheelchair up the three steps at our back door, but in my weakened condition it took more effort than I felt I could sustain. Also, I dreaded losing control and dumping the wheelchair and Shearlean into the bushes on either side of the steps.

I got on Amazon.com and ordered an aluminum wheelchair ramp that was delivered in just two days, and I installed it immediately to eliminate the obstacle of the steps.

Shearlean's symptoms and condition were swinging from one extreme to another now. She went from no appetite to a big appetite, but that was relative because she was continuing to lose weight. As perverse as it may seem, she was pleased that she was back at her college graduation weight of 118 pounds. I tracked what she ate so I could accurately report her diet to her doctors.

SAMPLE DIET

Jan. 6:

Small cup of tapioca pudding.

1/2 cup of applesauce.

Bite of leftover pizza.

Jan. 7:

1/2 frozen waffle with syrup and butter.

1 chocolate Ensure.

5 Cheetos chips.

Vitamin drink.

Mashed potatoes and meat loaf.

Ice cream.

Jan. 8:

Hash browns and a fried egg.

Cheetos.

Ensure.

Pasta with tomato sauce.

Shearlean's physiological symptoms varied, too. Two days after we got home, she resumed walking, with help, for a period of three days, and I was giddy with excitement. As suddenly as she started, though, she stopped. Painful seizures on her right side, lasting two to three minutes, came and went after this.

She became completely disoriented. She didn't know what day it was and couldn't name the day that follows Sunday. When I explained the day was Monday she argued it was Saturday. She became quick to anger. She asked, "What?" about almost everything and she answered nearly every question with, "I don't know."

And then she began to fall asleep uncontrollably. When she napped in bed she would sleep for 12 to 14 hours if I let her.

Just as after surgery, she could no longer use a fork or spoon. When she uncapped the toothpaste tube, she squirted toothpaste onto the plastic cap and tried to brush her teeth with it. If she tried to drink more than a sip, she choked and inhaled the liquid into her lungs, which contributed to pneumonia.

Before we'd left Palm Desert, I'd made appointments with Drs. Hinton and Kozlowski, as well as one for an MRI. Everything was scheduled for January 11, with an MRI at 8 a.m., an appointment with Dr. Kozlowski at 9:50 a.m. and an appointment with Dr. Hinton at 1 p.m.

For our umpteenth visit to Imaging, the receptionist wanted Shearlean to fill in a form saying the scheduled MRI was not requested as a result of an accident. I snapped. "We've been coming here for oncologist-ordered MRIs since August 2009," I said too loudly. "You know why we are here. It is right in front of you on your computer screen. I won't fill in or sign your form."

I dropped the clipboard holding the form onto her desk where it landed with a clatter that caught the attention of the whole waiting room. Remaining calm and even-tempered, the receptionist explained the insurance company's predicament if the MRI was not covered. "I don't give a damn about the insurance company's predicament. What about the patient's predicament, being treated with suspicion and like a stranger every time she comes here?"

The receptionist began to cry quietly as she put the clipboard away.

"I'm sorry I made you cry," I said without meaning it.

"You remind me of my father," she said as she dabbed at her tears, "when my mother was ill."

Her comment made me feel small and mean, but I was in no mood to back down. As I returned to my seat beside Shearlean, I thought: *There's never anyone responsible to vent at during these incidents—just some innocent following orders and being verbally abused by someone like me.* The only thing worse, to my way of thinking, though, was to remain silent.

I sat down heavily and took Shearlean's hand in mine as a silent apology for perhaps antagonizing the people she had to deal with.

When we met with Dr. Kozlowski a short time later, he already had a verbal MRI report from the radiologist who said there was basically no change in the image of the brain tumor. Shearlean's condition remained NED—No Evidence of Disease. Of course the MRI couldn't detect the be-

SURPLUS TEMODAR

Ironically, just as we had whipped Temodar provider RxB into shape we stopped treatment with Temodar. True to character, though, RxB then overreacted in the opposite direction (proving it was out of control no matter which direction it was going). As its finale it more than doubled the prescribed amount of Temodar it delivered. At that moment I had on my desk (when we no longer needed it) about $12,000 worth of Temodar. There was a surplus left over from the shipment for the previous treatment and a full dose (plus surplus) that had been delivered from Ohio for the currently scheduled treatment. And there was a shipment from RxB's Seattle pharmacy for the exact dosage quantity also for the currently scheduled (but canceled) treatment.

havior and symptoms the patient was experiencing. NED wasn't necessarily good news; it was more like no news. Dr. Kozlowski confirmed that he was canceling scheduled treatment with Temodar and Avastin because there were no tumor symptoms to be treated. Instead he wanted to focus on treating weight loss, dehydration, pneumonia and physiological maladies like difficulty swallowing, her ulcerated tongue and esophagus, and various bacterial infections.

Since she couldn't swallow reliably, Dr. Kozlowski wrote an order for installing a PICC (Peripherally Inserted Central Catheter) and gave her a prescription for home infusion treatment, using the PICC to provide nutrition, hydration and medication.

The PICC accesses a large vein in a patient's arm to facilitate ongoing infusion of large quantities of fluids—anything from medication to nutrients. It comes with a 32-page operation and maintenance manual from the manufacturer. Supplemental instructions were provided by the hospital where the insertion was performed.

The device is marketed as the "PowerPICC" solo catheter. With its sales literature and marketing language, it sounded more like a performance-enhancing auto accessory than a medical device.

A caregiver is allowed to use the PICC, but he is not permitted to maintain it. Professional nursing care is required to periodically care for the catheter insertion site by cleaning the area and replacing the dressing that secures the catheter in place. This seemingly harmless distinction would prove profound when we discovered its impact on our healthcare directive and end-of-life treatment.

At 1 p.m. we met with Dr. Hinton, who reviewed the MRI radiologist's findings and Dr. Kozlowski's new treatment plan. As usual, Dr. Hinton elevated Shearlean's mood and attitude, and she felt optimistic about the new treatment plan. I think we both experienced great relief from the MRI results, and Dr. Hinton and Dr. Kozlowski's positive outlooks about treating Shearlean's nutritional needs. With the tumor still in abeyance, we had to contend only with everyday medical issues. Death remained a distant threat so long as that bright spot on the brain MRI remained tiny.

Shearlean's immediate need was to increase her hydration and that could best be accomplished intravenously. It could coincide with the installation of the PICC that was required for the prescribed home infusion treatment. So on January 12, Shearlean was temporarily admitted to the hospital for several hours to install the PICC and to receive an initial hydration infusion. Altogether, we were there for about five hours and were discharged late in the evening.

UPDATE 20: Deceptive MRI

January 13, 2011

Hello All

Shearlean's recent problems were the result of her chemo side effects finally catching up with her. As supposed, her symptoms were not tumor-related. She had an MRI on Tuesday, January 11, 2011, and there was no evidence of disease. The tumor area was as tiny and insignificant as in earlier MRIs.

Shearlean's past reaction to chemotherapy has been no reaction. She has skated through Temodar and Avastin without any of the ill effects we all hear about chemo. Well, it finally caught up with her right after Thanksgiving. Dr. Kozlowski thinks the chemo stripped the lining off of her esophagus from her tongue down to her stomach. I could see that the outer surface of her tongue was gone and I guess the same thing happened at the back of her throat and on down the tube that is the esophagus that leads to her stomach. As a result she has been unable to swallow for a month without severe pain.

Being unable to swallow, she could not drink water and became dehydrated. She couldn't swallow pills and so missed most of her medication. She couldn't eat food either and lost 22 pounds in four weeks.

Treatment at this point will consist of her getting nutrition intravenously at home until her body can repair the damage to her esophagus. There is no other treatment to heal this damage. Hopefully, in a couple of weeks she will be able to get nutrition the conventional way, by eating food.

As for her getting pneumonia, there is no explanation. And there is no explanation for the near paralysis of her right side that caused the severe weakness that has crippled her and put her in a wheelchair for the time being.

On Wednesday we saw Dr. Hinton, who provides her primary care, and he concurs with Dr. Kozlowski. Dr. Hinton added that he thinks Shearlean has outlived her chemotherapy and no one can foresee exactly what will happen next. That is, most glioblastoma patients have died of their cancer before they have had this much Avastin and Temodar. There is little known about how such prolonged exposure to these chemicals will affect the patient. Dr. Hinton also said he thinks that the paralysis of Shearlean's right side is more a matter of weakness caused by malnutrition than by nerve or muscle damage. He thinks that with improved nutrition she will regain strength, which will enable her to better use her right arm and leg.

Chemo remains suspended.

Today she will receive her first at-home nutritional infusion to begin rebuilding her strength.

More later.
Bob Duke

Dr. Kozlowski had written a referral to Infusioneers for January 13, 2011, so Shearlean could have infusion treatments at home instead of traveling to an infusion center or being temporarily admitted to the hospital. At first glance this seemed like a blessing, but it proved to be more of a burden (even a curse) because of the equipment employed. The dismal service of the provider and the demands it made on the caregiver and patient was overwhelming.

The infusion service's chief representative made an appointment and interviewed us to see if we could handle the procedures, and to demonstrate the apparatus and explain actions that would be required of us, and to answer our questions. After we passed muster, a team of three infusion nurses arrived with canvas bags full of equipment and supplies to train me in using the equipment. Then they proceeded to prepare and administer the medications and nutrients to demonstrate the procedures.

Three was a crowd—literally too many people and too hard to deal with in the corner of our small living room as each professional clamored for attention. I was extremely irritated by them all, but tried hard to hide it so as to not upset Shearlean. She was already upset, though, and erupted into a rage when approached and "handled" by one of the three without prelude. All three froze and exchanged alarmed glances then nervous smiles as they eased back from Shearlean and settled onto their haunches to await a truce.

They attempted conversation. One nurse wanted to share her day with us. She talked nonstop about getting her kids off to school and ranted about making it to work on time and trying to find time in the day to take care of household chores. The other, a smallish woman with gray hair, wearing faded and worn floral scrubs, had to be busy the whole time, ransacking the equipment bags looking for items and never finding them. She gave the impression that she arrived without the necessary items. That didn't turn out to be the case; she just couldn't find them with her haphazard methods. The third nurse, continually fussing with her unruly hair, was too inarticulate to explain the process and left us wondering whether she knew what she was doing. None seemed to realize they were strangers to us—and guests in our home. The idea that they might not be welcome and that their presence was merely being tolerated seemed to have never occurred to them. They finally retreated from Shearlean, who had shrunk back into her chair to get out of reach, and turned to me to explain what my tasks would be for in-home infusion care.

The rocky start to our home infusion care was prelude to worse to come. Self-administered care by patient and caregiver wasn't the panacea the providers promised it would be. Contributing to the invasive nature of their service, infusion people would arrive at the door unannounced, which was very upsetting, and I complained to their company. I asked to have one nurse banned from visiting because she was too much of a drama queen in need of an audience. We required that they make an appointment and to show up on time, get on with their business and leave.

Home infusion turned our *home* into a clinical setting. The living room became an infusion suite, the kitchen was turned into a pharmacy-like preparation and waste disposal area, and the dining room, adjacent to the living room, became the infusion preparation site. Alcohol scented the air and dispenser bottles of hand sanitizer stood everywhere within easy reach. Debris from alcohol wipes, infusion tubing packaging, and expended infusion bags and medication bladders accumulated on the dining table, along with syringes and needles, until they could be disposed of properly. Now there was no escaping the "hospital" environment we all tend to associate with sickness and disease. We were now living in the midst of it 24/7.

Each day, morning to late evening, Shearlean sat in her recliner, in the corner of our living room, wearing a fleece vest and with a lap robe spread across her legs. A stainless steel IV stand was to the right and behind her chair. A plastic bag of nutrient mixture lay on the table at the end of the sofa while the infusion pump rested on the sofa arm. Clear plastic tubes led from the bag to the pump and the PICC in Shearlean's right arm. In theory the infusion bag and pump were to hang from the IV stand that the patient should be able to pull along with her to move about the room. In fact, mobility of the unit was nil. The stand was designed for use on a hard floor surface and would not roll on carpet because the wheels were too small, and all the weight of the device was at the top, making the stand inclined to tip over when the wheels got stuck on the rug. The pump was to be housed in a canvas bag closed by a zipper, however, the zipper operated so smoothly that it unzipped itself and let the pump fall to the floor repeatedly.

The pump sales literature showed a stylishly dressed woman, with a carefree expression on her attractive face, walking down a busy street unencumbered by the pump in its canvas bag while her infusion ran automatically as she went about her daily routine. Fact and fancy were far apart.

I could do this infusion procedure, I knew, but should I? "Wouldn't you rather do this at home than have to go to the hospital every day to have it done for you?" someone had asked when we'd made our original decision to invite this chaos into our house. Maybe, but was all of the disruption we were living with the best they could come up with? The emotional cost of having others constantly in our home was high, and there must have been alternatives.

After just a little experience with this whole process, it became clear that the pump and everything about the process was experimental. People like Shearlean and me were not the people for whom this pump was designed. The training hadn't been refined and, like the pump, the materials involved were being adapted from a hospital or clinical setting to the home, without having been modified or refined for home and unskilled use. I felt like a guinea pig and resented being experimented on at such a sensitive and vulnerable time in my life. *(See Appendix 1, Rants. Medical Equipment: Too Much Information and Home Infusion Services: Not Ready for Self-Administration.)*

Patient and caregiver were daily on the edge of despair and physical, mental and emotional collapse. Just one more thing or one more incident could push us over the edge of a precipice from which I feared we might not recover. Every day was a test and every day I worried I might fail. I wondered how much longer I could endure the strain. I would always say I could do whatever needed to be done, but not really knowing what I was agreeing to made my positive attitude dangerous. What might happen if I bit off more than I could chew?

How did anyone have the gall to ask all this of me or ask it of Shearlean?

The first infusion took me an hour to get the nutrients flowing. Hanging the bag that held the pump was the most difficult task. No instructions were provided about venting the pump line before connecting it to the PICC. Mistakenly, I had used the red instead of the purple connector. All minor stuff unless you were on the edge of losing your mind, like I was.

This whole service provoked me to complain—to engage in a battle with Infusioneers. As tired as I was, I didn't need any more battling, but I simply had to call them. I reached Infusioneers' president and its chief pharmacist to discuss problems with staff and equipment. While they listened attentively and were sympathetic, it was clear that one dissatisfied patient wasn't going to change anything in what was a successful business. I like to think, however, that I may have convinced them that in-home infusion was not appropriate for every type of patient.

Just as 17 months ago, I still had no clear idea of how much treatment was covered by insurance and what the financial limit of treatment was. For that matter, I didn't know what the clinical limit of the treatment was either. I didn't think any treatment should be open-ended. The Financial Responsibility Acknowledgement form said that the estimated cost of treatment was $1,865.20 per week (but may vary) and the estimated duration was TBD (To Be Determined). I had no idea what the treatment goals were and so could not tell whether progress was being made—nor would I know when treatment was complete. As it stood, Infusioneers could continue their profitable infusion process indefinitely. As things were, it delivered supplies and materials at a rate that suggested long-term treatment. I signed delivery slips, some two pages long containing

30 items, not knowing whether they were items I needed, whether the quantity was correct, whether I could return unused portions for credit, or whether all was covered by insurance. And I was too worn out to keep tracking everything as I had earlier in the journey.

I eventually persuaded Infusioneers to consult with Dr. Kozlowski to come up with a goal (pounds of weight gained, for example) at which point the treatment would be evaluated and a determination made about whether to continue or stop. Meanwhile, I told Infusioneers not to deliver any more than a two-day supply of nutritional supplement or anti-infective medication (because I had received a six-day supply of nutritional supplements without ordering it).

Once the goal was in place and weight gain and blood work indicated the infusion treatment had achieved its objective within seven (long) days, infusion treatment was terminated—January 21, 2011.

Shearlean would see Kozlowski only one more time—January 24, 2011. Since her January 11 MRI showed "no evidence of disease"—not the same as remission—and graphically, her tumor looked the same as in previous MRIs, whatever was wrong with her now was not related to the tumor. She had survived beyond the outer limits of what was known about the effects of Avastin and Temodar.

Having reached the limits of what chemo could do, cancer treatment was at its end.

CHAPTER TWENTY

Bad to Worse

"Woke up last night at 2:30 with an anxiety attack, wide awake, scared, mind racing, fearing return of my tumor."

I HAD BEEN so consumed with Shearlean's treatment and uncertain about what to tell anyone about her condition and status that I made no effort to write an update during this hectic time. From Thanksgiving 2010 through our race back home from Palm Desert, things had only gone from bad to worse. I finally realized that we might be approaching a crisis and dashed off a rambling update.

UPDATE 21: Deadly Treatment
January 24, 2011

Here are notes I've pulled together into a narrative about how Shearlean is doing and how things are progressing:

Though Shearlean is still very healthy when measured by blood tests and free of disease (other than cancer), she continues to decline. It is hard to put a finger on what is happening or what the cause is, but to sum it up, whatever it is results in a deterioration of her quality of life. Her tumor is not worsening. Her ulcerated esophagus is healed. She is putting on weight, and her voice has returned. But she is miserable and things that matter to her are being lost or slipping away for no apparent reason.

Recently, she wanted to get on Netflix and put some new movies in her queue. She used to do this often and spent a lot of time at it, and was proud of finessing the latest DVD release when it came out on a Tuesday. I was going out for two hours for errands and left her with the laptop. When I returned she was obviously disappointed about something. The first thing she asked me was how long she had been sitting there. I figured out she meant how long had it been since I left and I said two hours. That seemed to upset her even more, and I thought she was mad at me for being gone. Not so.

Rather, she was wondering how long she had been struggling with the laptop to change her Netflix queue.

She said she could not connect to the Internet. I asked if I could help and with two clicks we were on the Internet at Netflix's "Your Queue" page. I think my doing it so easily was even more discouraging to her than trying for two hours herself. It made her think, I believe, how much she had lost in the way of simple computer skills. She has realized for a long time it was becoming increasingly difficult for her to use a computer and now she couldn't even log on to a familiar site.

I sat on the floor beside her chair and watched as she attempted to modify her DVD queue to delete some rentals and to add others. Her hands were all over the keyboard and she couldn't use the mouse to click the correct functions. She became angrier and more frustrated by the second and began pounding on the keyboard and savagely jabbing various keys with her fingers. Of course this created havoc and resulted in her closing the window and the Netflix site, which made her frenzied for a few seconds. I tried to calm her and speak sympathetically, and to offer to do for her what she was attempting to do. She sagged in her chair and looked defeated. "I'm going to bed," she announced and roughly put aside the computer and started to get up out of her chair, careless of the infusion tubing connected to her and oblivious to the fact that she is too weak to get up without help.

She wants to forget this experience that reminds her of how impotent she has become and how frustrating ordinary activities are now.

This is just one recent anecdote, but it illustrates a general decline and loss of function that has been nipping at her heels every day since she began dealing with cancer and its treatment.

Is what is wrong with her the cancer? The surgery that removed the tumor? Residual radiation or chemotherapy? The narcotics and other medications she takes? Or is it psychological? Is it likely to pass, stabilize or get worse? I don't know.

In this same vein she has a terrible time remembering what day it is, when her appointments are, whether she has taken this or that medication, and when I leave, how long I am gone and when I returned. Sometimes five minutes and five hours are all the same, and when this dawns on her she is visibly alarmed by it.

Talking is difficult, too. She wanted to check out a CD at the Cancer Center one day, and the clerk asked her to confirm her name, address and telephone number, and it overwhelmed her. She became angry and tearful and walked off without the CD because she said, "They want too much information."

I went back and got it for her but she won't go back there for anything herself.

With increasing frequency she tries to communicate in sign language by drawing pictures in the air with her hands. She finally made circles around her eyes with the thumb and index finger of each hand and I understood she wanted her glasses. I don't recall her uttering a single whole sentence all day. She seems unable to get to the noun she is searching for and gives up resentfully, as though I am purposely being obtuse.

Sometimes I think I can actually observe her world closing in upon her with her options progressively becoming fewer. The effort required for her to keep functioning increases daily. Her condition seems good to everyone who sees her, yet the reality is a constant erosion of her abilities. She senses that and worries about it. So do I. I think her decline is the main source of her depression and discouragement. When I discover her weeping occasionally, I think it is caused by the realization of this irresistible slipping away of fundamental processes without anything to point to for a cause.

All of what I see is heartbreaking for me and I can only wonder how it is for her. It must be discouraging and depressing, but even with a lot of prompting and prodding, I cannot get much out of her about how she feels because her ability to communicate continues to slowly deteriorate. I think, too, the narcotic pain drugs may be suppressing her thought process and speech.

I watched a "CBS Sunday Morning" story about the reporter whose wife has advanced Alzheimer's, and I was distressed at the number of similarities in loss of mental function. It's not that Shearlean has ever not known me, but there is the drifting apart and declining communication. This is what most worries me.

The intense sadness I've felt since the diagnosis comes rushing back stronger than ever on days when I feel the weight of the inevitable pulling me down.

I did try to have a discussion with Shearlean today about whether she was okay with a stranger bathing and dressing her and helping her with the toilet and so forth. I explained to her that I was planning on finding a home care aide to come in daily to help care for her. I told her it would be the same sort of care an assisted living establishment provides, but it would be here in our home. She seemed to understand and said it would be okay with her. This will help me a little.

I've done some reading and have access to some local experts and will start seriously trying to find someone regular to help out. I can't keep this up myself and don't want to wait so long that I am too far gone before I cut back. I want to recover sufficiently so I can remain healthy and continue doing other work that has to be done. I think I am looking at something in the range of $20/hour for 20 hours per week. I'm going to compare hiring someone directly versus someone through an agency.

I hope I am not upsetting you all with this news. While there have been some genuine improvements in aspects of her condition, there is also this slow inevitable decline that continually creeps into every day. I can't seem to hold it back nor can anyone else. It is an irresistible force, and about all I can do is impede it momentarily and then get out of the way until the next wave comes along.

Bob Duke

CHAPTER TWENTY-ONE

Emergency

"I was scared, stressed, and sad to be scared, but I believe this was merely a small test of my faith."

ON MONDAY, January 24, 2011, Dr. Kozlowski confirmed that Shearlean's weight gain and hydration were satisfactory, and he ordered lab tests for the next day, Tuesday, January 25.

On the morning of January 26, 2011, Shearlean awoke complaining of pain in her groin and bladder areas. She had a dry barking cough and had spit up her Ensure nutrition drink and pills. She was frantic about something—I didn't know what—and kept repeating, "G! G! G!" but I didn't understand what it meant.

I gave her a scheduled pill but told her to take it when she felt she could. I was still waiting for her to take it two hours later. I had a backlog of five more pills for her to take. I hated this duty of forcing pills on her and checking on her every 15 minutes or so, knowing that if she took one pill I would only force another on her. At least she no longer hid pills she refused. She just left them in plain sight and ignored my repeated urging.

To distract her, I decided to get her out of the house. I asked her to ride with me to do errands that day. We stopped at the retail pharmacy to pick up a prescription that she was told to start immediately (another pill!). When I returned to the car I handed her a tablet and opened a bottle of water so she could take the latest pill. She choked on it when she tried to swallow, spitting it and the water into her lap. There was a long pause in her breathing and her eyes grew large as she made an awful strangling sound. She still hadn't taken a breath as far as I could tell and started jerking about, convulsing. I studied her closely to see whether she was truly in distress or was merely reacting to a powerful reflex of gagging on the pill. I pleaded with her to give me a sign as I tried to calm her down. Waiting much longer didn't seem to be a good option, and I had to decide to do something: call 911, run into the pharmacy to ask for help, or drive like a maniac to the hospital. Finally, I heard a weak inhalation, but more strangling followed it. I thought she might die right there in the passenger seat right then. I dialed doctor Dr. Hinton's office on my cell phone and left word with reception that I was taking Shearlean to the emergency room.

On the way Shearlean started breathing—with difficulty—but had a terrible distressed expression on her face. I pulled into the emergency entrance driveway and parked to one side. In the emergency room, I expected a TV-show type of reception by a half-dozen people in scrubs, but no one paid any attention to me. I might as well have walked into a bank and gotten in line for a teller. I was determined to remain calm and not create a fuss. In a real crisis I believed it was essential to remain calm and coherent, to be in control of the situation and myself. My rants and assertive behavior were calculated to have maximum impact in routine circumstances in order to provoke a response from an otherwise indifferent audience. I hoped someone behind the counter would notice me or step up and volunteer to talk to me. I waited maybe two minutes, while the three people there spoke with each other and shuffled papers. Finally, I said, "I need help with my wife in the car."

"Bring her in," was the reply.

"I can't get her out of the car without help," I explained.

Finally, casually, a man grabbed a wheelchair and started for the door with me following. The two of us got Shearlean into the wheelchair. Her distressed breathing was obvious enough for the man to pick up the pace and get her inside. From this point on, the anticipated action unfolded and people appeared out of nowhere to take charge and provide care. It all became a blur to me as I tried to stay out of the way and respond to questions.

Soon four or five people surrounded Shearlean. An overhead

electric hoist lifted her from the gurney she'd been placed on and deposited her into a standard hospital bed. A suction tube was used to remove fluid from her mouth and throat. Someone was listening to her heart while another person started an IV and someone else removed her clothing and dressed her in a hospital gown. The flurry of activity continued for about five minutes while I watched from the periphery. The response was now overwhelming and I feared things were worse than I had been told and that I had arrived at the hospital too late. Then someone pushed a clipboard at my chest and said, "Sign here." The clipboard person said Dr. Hinton had called. Shearlean was stabilized; she would be taken to intensive care (ICU), and she would be admitted to the hospital. I was handed a bag containing her clothes, earrings, wedding ring and wristwatch.

As fast as they materialized, the people disappeared. The frenzy of activity had subsided suddenly and I was left wondering what would happen to her. Exactly where would she be taken? Should I stay or should I go? Could I see her later in ICU? Who in emergency was in charge? I stood outside the curtained area enclosing Shearlean's bed hoping someone would approach and tell me something. I scanned the room trying to meet someone's gaze, anyone's. The room was full of milling medical people, but I could not make eye contact with anyone. I was amazed how invisible I had become.

Two orderlies arrived, promptly released the brakes on Shearlean's bed, and began to wheel it toward the double swinging door at the back of the room, which, I guessed, led to the main hospital building. They said nothing to me. Someone I recognized from reception walked directly up to me and said I would have to move my car.

When I moved the car, I must have driven home, but that part blurred in my memory. I made no notes from that part of the day. I don't remember what transpired until I saw Shearlean again in ICU about two hours later. The very experience we had worked so hard to avoid—Shearlean snatched from my care and confined to a hospital room—had happened. I was on the outside now and she was with strangers—at least temporarily.

When I got back to the hospital, she was asleep and appeared to be breathing easily. An array of monitoring and treatment equipment surrounded the head of her bed. She was getting oxygen from plastic tubing draped across her upper lip. She was taking all meds and nourishment through tubes connected to her PICC. The head of the bed was tilted up at an angle to ease her breathing. The bed was heaped with layers of blankets and she was fitted with a dainty skullcap. Just the circle of her swollen face showed there was a human being beneath all that bedding. She was now transformed from my Shearlean sitting next to me in the car to this institutionalized object in the charge of big Impersonal Medicine. Here I stood, my presence subject to the toleration of strangers. But my resentment and insecurity faded as I embraced what I thought must be Shearlean's feelings about this sudden shift in fortune. This wasn't about *me,* rather it was about me helping her make the best of this calamity.

Over the next four days I visited Shearlean in ICU three times daily: morning, noon and night. Mostly she slept. When she was awake, though, she complained of discomfort, mainly the same complaints she had suffered from for the past few weeks: ulcerated tongue, difficulty swallowing, dry mouth, cracked lips, chills, and itchy skin. Blood was being drawn every two or three hours around the clock and poor Shearlean's arms were black and blue with puncture wounds. But at least when she was awake, she was always coherent and willing to talk. She knew I was there.

Each evening, I put lotion on her face and applied balm to her lips and gave her a fresh moistened Toothette (foam tipped toothbrush) to soothe her dry mouth. When she became quiet and slept, I left.

Every day seemed the same as the one before and as far as I could tell, time was meaningless for both of us. A feeling of helplessness overwhelmed me because of Shearlean's pathetic appearance and condition. After only 20 minutes with her, I usually felt completely drained. I wanted to lie down or leave and was ashamed of how I felt, but I often left anyway. I was conflicted about staying when I wasn't sincere about wanting to be there. What I really wanted was for Shearlean to be back at home.

My notebook pages during this time contained only incoherent scribbles of names and numbers: nurses and aides Kari, Ivy, Lynn, Jo Ann, Joe, Di, Jesse, Tammy, Salome, Brian and Taylor; Drs. Lowry, Brockman, Brown and Hinton; and room numbers, 4-digit hospital extensions and 7-digit office telephone numbers. Looking at them later I could only ask myself, "So what?" Recording such information was a habit and was the only remotely constructive thing I could think to do.

Nurses came and went, and we exchanged pleasantries while each took her turn fussing with this and that in the room and at Shearlean's bed. As the days in ICU passed, my most frequent question became some version of, "When will she be discharged?" Typical answers were: "Soon." "That's up to her doctor." "Check with the nurse's station." "When she's feeling better."

I had begun to fear Shearlean might die in the hospital. She might die alone. She might die before I could get there even if I were summoned. She might die in the hospital despite 17 months of heroic efforts by both of us to guarantee she would die at home.

When I arrived at her ICU room early in the morning of January 30, she was panting. It was hot in the room. She was agitated and wanted something, but I couldn't figure out what. I pulled her blankets off (because she couldn't) and tried to distract her by talking about flowers someone brought during a visit yesterday. When she remained agitated, I offered a Toothette dipped in cold water. This seemed to help and she concentrated on brushing her teeth.

With everything we'd been through, I had talked to enough medical people to learn the language of administration. Over the months, I'd memorized all the platitudes they'd showered on me. Now, when I heard nothing but placating statements without specifics about discharge dates, I knew I was being put off because they couldn't do anything for her. It was not okay with me for her to die in the hospital. I decided I wouldn't settle for anything less than a date or a damned good reason why the discharge plan was so nebulous.

With a little nosing around I discovered that Shearlean had no discharge date because no patient could be discharged from ICU, according to hospital policy. Patients could only be discharged from general care.

"So move her to general care and discharge her," was my peeved response.

"We don't have any beds available in general care," I was told.

"Then put her bed in the hallway in general care and discharge her immediately. She doesn't need a room if she is going home," I said.

"We can't do that," was the answer.

Well, at least now I had a specific objective I could work with—something I could do: Get Shearlean moved to general care ASAP. I started lobbying and pleading with everyone who came within the sound of my voice. The next morning (January 31) Shearlean's ICU room was vacant when I arrived. I thought the worst—she had died and I had not been summoned. I zoomed from despair to elation when I was told she had been moved to general care.

When I found her room on the general care floor, I was surprised to run into Dr. Brockman, the original primary care doctor who had made Shearlean's diagnosis. What was *she* doing here, I wondered? She must moonlight at the hospital. With a glance toward Shearlean's room, Dr. Brockman said Shearlean would be discharged tomorrow, February 1. Following the direction of Dr. Brockman's gaze, I saw a group of white coats clustered around her bed with everyone seemingly talking at once.

Before Dr. Brockman could scurry away on her hospital rounds, I wanted to find out what to expect of the discharge process. "Oh, you don't have to worry about that, you will be given a folder," Dr. Brockman said as she turned to go.

"But who is responsible for discharge?" I asked, thinking ahead about whom I might have to pester to get the paperwork together.

"It is just a routine matter, they do it every day. Various people have to sign off, but it is up to the admitting physician and the floor supervisor," she said sounding (familiarly) exasperated when questioned about anything.

I got out my notebook and pen, and said, "Let's sit down over here and you can tell me exactly what the procedure is." I tried to maintain my civility.

"You can take that up with the hospital," she strode away. On her heels, I said, "That's the whole point. I'm trying to get you to give me names I cannot get any other way so I *can* take it up with the hospital and get out of here as soon as possible," I said too loudly. We stopped walking and glared at each other. "Give me a name or two," I demanded.

She spit out two names at me and took off, but I kept after her and asked, "How do you spell that?" Without slowing or turning, she spoke a string of letters that I copied into my notebook. And she was gone. "Good riddance," I muttered to myself as I turned back toward Shearlean's room and the meeting going on there.

When I walked into Shearlean's room, no one paid attention, and I made no effort to be noticed. I wanted to hear what the discussion was about. I recognized Dr. Hinton, of course, and a hospice representative I had spoken with a few times. Another individual looked like the floor or duty doctor I had seen but never been introduced to. I noticed a familiar nametag and figured he was from Dr. Brockman's office (probably standing in for her). The other two white coats were strangers. No floor nurses were present. Noticeably, Dr. Kozlowski was also absent, and as far as I knew had never attended Shearlean while she was hospitalized. Just as well, I thought, because he might have her in tears.

I finally focused on Shearlean and saw the happiest expression I had seen since before she was admitted to the hospital. She was smiling broadly and actively engaged by the conversation with the group gathered around her bed. I studied Shearlean for a moment and had to wonder whether she could really comprehend what was being said. She didn't look to be fully tracking the discussion, but rather intent on being gracious to her visitors. Her eyes darted from person to person as though hoping for a clue about why everyone was there. She finally saw me and I could see the relief she obviously felt.

Yes, the discussion was about discharge, but there seemed to be controversy over treating her with antibiotics.

This was when I learned about the definition of "skilled nursing care" and the significance of antibiotics as they apply to the terms and conditions of a patient's healthcare directive. This whole topic came out of left field for me. I was stumped trying to imagine how we—how anyone—could foresee circumstances like we were facing now when we signed off on our POLST form, or healthcare directive, almost two years ago.

I actually recalled wondering about a particular clause in our POLST form, which required a decision about administering antibiotics at the end of life. To me antibiotics were an everyday treatment that had nothing to do with end of life. So we both answered yes to the question about whether we would accept treatment with antibiotics if we were terminally ill. I didn't ask for an explanation, though someone—a doctor—could have explained it to us when we signed our directives.

I was discovering now that if antibiotics could not be taken orally then they had to be administered intravenously, which would require skilled nursing care. Since Shearlean could not swallow

POLST – PHYSICIAN ORDERS FOR LIFE SUSTAINING TREATMENT

Many states, but not all, have some version of this form. The one discussed here is Shearlean Duke's for the state of Washington.

In 2007 or 2008, Shearlean and I filled out this form mainly to humor our primary care physicians. At the time, we were each offered counseling about the form but frankly we didn't know what to ask. Or more to the point, we erroneously assumed we understood what seemed like simple or obvious choices or instructions. It turned out in 2011 we were wrong.

Another mistake was that we thought this form was redundant with our Health Care Directive. There is some overlap, but the directive covers much more than the physician's orders. In fact that's one reason the Washington State Medical Association created the POLST, to separate physician orders from the non-medical contents of the directive.

Shearlean's POLST was actually used in her hospital room to confirm her decision about her care in 2011.

medication, her only options were to take it intravenously or by a tube inserted through her stomach for administering antibiotics with a syringe. Antibiotics by stomach tube were considered the same as taking them orally. But this required being fitted with one of the dreaded end-of-life tubes all of us hope to avoid by having a healthcare directive in place when the time comes.

I listened and watched closely as the doctors surrounding her bed conversed with Shearlean. To my surprise, she nodded at all the right moments, seemingly comprehending at least some of what was being said. She even mouthed an appropriate "yes" or "no" to a handful of questions. Perhaps she understood what she was being asked to decide. I was grateful for that at first.

But I noticed that each doctor spoke to her like a prosecutor cross-examining a key witness: Did she understand she was being asked to modify her directive? Was she sure she wanted to do this? Was she making this decision free of coercion? When she emphatically agreed to the tube in her stomach, I silently said "Oh no!" *Sweetie, why? What have you begun? Where might this lead? More tubes and more last-minute reneging on early decisions?* Everyone seemed pleased with her decision, except me. And then all the white coats dispersed.

An orderly showed up quickly to take Shearlean to surgery for her tube. Snap. Just like that and it was done. It seemed it wasn't 30 minutes and she was back with the new tube in place.

While Shearlean was in surgery, the hospice nurse briefed me on hospice services and discharge. When she came home it would be by ambulance. Hospice had ordered a hospital bed and oxygen to be delivered to the house. The services of a social worker were offered, but I didn't know for what, so I declined. A nutritionist wanted to talk to me about the formula she was prescribing that I would have to administer by way of the stomach tube (now that one was available). This would replace the nutrition supplement she now took by PICC infusion.

I overheard a nurse describe to someone whose function was unknown to me that Shearlean's condition was frail and fragile. She classified her swelling at number 3. I didn't know what the swelling scale meant, but what little of Shearlean's body I could see was definitely swollen. Her face was puffy, barely recognizable as the approach of death began to transform her even while she lived.

Last minute instructions sounded urgent and ominous: Don't give anything by mouth. To be fed by tube six times daily. Meds to be given two times daily. Diapers required at all times. Lookout for bedsores. There was a high potential for bleeding because blood platelets were low. Platelets that were earlier at 40 were now 12—whatever that meant. If bleeding occurred, use dark towels so blood doesn't show and frighten the patient.

I didn't take it in. I just couldn't.

While Shearlean's decision about the stomach tube had inflicted my first stab of disappointment with her, I was now stricken with shame at being so critical at such a time. Once more I was grateful we'd been so intentional in our discus-

HEALTHCARE DIRECTIVE

With the advent of the POLST form, the Healthcare Directive has been relegated to stating the patient's end-of-life wishes on matters of quality of life, comfort, religious or cultural practice, and dying. It is intended not only to instruct healthcare providers, but also family and others near to you. It can be amended by the attachment of a letter to include anything the patient wants those caring for her to know about her and her care. For more information about end-of-life documents see Appendix 1: Rants. Critical Documents: Little Help, But Essential.

sions at the beginning stages of this journey. I was glad to have a first principle to fall back on to save us both from overreacting to transitory events. We had earlier agreed upon a strategy that protected us from tactical setbacks: As long as I believed Shearlean was competent to make her own decisions, I would not interfere. If she understood what she was being told and if she could process the information and arrive at a rational decision (without me), I wanted her to do that. If her last breath was to speak for herself, then she should have the last word—literally—about her care and treatment.

Here for the first time, we had almost reached a tipping point. I didn't like her decision, but it was her decision, and I felt she was capable of making it in the moment. We had our ground rules in place and had been adhering to them for many months of hardship and we weren't going to abandon them now.

I called my friend Tim, with whom Shearlean had traveled to Kenya in 2008 and 2009, to help me move furniture to make room for Shearlean's hospital bed in our bedroom. We were fortunate to have a large enough bedroom to allow me to move our queen-size bed to one side to make room for the hospital bed to be set diagonally in the opposite corner, close to the connecting bathroom. There was a window near this corner with a view of our deck and landscaping, and it had the sun for half of the day. Situated diagonally, I could easily walk around the sides and foot of the bed to tend to Shearlean.

Later that day the hospital supply service (arranged by hospice) arrived and set up a rented hospital bed in the corner and demonstrated how to operate its mechanical and electrical adjustments. They set up an electrically powered oxygen generator and showed me how to operate it and pointed out the supplemental oxygen tank attached to the foot of the bed that was to be used in case a power failure knocked out the generator. Next, they installed an air mattress that automatically inflated and deflated periodically to prevent bedsores. And they left a change of bed linen. The hospital supply people were quick, businesslike and efficient; they were there and gone with no fuss or wasted effort. It all took less than 15 minutes.

I stood at the door looking across the transformed bedroom. It had now taken on a menacing appearance that the sunshine through the window could not dispel. The good feeling I had enjoyed at the prospect of Shearlean coming home vanished and dread replaced it. Nevertheless, imminent death was not what was on my mind. Shearlean was stable. Every symptom was being treated. Nothing she was suffering from was related to her tumor. Most importantly, no one had taken me aside to counsel me about signs that the end might be approaching. Medically, it seemed to be business as usual. A part of me still believed we could be on our long-sought path to recovery—the one we had been pursuing since the beginning of December. I was thinking again beyond tomorrow.

I recalled that I owed Dr. Hinton an email and so sat down at my computer:

> Good Morning Dr. Hinton
>
> When I remembered last night that I was going to email you, I could not remember what the subject was to have been and so I didn't email.
>
> I am glad you were able to see Shearlean yesterday.
>
> She is coming home today at about 1:30 for home hospice care. I will be the 24-hour caregiver, but there will be plenty of other help coming and going. She is coming home by ambulance on a stretcher and we have a hospital bed for her.
>
> When I was at the hospital this morning I did all the treatments for her with my own hands with a nurse watching and we were both satisfied with my performance. Dealing with the stomach is so much more forgiving than the blood system. I even got my own pill crusher.
>
> The nurses describe Shearlean as fragile and frail. If she remains this way or worsens I don't see how we can keep doctor or imaging appointments. I think I will cancel our next appointments with you and Dr. Kozlowski until she is stronger.
>
> I in no way mean it as a criticism of the hospital, but I think Shearlean will get somewhat better care at home, plus she will have the added comfort of being in her own space.
>
> If you have questions or suggestions I would be pleased to have them.
>
> Sincerely,
> Bob

Shearlean arrived home at 1 p.m. February 1, by a van ambulance. Attendants brought her in through the back door, through the kitchen to the master bedroom off the living room. I could barely see her on the gurney, buried as she was under a heap of blankets and miscellaneous medical paraphernalia. The attendants wheeled the gurney alongside the hospital bed, dropped the safety rail, raised the gurney to the height of the bed, and transferred her smoothly across, bedding, pillows and all. They raised the safety rail back up, collapsed the gurney and handed me a clipboard to sign and initial for delivery of the patient—and then they left. Perhaps five minutes had elapsed from arrival to departure.

I couldn't say I actually saw Shearlean all the time they'd been transferring her, but I was certain she was in there somewhere. I hurried back into the bedroom after seeing the ambulance attendants out and went to the head of her bed. There she was looking cheerful, though obviously fatigued by the travel and handling. I leaned down and kissed her, but had no ready words. I just gazed at her and enjoyed the pleasant sensations surging through me. She was home, where she should be.

My good feeling didn't last long. I realized I better get busy. I had a lot of care responsibilities to fulfill. Adjusting the head of the bed to the prescribed 30 degrees, I checked that the green light was lit on the oxygen generator, adjusted her pillows so they were not obscuring her face or vision, and arranged her blankets neatly. When I was finished, she was asleep. I listened to her breathing and was relieved that it was effortless and regular without any alarming noises.

I stood back to view the overall arrangement. I had been strongly warned about the patient's position in the bed. While it didn't seem like such a big problem as the nurse made it out to be, I wanted to comply with every instruction just to be on the safe side since this was all new to me. Everything looked fine, so I left Shearlean dozing and went into the kitchen.

I was tired. Drained. I needed something to eat and needed to sit and rest before I began the scheduled treatment and other care chores. Taking care of Shearlean at home was mainly going to be a continuation of the simple things I did for her in the hospital, a combination of comfort and medication. I had to wipe her face and hands with the moist washcloth, apply moisturizer and lip balm, keep her supplied with Toothettes, and give her ice to suck on. Her mouth was dry and still ulcerated, so she needed to rinse regularly to maintain moisture. I now also had to give her medication through her stomach tube, which didn't require her participation. I could crush a pill, mix it with water, suck the mixture up with a syringe and shoot it into her stomach through the tube by simply lifting her bedding out of the way to expose the tube. I suppose I could have done it while she was asleep, but that seemed too intrusive, and so I would wait until she was awake or I woke her.

I had purchased a baby monitor and set it up on a bedside stand and placed the receiver in the living room on the end table beside my TV-watching chair. It was sensitive enough that I could hear her breathing with the volume turned up high.

Within a few hours, things had settled into something of a routine, and I was settling into a comfortable situation in which everything seemed safe and secure. As evening passed, Shearlean remained quiet and apparently comfortable. The strain of the day's activities was catching up with me and I was feeling ready for bed.

I went into the bedroom and stood beside her bed and watched her sleep. What did I need to do before I went to sleep myself? It dawned on me I hadn't checked her diaper since she had arrived home and she hadn't indicated that she might need it changed. I shook her shoulder gently until she opened her eyes and then I lifted the blankets from her lower body to expose her diaper. The odor was unmistakable, and I immediately regretted my negligence in not checking sooner. I untaped the diaper tabs and paused, wondering how to proceed.

I understood the problem. I would have to pull the diaper out from underneath her, clean her, and put a fresh diaper in place, but I didn't have a plan or a technique in mind.

Unwittingly, I began a clumsy wrestling match. Shearlean could do nothing to help. The challenge was to lift the lower half of her body to take her weight off the diaper so that I could pull the diaper out from under her. But when I tried to lift her with one arm while trying to pull out the diaper I merely pulled her down in the bed without gaining control of the diaper. It was just as well. If I had been successful, the diaper's contents that coated her underside would now be smeared across the bedding beneath her, making her situation worse. I couldn't possibly change the whole bed.

I now realized that before removing the diaper, I needed to put a disposable pad under her. If I managed to do that, I would have to lift her high enough and hold her there while I separately removed the diaper without dragging the disposable pad with it. Next, I would have to lift her again or roll her over to clean her before putting a new diaper in place.

I was physically unable to do any of it. I simply was not strong enough. As big, strong and able as I fancied myself to be—six foot four, physically fit for my age—even with all of the mechanical contraptions around us to make Shearlean comfortable, I could not do it.

Of all the obstacles I could have imagined facing for the duration of Shearlean's illness, changing a diaper never occurred to me. Whereas I started out utterly confident I could deal with anything demanded by caring for her, being physically too weak was unfathomable.

I had provided every second of Shearlean's personal care throughout 18 months and thought I could do so up to the moment of her death. Now, here I stood impotent. Totally defeated by a simple physical task.

It dawned on me that in the hospital three nurses or aides were required to move her around in bed to change bedding or a diaper. Apparently, that had never registered with me. I likely thought they were three small women doing what one stronger man could do. And maybe one strong man of 30 could have done it himself, but I was a weak old man, now 72, unsteady on my feet—and it was impossible.

I stood there momentarily looking down at Shearlean wet with urine and smeared with feces, pitying her and pitying myself. I burst into tears, convulsively sobbing and choking on each attempted breath. The only thought I was capable of was that this was the end: shockingly... disgustingly... humiliatingly. *I'm defeated. I'm incapable of doing anything more.*

I've failed her.

Suddenly her labored breathing snapped me out of my emotional collapse. She was so doubled up by sliding down in the bed now that she was suffocating. An even greater terror seized me. If she fainted or passed out or had some sort of seizure from all of my strenuous effort to change her diaper, and I left her like this, it could kill her.

I could kill her.

That thought sobered me instantly and brought me back to the then and there.

I moved to the head of the bed and tried to pull Shearlean back upright by gripping her under her armpits, but the angle from the side was poor and I couldn't put my weight behind my effort. I tried to get behind the bed, but the headboard was too high for me to lift her and pull efficiently. Her breathing remained labored. I was breathing heavily and sweating from the effort. I could feel desperation creeping up on me.

I finally thought to lower the head of the mattress so it was flat, and I pulled on Shearlean, first on one side and then the other, until I wiggled her all the way up in the bed. Then I raised the head again to 30 degrees and rearranged her pillows until I saw that she was breathing easily.

I was shaking from the effort and feeling weak. The tears were still flowing; I was on the verge of hysteria.

This was the end. She would not be able to die at home as we both wanted. Tomorrow I would have to put her into the hospice facility. She would die in hospice. I choked back the urge to shed more tears and took several deep, shuddering breaths.

I used the disposable pad to dry and wipe off Shearlean as best I could and refastened the tab on her diaper. She seemed pretty much unfazed by all of the commotion I had just caused and nodded off to sleep again. Blessed sleep.

I silently apologized to her for leaving her in this condition. I told myself I would take care of all of this tomorrow. I reminded myself that the hospice facility and staff were great, and much better than the hospital. She could go there.

Still staggering under the burden of having failed this simple caregiver trial, I undressed and fell into bed.

III

Life Celebration and Memorial

CHAPTER TWENTY-TWO

Final Update

"Oh Bob, what are we going to do without her?"

Shearlean's sister Janet.

NOW, FEBRUARY 2, 2011 at 5:50 a.m., there would be no tomorrow. We had been told 531 days ago that this day was certain. We had 75 weeks, 12,744 hours, 764,640 minutes and 45,878,400 precious seconds.

Waking up dying as she did suddenly ended the long struggle. I had prepared for this for so long, and I knew what had to be done and I was doing it, but everything felt unreal. Or rather, the reality kept fading in and out like waves breaking over me, tossing me this way and that, flinging me up onto a beach and then pulling me back into a drowning sea.

I was waiting for the mortuary service to arrive to remove Shearlean's remains, I reminded myself. And then I held my breath as the concept hit me—of some stranger coming to take her away to someplace I couldn't reach her, to incinerate her flesh and return what remained of her in an urn.

It was only 9 a.m. I just sat, trying to rid myself of morbid images and trying to focus on the tasks and responsibilities I now faced, but those thoughts couldn't take hold. Instead, I picked up one of Shearlean's abandoned journals that had gathered dust on a dresser since she could no longer write legibly or had lost the will to make the effort. I thought making a final journal entry on her behalf might be a meaningful thing to do now that the end was known.

When I picked up her journal it fell open to words Shearlean had committed to her journal after her diagnosis infinite months ago. There, in her fluid familiar script, were words that were a fitting final tribute to how she lived her life right to the end. I saw she had ideas back then to write a book about her experience with cancer and had adapted a title from the draft of one of the mystery novels she hoped to finish writing in retirement one day. I read possible titles she had toyed with:

Once Upon A Dying Time

Surviving Terminal Cancer

The Day My Life Changed

By Shearlean Duke

Friday, Aug. 21, 2009, the day my life changed. That was the day my doctor told me I had a brain tumor. But it gets worse. It is an aggressive type of brain tumor, and I may have only a year, or even a few months to live. I still can't believe it. I can't breathe. I am in shock. I am angry. I am terrified, and profoundly sad.

Mostly, I am confused: Why me? I knew I would live until 80. I had that vision of growing old, seeing my nephews, Jake, 6, and Ryan, 4, grow up. Growing old with my husband, Bob.

This can't be happening. I don't believe it. So many decisions to make. I go to see a specialist Wednesday, but whatever treatment I receive is temporary: There is no cure.

I have not read about my disease yet. Bob did, and was so depressed he warned me not to, and I agreed. My diagnosis? The worst of the worse: A glioblastoma, the most deadly brain cancer.

Always terminal.

I have not even told my sister, Janet, who is also my best friend. I know the news will devastate her. And my nephew, Jeff, who is like a son to me. For some reason, I feel ashamed to tell. What did I do to deserve this? I don't want anyone to

> *know about my dying, my weakness. My mortality. I don't want people's pity, especially my co-workers. I don't want to see the "Glad it is not me" in their eyes, feel their relief in knowing their life will go on while I will cease to exist. Now, I understand why some people feel shame with cancer. It is irrational, but there it is.*
>
> *But this is part of my truth. As a writer, I kept this journal you are reading now. Writing keeps me sane. I wrote during sleepless nights, I wrote through tears. This is a private journal, but now after one year of surviving this terminal disease, I want to share my story with you. This, I hope, is my gift to you.*
>
> *Because, above all, I have survived!*
>
> *Not only have I survived this disease, but also my life is a story of survival. I have overcome great obstacles, beat tremendous odds, and accomplished the impossible.*
>
> *So, this is not my ego, but my heart offering you evidence of inspiration to meet your own challenges—even the most terrifying.*

She really thought she could survive and she worked hard at it every moment right up to the end. She gave it her best and was pleased that she had earned six more months, and good months at that. She died as she had lived: excelling, determined and optimistic. I'd admired her from when I met her at age 22 right up to the moment of her death at age 64.

I closed the journal without adding a postscript. I couldn't think of anything worth saying. The effort to think of something was overwhelming. I looked over at her, my eyes brimming, looking at her intently as though if I blinked she would disappear.

The pallid early dawn light that matched the blue-gray pallor of Shearlean's face illuminated the bedroom. The light created the effect that she was slowly fading away, blending seamlessly into the ether. I sat with her, urging my mind back over the months to the beginning of the end. I was attempting to consolidate all that had transpired into a single neat package—a beginning, middle and end. I think I wanted to make the experience a book neatly bound between two covers, or a play in three acts, with the curtain drawn at the end. But I failed to bring any order to it all. My memories remained chaotic; none of the pieces would neatly fit together into a whole. So I just sat, letting images and recollections swarm, some lingering and others zipping past like meteors, barely recognizable.

Just let it be, I told myself. Don't try to manipulate it. Just experience it as it evolves under its own momentum.

A knock at the back door startled me. I opened the door to the mortician, a portly man made more ponderous by his burden of solemnity and deference to what he was stepping into. He clutched one hand in the other, poised to respond to whatever might be coming. I smiled, extended my hand. As we shook I turned briskly and walked across the kitchen to the door to the bedroom. Like two men preparing to move furniture, we silently acknowledged that there was adequate space for maneuvering the *load*. Satisfied that I appeared stable and ready for Shearlean to be removed, the mortician went to the kitchen door and returned with two young men wheeling a gurney. Somehow I was maneuvered out of the bedroom as they entered and the door was closed behind me. Shortly afterward the door opened and the gurney sped along with a bulging black plastic bag strapped securely in place.

I would never see her again. She was gone. She wasn't just dead now, but she was also gone. Disappeared. I realized we were now talking about procedures and papers and schedules, and I agreed to meet at the mortician's office later that day. I heard the heavy doors of the van slam shut, the engine start and then stunning silence. Powerful silence such as I had never experienced before, even in the remotest Alaskan wilderness I had explored. I realized it was the sound of utter emptiness. Emptiness had a sound and this was it. *Was the house always going to sound like this now?* I listened intently and shuddered.

That's all I can vividly remember of that morning. Nothing else was transformed into a memory I still carry with me. Somehow, I pulled myself together and the day passed into oblivion. And so did the next day and the next, with none of them leaving any impression on me.

I telephoned Janet and, choking back tears, told her Shearlean was dead. I managed a few essential details about the morning and, barely audible, asked her to call her son Jeff and break the news to him. I said I couldn't talk anymore and without waiting for an answer, hung up the phone.

Then I telephoned my sister and asked her to tell my nieces and nephews. As I hung up, I heard her saying, "Be strong, Robert." Next, I wrote the perfunctory emails. I sent the following message to Dr. Hinton. I wanted him to know on a personal basis, but I also was hoping he and his office would get the word around to all the other medical providers, so I wouldn't get any calls about appointments or have to call to cancel anything that was scheduled.

> Good morning Dr. Hinton,
>
> Shearlean died at 5:50 a.m. this morning, Feb. 2, 2011, after a brief coughing spell that produced copious blood. Hospice came and helped me with confirming her death and preparing her for cremation. She had arrived home yesterday at 1 p.m., and I was sleeping beside her and awoke to help her and tell her I loved her.
>
> I don't think she suffered and I believe she was fully prepared for this. She had 16 great months of high-quality life after her diagnosis.
>
> You have been an enormous source of comfort and security to her throughout her illness. We have both been very grateful to have you with us during this trying time of life. It is rare for a doctor to become a friend, but that is how we came to think of you and I hope we have reflected that attitude from our side.
>
> Thank you so much.
> Bob

UPDATE 22: The End
February 2, 2011

Hello All

Shearlean died this morning at 5:50 a.m. at home with me. She was discharged from the hospital yesterday and came home under home hospice care. She had a hospital bed in our bedroom and she slept peacefully until about 5:30 a.m. when I was awakened by her coughing. It sounded especially bad, and I jumped out of bed and turned the lights on and discovered her bleeding heavily from the mouth.

I had been told to expect bleeding that could be fatal because her blood platelets level was extremely low. If she started bleeding internally, it probably would not stop because clotting was impaired. She hasn't been able to speak for a long time, but she could understand everything said to her. I got towels to mop up the bleeding and spoke to her and she understood me. I was able to tell her I loved her and was assured that she knew she was at home and that I was the one caring for her. Her distress lasted only about 10 minutes and then she closed her eyes and lay quietly. I checked for a pulse and breathing and could not detect anything. I called hospice and they dispatched a nurse who arrived at 6:30 a.m. The nurse confirmed that she had died.

The nurse and I cleaned up everything and put Shearlean into clean clothing and arranged her to look natural and comfortable.

Hospice called a funeral home and they removed Shearlean at 10 a.m.

It was Shearlean's desire to be cremated and that will take place in a day or two. Meanwhile, friends and family are helping. I must admit that seeing the end of her suffering is consoling to me. I am planning a memorial and celebration of her life to take place in the next two to four weeks.

Bob Duke

~

Sometime that day the hospital supplies company that delivered the hospital bed the day before returned to pick it up. Shearlean had died just 15 hours after returning home from the hospital. As when they delivered, they were in and out in less than 10 minutes. It was business as usual for them, but profound for me.

With the hospital bed gone, I wanted to put the bedroom back into its original configuration, with our (my) bed centered against the wall between the windows and with other items moved back to their familiar spaces. I called Tim, who had helped me prepare for Shearlean's return home, and told him she had died and asked him to help me move the furniture back. He came over that afternoon. Tim had been a nurse for several years, and his presence was stabilizing and calming.

With Tim's help, we also moved sickroom furniture that I owned or had borrowed into the garage to get it out of sight, and we picked up all of the treatment and care materials and paraphernalia. I bagged and boxed it and put it in the garage in preparation for donating it to hospice.

After a few days passed, I picked Janet up at the airport and we drove home with no tears and few words. When we entered the house and set the luggage down in the living room, Janet threw herself against me, letting her tears flow freely, and with her head on my shoulder and her face pressed against my neck, she said, "Oh Bob, what are we going to do without her?"

Janet and I had never had such a moment together before and it had a powerful impact on me. It jolted me back to life, I think.

While Janet visited, we cleared out all of Shearlean's clothing and other possessions. I wanted Janet to take whatever she wanted as a remembrance and to give things to her son Jeff's family. Shearlean had willed a couple of things to her niece, nephew and their children.

I had decided long ago that I would dispose of everything of Shearlean's immediately after her death, because I thought it would be harder the longer I waited. Experience with clearing out my mother's house in preparation for selling it demonstrated the volume of material a person accumulates. Even a serious effort at a thorough clearing still leaves plenty behind to be discovered and disposed of later. I recalled how my mother had left my father's clothing in the closets for several years, despite frequent reminders from my sister that it should be disposed of.

Janet and I shopped for urns for Shearlean's ashes and agreed on two identical metal urns that we purchased online. In the process, we marveled to find we could have purchased them from Costco. Who would have thought?

According to Shearlean's wishes, we planned two memorial services, one in Washington and one in California. We discussed obituaries and selected photos of Shearlean for them, one professional and one personal, depending on the audience for the publication or Web site. Then Janet was gone.

With Janet's departure came the finale to Shearlean's death. For a few days it had been a process, but now formalities were complete and plans had been made that emphasized Shearlean's absence. She was now adrift on an ebbing tide of memory, moving inexorably away from us. The whole preceding 18 months was slipping into the past more quickly than I would have thought possible.

More than her mortal remains were gone. Her presence had disappeared, dematerialized. For so long I had been alert to her every need. Now I had nothing to do. Besides missing her, I missed the responsibility of caring for her.

CHAPTER TWENTY-THREE

Celebration of Life

"She never stopped trying. She never gave up. She never complained. She always faced every fear. She was brave even to the end,"

husband Bob.

I WROTE an "official" obituary for Shearlean, producing it in good professional PR fashion and distributing copies to anyone at the university or elsewhere that might need it for an announcement, the student newspaper or a department press release. Shearlean had been a staff writer and editor for 12 years with the Los Angeles Times Orange County View section and had worked for the Times as a freelance columnist and feature writer for another 13 years. I felt determined that her obituary should run in the Times, even though the Orange County edition was long defunct due to the terrible attrition in the newspaper business nationally.

Dennis, a reporter whom Shearlean had hired 30 years earlier, was still with the Times and wrote obituaries. I contacted him to tell him Shearlean had died and to ask that he pass the news around to Shearlean's former Times associates. And, oh by the way, I asked, do you think you could get permission to run her obituary in the Times? I was sure she would be pleased to have the Times publish her obituary. I also knew that if there were space and time available, the Times would willingly accommodate my request.

On February 13, 2011 the following obituary appeared in the Passings section of the Obituaries page of the Los Angeles Times.

That day's section also featured the obituary of MGM musicals star Betty Garrett. Since she was a huge fan of old movies, such serendipitous company would have pleased Shearlean.

Shearlean Duke, former Times writer and editor

> Shearlean Duke, 64, a former Los Angeles Times features writer and features editor in the Orange County edition who later became chairwoman of the journalism department at Western Washington University in Bellingham, Wash., died of brain cancer Feb. 2 at her home in Bellingham.
>
> Hired as a reporter for the Orange County edition of the Times in 1972, Duke was an award-winning feature writer for the old View section from 1974 to 1981.
>
> She became the edition's assistant city editor in charge of features in 1981 and its View and Calendar editor in 1982.
>
> After she left the Times in 1984, Duke and her husband, Bob, spent more than a year sailing in the Gulf of California on their 35-foot cutter.
>
> Returning to Newport Beach, they established a public relations business in Costa Mesa. Duke also wrote education and boating columns, as well as feature stories, for the Times' Orange County edition.
>
> After earning a master's degree at Chapman University in Orange when she was 50, Duke taught journalism at East Carolina University in Greenville, N.C., and at Western Washington, where she established the journalism department's public relations program.
>
> Born June 21, 1946, in Copperhill, Tenn., Duke earned a bachelor's degree in history at Tennessee Technological University in 1968. She worked at the Cookeville (Tenn.) Herald Citizen, the Houston Post, and the Orange County Register before joining the Times.

Shortly after her diagnosis, her counselor had asked Shearlean what she regretted not doing during her life. Shearlean had replied, "Nothing. I've been everywhere and done everything I wanted. I'm ready to be home." Knowing she had lived life to the fullest and lived it so as to have no regrets, I knew she was sincere in what she said. There was peace in this for me.

With cremation there would be no body to view or casket to bury—no place for people to gather to say farewell or to mourn. The few funerals we had attended over the years together had been dismal affairs; memorial services impressed us as too solemn and out of character for us, so what I thought Shearlean would approve of would be a celebration of life. This would conform to her upbeat and positive outlook. I believed she had a genuinely interesting story to tell, and I would tell it for her. I would stage an open house, with exhibits and displays about her life and accomplishments where people she touched and who touched her could mingle and talk about her.

As for her ashes, at one point, I had planned on taking family and close friends aboard our friend Jim Kyle's boat, Home Shore, a 65-foot salmon seiner, and scattering her ashes at sea. Shearlean never expressed approval nor disapproval of popular notions about burial at sea, yet it was clear to me she was not enthusiastic about it. Finally, one blustery winter day, without prompting or obvious motivation, she'd volunteered that she couldn't bear to think about her ashes being spread in the cold, gray waters of the Pacific. "I'd like someplace warm and sunny," she said, "like California. Up on a mountain top—like at Janet's."

I could see she had given it a lot of thought, and I was pleased with her idea and relieved that she had finally voiced it. "That's a great idea," I'd said. "We'll do that. We'll do both."

Shearlean knew that I saw the ocean as more benign than she did, and she knew I wanted to think of her and our boating life when I looked at the ocean. Spreading some of her ashes on the sea was important to me. But I knew that if it had been up to her alone she would have never left California and so returning, even symbolically, was meaningful. She liked it there far better than I did. She told me once how much living in California had meant to her because she had lived more than half her life there. She had told me that if I died first she would move back to California immediately.

The day before our Celebration of Life, the Kyle family (who owned Home Shore), Janet and Martin, nephew Jeff Bain and family (Kristin, Jake and Ryan), our friend Lisa and I motored out into Bellingham Bay and ceremoniously spread tokens of Shearlean's ashes on the waters of the bay.

I had seen so many snafus with people trying to scatter ashes (TV's home videos) that I was determined not to have Shearlean's ash scattering turn into a fiasco. I didn't want to lose her urn overboard, for example, so I devised a plan to put small quantities of ashes into tiny individual boxes for each person so they could be opened easily to spread the ashes when they were ready. If a box fell overboard that would be okay because it was biodegradable. Kathy Kyle brought some long-stemmed roses and gave each of us one to throw into the water with the ashes. We had a moment of silence and watched flowers and ashes drift away before returning to the harbor where we concluded our family ceremony with lunch at a waterfront restaurant.

For me, this private ceremony was what I needed most. I wanted all of us to whom she was closest and who were closest to her to share our thoughts and feelings in an intimate way that couldn't be accomplished in the larger setting of a public celebration. I needed to be with friends and family and to know that we'd said goodbye to her properly. It came to me as a great relief to formally and publicly acknowledge the finality of her departure with these sympathetic and sharing witnesses. Spreading her ashes and having them carried away on the wind and tide was truly letting go.

Back at home, I had decided to set up 10 displays of artifacts from her childhood, education, teaching, reporting, freelance writing, public relations career, marriage and family, travel and boating to serve as a celebration of her life story. I recruited Tim, with whom she had traveled to Africa twice, and Carol, Shearlean's friend and the Western Washington University Journalism Department's administrative manager, to help me create these displays. We worked as a committee for three weeks gathering, sorting and assembling material on each subject and then mounting the material on foam boards before organizing the boards by subject. We displayed them on tables arranged around the floor of the Boathouse meeting room in Squalicum Harbor in Bellingham.

I sent out an invitation to about 120 persons for an open house with catered hors d'oeuvres, wine, beer and soft drinks. Scattering her ashes had been private, but there were many people who needed to say goodbye to Shearlean.

On March 6 at noon, her friends and colleagues gathered to bid her farewell and to celebrate her life. It was an incredibly diverse crowd ranging from fellow cancer victims to doctors who treated her to fellow Kenya travelers to journalists from Bellingham and Seattle to university colleagues to journalism department students. And as no surprise to me, there were a dozen or so strangers that Shearlean-the-constant-networker had befriended from all over Bellingham. Each expressed to me his or her fond connection with Shearlean through some good deed she had done.

I learned that everyone knew a different Shearlean and each was amazed at how little they knew of her whole story, which reassured me that she did indeed have an impressive story to tell.

I thought I knew her whole story, of course, and was as impressed with it as anyone else; there was so much to cover. That's why I'd had difficulty coming up with an appropriate eulogy for her. There was too much to say and every attempt to shorten my talk left out too much. I finally realized, upon hearing from so many people that even I didn't know the whole of her life (I was still discovering her at her wake).

I decided that there had to be one word powerful enough to capture how I felt about her essence as I had experienced her and I finally settled on "admiration." The more I'd mulled the word, the better I felt about using it.

Yes, I loved her. Yes, we managed to stay together and be happy for 40 years. And there were other proofs of the strength of our relationship, but what I saw as so powerful about my relationship to Shearlean was that I admired her from the day I met her in 1968 until the day she died in 2011. I knew others admired her too, and I could see why, but no one else had ever been through what I had been through with her—life itself—and could lay claim to continuously admiring everything about her as I did.

For four hours I circulated among the exhibit tables greeting visitors and listening to tender anecdotes from strangers who had come into contact with Shearlean in various ways. I overheard exclamations as people who thought they knew her well discovered some new facet of Shearlean's life and accomplishments. At times I was overwhelmed and disappeared into the catering kitchen or the men's room to wipe away tears or regain my composure. At last I asked Shearlean's musician friend, Marie, to call the group to attention by playing her guitar and performing a song she'd composed. When the song ended, I stood on a chair set close to a wall so I could lean against it to keep my balance. I tried hard to hide my trembling and prayed I could make it through the eulogy I had prepared.

I thanked everyone for sharing this celebration with one another, and me and explained my quest for a single word that I felt would do justice to Shearlean.

"Admiration," I said was the single word worthy of the Shearlean I knew. Just getting that word out nearly knocked me off my chair and I was glad the wall was at my back for support. I paused and surveyed the room, letting my heart slow down and allowing my breathing to even out, before launching into my eulogy:

"Shearlean had an adventurous life in every sense of the word. You glimpsed that in the exhibits displayed here today.

"She had terrible fears to overcome from these adventures.

"Physical danger: 'I don't want to drown,' she said on more than one occasion on a boat somewhere in the world. But she overcame her fear and never refused to go out on the ocean. And she couldn't swim.

"Academic fear: She feared getting any grade less than A and maintained an A-average throughout school including her master's program. She finally admitted to an addiction to perfection.

"Professional failure: She was afraid she would be doomed to live the hillbilly life she was born into, but she overcame every obstacle to lead a highly public upscale life beyond her dreams.

"Personal ruin: She feared she could not overcome her faults and improve her character, but she never stopped trying. And every time she stumbled, she got up again and plunged on, determined. She often regretted doing what was expected of her, but could never do less.

"She never stopped trying. She never gave up. She never complained. She always faced every fear. She was brave even to the end.

"This is why I admired her so."

Others followed me with brief remarks and after about 10 minutes, I took the microphone and thanked everyone for coming and concluded the celebration.

~

Janet and Martin owned a home in Idyllwild, California, in the San Jacinto Mountains, about 6,000 feet above Palm Springs. Even in mountaintop Idyllwild, their house sat up high overlooking the town and a western vista of peaks, valleys and forest. They had a spectacular and sprawling view; this would be a glorious place to rest for eternity. Since I'd assured Shearlean that we would put some of her ashes there in a separate memorial ceremony, I drove down to Janet's in Idyllwild where we had a small ceremony that included people who couldn't get to Bellingham for the main ceremony. Family and friends scattered some of Shearlean's ashes in a small garden circle among the giant boulders and trees on the west side of Janet's house. She had leveled a small area for the gathering and put an unused iron fire ring around it. Each of us present took turns mixing Shearlean's ashes into the loose soil. Then we planted some starter rose bushes inside a wire barrier intended to keep out the hungry deer.

Close friend Skip, (Shearlean's longtime California PR associate) and Skip's husband Jerry, my daughter Rebecca, my grandson Chad, our hosts Janet and Martin, and I assembled and performed our ceremony.

Shearlean's dying was now complete, and I felt satisfied that everyone had the opportunity to honor her sufficiently and achieve the closure they desired. There was just one more thing I needed to do.

~

I felt that celebrating Shearlean's life would be incomplete without an ongoing way to honor her memory. It should be something that symbolized the role model qualities I had seen her demonstrate throughout her life.

The following front-page story appeared in the March 2011 issue of the WWU Department of Journalism's "Alumni News" publication, announcing her modest legacy.

Scholarship helps keep Shearlean Duke's memory alive

The Shearlean Duke Memorial Scholarship was founded in spring 2011 to honor Shearlean Duke, the former journalism department chair.

Shearlean died of brain cancer Feb. 2, after battling cancer for about a year and a half.

Her husband, Robert "Bob" Duke, set up the scholarship to commemorate Shearlean's dedication to journalism, public relations and education. The scholarship grants money to journalism students on the public relations track.

"Shearlean Duke had a huge influence on a lot of students, and I couldn't see why that should end with her death," Bob said. "The scholarship, if it gets fully funded, will influence students in perpetuity in her name."

Department manager Carol Brach said she began receiving phone calls from alumni the day after Shearlean died; they were asking how to donate to a scholarship fund.

"I can't imagine not honoring her in some way," Brach said.

Brach soon approached Bob with the idea to set up a scholarship, which he had already been considering.

"My personal reason for creating the scholarship was pretty simple," Bob said. "I admired her a great deal and wanted to express my admiration in a charitable way."

Shearlean and Bob loved to travel, and Shearlean visited Kenya twice to help set up a service learning project between Western and the Ombogo Girls Academy, which mostly supports girls orphaned by AIDS.

When Shearlean found out she had cancer, she looked at it as a new adventure, Peggy Watt, journalism department chair, said.

"She handled it with a lot of grace," Watt said. "So long as you have to do something, you have to embrace it, and that's what Shearlean did."

In order for the scholarship to be endowed and become a permanent fixture, $20,000 must be donated. Once it is endowed, the money will be invested and the scholarship funds will come from the investment returns every year.

Amber Asbjornsen, the leadership annual giving officer of Western Washington University Foundation, said about $17,000 had been donated so far.

Asbjornsen said all the donations have come from journalism alumni, staff, friends and family.

"We've all been really touched by the outpouring of support and generosity," Asbjornsen said. Donations have been pouring in at a quick rate, she said, and Asbjornsen expects the $20,000 will be met by spring 2012.

On average, endowed scholarships generate a 4.5 percent return, meaning the scholarship would be about $900 each year. If the endowment amount is larger, the scholarship will be larger.

Although the scholarship is not endowed yet, Bob decided to give the first scholarship for $1,000 this year.

To receive the scholarship, applicants must include a 600-word essay with their applications, detailing something they are passionate about.

Public relations senior Alex Bacon received the first Shearlean Duke Memorial Scholarship in June (2011). Bacon said she was thrilled when she found out she had been awarded the scholarship.

"I was incredibly honored to be selected to be the first recipient of the scholarship," she said. "I bawled my eyes out."

She said she thinks it is vital that the scholarship continues.

"It's important that her legacy outlives her," Bacon said. "The people who come to the department in five years need to understand her generosity and impact on the department, and the scholarship is a great way to do that."

The scholarship will honor Shearlean and all the work she did for the department and the school.

In 14 months we were able to fully fund what was eventually formally titled the Shearlean Duke Memorial Scholarship for Public Relations. With the generous help of just 44 friends, relatives, colleagues and the Western Foundation, we were able to match the initial $10,000 I donated as seed money for the scholarship. Subsequently, contributions have continued and now the scholarship exceeds it minimum for endowment.

Last Word

Being a caregiver to a terminally ill patient gives you the authority to speak on a variety of topics important not only to you and your patient, but to the public at large that may someday be in your shoes. We all come to the end of life and being prepared is critical to the quality and dignity of the end of one's life. You can help yourself and your loved ones through an important part of life by simply talking about what you want and don't want when your time comes. The alternative is too unthinkable to even consider, so act now—while you can.

Epilogue

I'D STUMBLED through 18 months of caregiving without resolving my questions about my rights, duties, authority and entitlements as caregiver to a terminally ill patient. I relied mainly on a sense of outrage, indignation, commitment and protectiveness to sustain me.

Throughout the process itself, I had no time or energy to invoke legislated, approved or negotiated patient's rights or standards of care that might empower caregivers such as me to exercise or express his will over the care received by his patient.

All I could do was keep moving forward as best I could because there was never a moment to be squandered in parsing out rules and policies. It wasn't until my caregiving duties terminated with Shearlean's death that I could reflect on my experience. And though I was pleased with what I had accomplished and felt I could not have done more or better regarding her outcome, I continued to be disturbed about how difficult caregiving had been for me and how stressful the healthcare system had been on the patient. Surely, I've mused many times, things could be improved. And just as surely, I can't be the only person thinking like this.

When this gnawing, aching feeling about the state of caregiving and the healthcare system's deficiencies didn't lessen with time, I decided to write this book. With a well-documented story, I hoped I might spur needed changes—or at least let other caregivers know they aren't alone when they feel they've been abandoned, ignored, mislead or dismissed.

But for change to happen, I thought I would need to hand the healthcare system a journalistically compiled record of care and treatment full of names, places, times, dates and documented circumstances. This they could not disregard as the vague complaints of a disillusioned and grief-stricken spouse. That is the reason that, in addition to my story of caring for Shearlean, which you have just read, I've included such detailed appendixes. Now that you've read my personal story, I hope you'll give plenty of time to the appendixes and glean the benefit of the raw facts you may have to grapple with yourself at some point.

~

I can't perfect my story beyond how Shearlean and I lived it, but I can backtrack and offer our experience through the system we had to traverse. With the draft of this manuscript in hand and questions deserving answers, I tried to bargain for a dialogue with identifiable components of the healthcare system, locally and at state level.

I gave myself two months (December 2012 through January 2013) to find answers to about three dozen local questions that were to be the basis of my interviews with healthcare experts and providers. *(See Appendix 1: Rants, Original Fact Checking and Interview Questions.)* I also had about a dozen questions for state-level healthcare providers. When I realized I was facing substantial resistance to interviews, I extended my effort by a month, through February 2013.

At the end of three months I got only a single face-to-face interview about how to correctly complete the Community Hospital's "Authorization to Use and Disclose Health Information" form. I accomplished this, not through official channels, but by hearsay from administrative staffers I approached personally. I got nothing from management or supervision. Very frustrating.

Except for surgery at University Medical in Seattle, Whatcom County's healthcare system and providers delivered most of Shearlean's care in our hometown of Bellingham. It was this system that we relied on most heavily and to which we had the greatest exposure. Since arriving in Bellingham in 1999, we'd been in the local healthcare system nearly 12 years at the time of Shearlean's death. After her diagnosis on August 21, 2009 until her death February 2, 2011, we were in daily contact with the system, sometimes several times daily. Despite this exposure there was much we did not know or were unsure about regarding its functioning. For example, during my caregiving I never knew to whom (or what entity) to turn to for help resolving conflicts between providers, even when they were in the same system. When care is urgently required for a patient's acute condition (such as terminal cancer), who can quickly respond to solve a problem? During fact-checking, this was my number one question. I compiled a list of 22 persons (job titles), but was unable to identify a single candidate who could be called upon to promptly advocate for a patient confronted with a severe problem. That the need for an advocate was a serious issue was confirmed during my fact-checking by my discovery of the recent appointment of the position of Care Navigator for lung cancer patients in the cancer center. Why? Because diagnostic and administrative obstacles to treatment were delaying treatment of lung cancer patients to a dangerous degree. Lung cancer victims were being denied weeks of critical treatment because of bureaucratic obstacles and administrative delays that kept them from entering care as soon as they should.

At the outset of my research I provided my list of 36 questions to the hospital's public relations department to alert them to which interview topics I had in mind for fact-checking. While waiting for a response from the hospital, I was able to get many of the questions answered by an unexpected source, Whatcom Alliance for Health Advancement's (WAHA) project manager who, by necessity, knew the local system intimately.

Sensing that my hospital contact was stalling, I revised my now shortened list. I divided it into three categories—administrative, patient records, and financial services and billing—so I would need to interview just three people to do my fact-checking.

More time passed with no response.

I emailed my contact to tell her I was running out of time and to not spend any more time trying to help me. Instead, I went to the hospital every afternoon, questions in hand and approached staff about whom to ask these questions. I met a lot of nice, friendly people, but it was clear that anyone who knew anything, while they might talk to me initially, would never get back to me with answers. Next, I went to public meetings where hospital staff were speakers and tried to interview them after the meetings ended. They told me they couldn't speak to me without their boss' permission.

At last I ran out of time and gave up. I decided I had to accept the fact that my book might contain errors and omissions. I apologize to readers for this, but there would be no book otherwise.

For more information about healthcare reform and a comparison of reform goals to the reality of my experience with the existing system. *(See Appendix 2: Healthcare Reform: State and County Level.)*

Additional information can also be found at the Waking Up Dying blog at robertaduke.com.

Acknowledgements

EVERYTHING THAT WAS WRONG with this book in its early stages was put right by my editor, Cami Ostman, through hard work, wise advice and deft skill. For her help, both readers and I can be grateful. For what remains awkward, difficult or erroneous, I am responsible.

Larry Thompson, executive director of Whatcom Alliance for Health Advancement, and his caring and helpful staff broke the log jam I faced with Whatcom County's healthcare establishment. In particular, Julianne Dickelman, who supplied numerous facts about the healthcare system and lent a patient ear for wide-ranging discussion of the need for healthcare reform and end-of-life preparation.

Professor Marie Eaton, PhD, former Dean of Fairhaven College, was Shearlean Duke's companion for the 2008 and 2009 service learning programs to the Ombogo Girls' Academy in Kenya, Africa. Professor Eaton's early review of a draft of "Waking Up Dying" was instrumental in improving its tone and direction. Her singing and guitar brought warmth and joy to the celebration of Shearlean's life.

Many of Shearlean's friends, relatives, admirers and colleagues contributed generously to bringing this book to fruition. Without their help and support I may not have been able to sustain the effort required to complete this publishing project. Most importantly, these were the people who did so much to comfort and support Shearlean during the 18 months she battled cancer and confronted the healthcare system. All are celebrated in the pages of this book.

Appendices

APPENDIX ONE

Rants

Medical Equipment: Too Much Information

Home Infusion Service: Not Ready for Self-Administration

Critical Documents: Little Help, But Essential

Healthcare Providers—Good, Bad and Ugly

Original Fact-Checking and Interview Questions

Washington State Health Care Authority Q&A

Medical Equipment: Too Much Information

As with the PICC catheter discussed in Chapter 19, we received a crash course in computerized self-infusion, with lectures, demonstrations, and a practical test of ability and comprehension. There was even more equipment literature to read—reams of it—about infusion pump operation, Total Parenteral Nutrition (TPN) that uses the catheter to bypass the stomach, infusion practices and procedures, IV supplies, and proper liaison with the infusion provider. Here are the titles and contents of the publications that patient and caregiver were expected to master:

"Flushing Your Central Line with Sodium Chloride"
22 steps, 1 page.
- Wash Your Hands
- Gather Your Supplies
- Clean Your Work Area
- Flushing the Catheter
- When to Call Infusioneers
- When to Call 911

"Patient Quick Guide for TPN Therapy" 13 steps, 1 page.
- Responses to screen prompts:
- To Resume – 4 screens
- To Repeat Rx – 5 screens

"Fluconazole Patient's Education Monograph" 3 pages.
- No subheadings

"Patient Guide Ambulatory Infusion Systems" 10 pages.
- Introduction
- Preparing Your Therapy
- Installation of Administration Set
- Removal of Administration Set
- Priming the Administration Set
- Starting the Pump

Information on Demand
Power
Alarms – 11 alarm conditions.
Frequently Asked Questions – 13 questions and answers

"Financial Responsibility Acknowledgement" 1 page legal/financial agreement.
No subheadings

"Patient Consent, Authorization, and Assignment of Benefits" 1 page legal/financial agreement.
No subheadings

"TPN Instructions" 4 pages, 71 steps.
General Information
Caring for Your IV, TPN Solution and Supplies
Washing Your Hands
Prepare Your Work Area
When to Call the Nurse
Gather Your Supplies
Prepare Your Medication
Prepare Your Needle and Syringe
Remove Any Air Bubbles
Add Medication to TPN Bag
Connect the IV Tubing
Consult Pump Manufacturer's Directions
Starting the Infusion
Stopping the Infusion

"Instructions for the Elastomeric Pump" 1 page, 11 steps, 5 illustrations.
Before You Begin
Giving Medication

"Infusion Pump Administration Set" 2 pages, 21 steps, 5 notes, 2 cautions.
Note
By Gravity
By Using the Pump "Prime" key
By Gravity and Using the Pump "Prime" Key
Untitled 4 – illustrations and 3 steps

"Welcome Packet: Infusion Therapy Services" 9 pages.

Welcome
Services
Products
Emergency Preparedness
Bill of Rights and Responsibilities
Preventing Infection
Safety in Your Home
Advance Medical Directives
Patient Satisfaction
Disposal of Medications and Supplies
Notice of Health Information Practices

Can you picture yourself reading all of this and performing the procedures for a terminally ill patient late in the course of care?

Home Infusion Service: Not Ready for Self-Administration

The infusion equipment and supplies (discussed above in Medical Equipment: Too Much Information) were provided by a local business, Infusioneers, which operated a commercial infusion center and provided home infusion equipment and supplies. While Infusioneers' services benefited many patients, they were not appropriate for every patient. Infusioneers and its equipment suppliers, though, seemed oblivious of the circumstances of a patient and caregiver such as Shearlean and me as explained in Chapter 19.

In an effort to persuade Infusioneers why its "one size fits all" approach to home infusion didn't work for us, I prepared the following list of problems and suggested improvements from the patient's perspective. I had a long telephone discussion with the owner of Infusioneers and sent her and the infusion pump's manufacturer a copy of this list:

- Equipment needs to be refined. *This combination of equipment could not have been field-tested prior to release for home use by patients because it has too many flaws.*
- Alarm's too shrill and frequent, can't turn off and keep off. *Alarms are alarming.*
- Pump should be a black box. *Too many controls to be mastered for in-home use by persons with limited abilities. The unit must be foolproof.*
- Documentation is incomplete. *Documents need subject indexes to be more useful and for quick reference (when alarms are sounding and messages flashing) and operating instructions need to be proven by testing against procedures.*
- Infusion kit includes surplus or unidentified parts. *Every part is important unless you know otherwise.*
- Tubing is too awkward to handle. *It causes problems by catching on obstacles and kinking and setting off an alarm.*

A means of coiling or rolling up excess tubing is required to keep it out of the way.

- Unsuitable technical language is used in onscreen pump help instructions. *For example: "occlusion." This is the precise medical word to define the cause of an alarm, but to lay persons the alarm is caused by supply tubing being kinked or blocked—not* occluded.
- Home infusion service providers need to offer individual treatment. *Somewhere between do-it-yourself and skilled nursing care in a hospital, there needs to be a service priced for having a skilled person provide the service at home.*
- Complicated equipment and disorganized procedures cause information overload. *Too much information is reported to the patient. Everything needs to be simplified at every level.*
- Trying to use clinical equipment at home is stressful. *Equipment not designed for home use requires actions some ill people are unable to perform. So much infusion plumbing creates a very negative image of the "tubes" that sick and dying people dread.*
- Current equipment and procedures create too much work and effort for too little or no patient benefit. *Though infusion is done in the home, the process—as it is currently implemented—does too little to improve the patient's circumstances to justify widespread use. Patients in Shearlean's condition are ill-equipped to deal with this sort of procedure and complex equipment.*
- Handling the infusion pump is the worst feature of this system. The canvas bag intended to hold the pump is impractical. Getting the pump, with tubing attached, into the bag is the most difficult single infusion activity. Tubing length is too short between pump and infusion bag. *The unit we were provided with was designed and outfitted for mobile infusion treatment, where patients can go about their daily activities while receiving their infusion from this portable device—far different circumstances than Shearlean's home infusion situation.*

- I could not check the pump battery status using power check key as instructed. *This function did not work the way it was said to and so batteries died mid-infusion, inflicting yet another alarming event.*

- The fourth tubing kit I used repeatedly gave an air-in-line warning. I removed the line, purged it and reinstalled it and got the warning again. I tested all fittings and found nothing wrong. I removed tube from nutrient bag #3 and installed it on bag #4 and had no more alarms. *Inadequate quality control during manufacturing may have resulted in defective fittings being delivered for patient use.*

- With the external power supply plug connected at the bottom of the pump, it is too difficult to put the pump in its canvas bag. If not fully closed, the bag's zipper unzips itself. The high level of stress and irritation under which the caregiver and patient are living magnifies a small problem such as this. *Nothing can be tolerated that adds to this condition because these individuals are so close to the edge of collapse.*

- The batteries supplied with the pump lasted for only one nutrient bag. When new batteries were installed in the pump, it indicated the batteries were partially discharged. Before one bag was administered there was a low battery warning. That happened without touching the monitor during treatment. *Infusioneers or the pump manufacturer's equipment performance expectations are too high and mislead the patient into thinking there is an equipment malfunction (more stress).*

- When these problems happen during dinner it is nerve-wracking, annoying and scary. *Though the patient is being fed by infusion, she and the caregiver try to "eat" together for the sake of a little normalcy, and the timing of alarms is especially unfortunate. Even one alarm is one too many.*

Critical Documents: Little Help, But Essential

It wasn't until November 2012, while fact-checking this book, that I better understood the purpose and scope of three critical legal and medical documents: Physician Orders for Life-Sustaining Treatment (POLST) form, Healthcare Directive (also called Advance Directive or Living Will depending on what state you live in), and Power of Attorney for Healthcare (also called Durable Power of Attorney for Healthcare depending on what state you live in). More about these documents is presented in Chapter 21. In this appendix, I deal only with my use of these documents while caring for Shearlean between August 2009 and February 2011.

While I was Shearlean's caregiver, my understanding of these documents was pitifully inadequate. I was under the mistaken impression that these documents provided me, as caregiver, all the authority necessary to fulfill my objective and mission to care for Shearlean.

Unfortunately, these documents were of little practical help in providing care for three principal reasons:

1. Healthcare providers themselves had little or no in-depth knowledge of the application of these documents as they applied to patient care or caregiver authority. And because providers were uninformed, they were unable to advise caregivers in their use.

2. Patients and caregivers were basically ignorant (as was I) about the legal and medical implications of the documents as they applied to clinical situations where treatment was taking place or being planned. Combining this ignorance with poor provider knowledge led to inaction and confusion.

3. An average of only 27 percent of the public had these documents and those who had them (including Shearlean and me) *assumed* they conferred protection and powers that they did not provide.

If the caregiver and patient are to have any control over the care they receive, they must prepare these documents and have them on file where they are accessible to healthcare providers the instant they are needed. The patient and caregiver must understand the extent to which these documents affect treatment and care decisions.

Put another way, without these documents the caregiver is impotent, but with them the caregiver is merely handicapped. All else about caregiving is subject to personal grit, organization, knowledge, persistence and dedication.

Healthcare Providers—Good, Bad and Ugly

For the purposes of this book I defined everyone employed within the healthcare system as *providers*. Providers were the *they* versus the *us*—the patient and caregiver. Providers were all of those who, in some fashion, were in the business or profession of providing care to a patient. Providers included state and county governments, insurance companies, pharmaceutical companies, clinics, medical care management companies (such as PeaceHealth in Washington) and a host of other businesses. Besides who they were and what they were was more to the point: they were businesses first and their primary outlook was a corporate one, aimed at profit and cost containment. Corporate thinking, profit and cost control dominate our healthcare system, which puts the patient far down the list of priorities and makes him or her an object to be managed for the provider's benefit. Medical corporations unfortunately care for patients using the same methods and practices as AT&T, Comcast or General Motors use in their businesses. Does thinking about your cell phone, cable or car suppliers inspire you to want the same service and management for your healthcare? Government cares for patients along the same lines as TSA (Transportation Security Administration) and IRS (Internal Revenue Service) do their jobs. Would you like similar methods applied to its caring for you and your loved ones?

The hands-on providers—the doctors, nurses, technicians and clinical staff—are also at the mercy of the system they are in, but to a lesser degree than patients and caregivers.

Providers—all providers—were one of the audiences I had in mind for this book. Arguably, Shearlean Duke was well cared for and had a successful outcome, given her condition. In the American legal system, since Shearlean was not harmed there were no grounds for legal action against the healthcare system. True! But I believe that Shearlean the patient and I the caregiver were wronged by the healthcare system by all the hardship, stress, complexity, threat, fear, manipulation and unnecessary demands placed on us by the "system." We could have done without all of that and had a much better experience even if the outcome were the same.

By painstakingly documenting the defects and problems I encountered in the healthcare system, and defining them in terms of their impact on patient and caregiver, I hoped to give providers understandable examples of what was wrong with the system and their role in it. The adverse effect of the healthcare system on patient and caregiver was not that of a tsunami but rather of erosion—slow, irresistible and subtle, but something that could carve a Grand Canyon.

Because this is not a corporate book—on managing for results, maximizing profits, increasing sales, Internet marketing or business strategies, it is likely to be ignored by most of the corporate healthcare providers because of their corporate worldview. That's too bad because it will delay much-needed reform that the providers themselves will one day wish had been implemented before it was their turn as patient or caregiver.

What am I trying to say?

Despite being intensely involved in the state, county and university healthcare systems continuously for the 18 months of Shearlean's treatment, I learned little about those systems and understood less. I did, of course, accumulate more information about them after 18 months than anyone just entering the systems would possess. I thought that with such knowledge I could sort out all of these systems and describe and define them for readers of this book, but I was mistaken. After my experience, the systems remained nearly as confusing, convoluted, defensive, obstructive, indifferent and complicated as when I started.

As a result, this book contains tales of failures, frustrations, troubles, problems, issues and so forth. It is short on solutions, answers, explanations and advice. I hope it nevertheless succeeds at defining and illuminating some of what confronts patients and caregivers in our current systems of healthcare.

While I was writing this book and trying to get explanations about issues I encountered as a caregiver, I did make one important discovery: individual providers were not the heart of the problem. It was the system that we—provider, patient and caregiver—were forced to function in that confounded, debased and victimized everyone and everything it touched. Remarkably, the 30 to 40 clinical providers who cared for Shearlean and whom I interviewed when writing this book agreed we had a bad, broken system desperately in need of reform. Any apologists for and defenders of the current system were mostly administrative and corporate interests deeply invested in the status quo. The main fault I found with clinical individuals was their passive acceptance of the system they found themselves a part of. They defended their unwillingness to confront the system as their obligation to put patient care ahead of all other interests. My view, based on my experience, was that reforming the system would do the most for patient care. The healthcare we have is the system we created to provide it. If we want to change healthcare we have to reform the system. The bad system we have is only made worse by every effort to repair it instead of replacing it. So this book, which started out to be only about caregiving and the end-of-life experience, morphed into a plea for reform.

Original Fact-Checking and Interview Questions

The following are the original questions I hoped to get answered during the three-month fact-checking process described in the Epilogue. Answers to these questions would have filled in voids in my knowledge of the healthcare system I inhabited for 18 months and validated conclusions I drew from my experiences as a caregiver. Aside from the value of these questions to me as an author and to the thoroughness of the contents of this book, the questions may benefit readers taking on the role of caregiver.

These unanswered questions demonstrate how uninformed a caregiver can remain even after completing an intensive caregiving experience.

ADMINISTRATIVE

1. Who is responsible for coordinating patient treatment that involves three or more departments? For example: hematology, hospital pharmacy and infusion center?
2. Do the terms "caregiver" or "advocate" appear anywhere on forms or literature within Community Hospital? Where can I find samples?
3. Are computer terminals accessible to the public for reading or researching hospital policies and procedures?
4. Is there a Community Hospital ombudsman function or case manager who can assist a patient or caregiver to cross all department lines to resolve complex care issues?
5. Who—title or management position—is responsible for **compliance** with HIPAA rules? Hospital? Independent practice? Who coordinates? Who to challenge?
6. Where do you draw the line between the patient's privacy and the caregiver's authority designated in the power of attorney and healthcare directive?

7. How is excessive (overzealous) privacy enforcement remedied? What privacy waiver options are there? A directive states: "A covered healthcare provider with a direct treatment relationship with individuals must make a good faith effort to obtain written acknowledgement from patients of receipt of the privacy practices notice." Badgering?
8. What is the extent of care provided to patients by Community Hospital? That is, where are the borders? What defines the limits of service provided by Community Hospital versus where the patient must represent herself and cannot rely on her hospital or doctor to resolve issues?

PATIENT RECORDS

1. Does Imaging, for example, have access to Community Hospital electronic (computer) patient medical records?
2. Where are all lab results posted and accessible to providers? Why would three providers need to take blood in one day?
3. Can patient records be accessed from home computers?
4. Can a patient obtain a copy of his Community Hospital medical file to audit its contents? Online?
5. What is the patient information relationship between Community Hospital and an independent medical practice such as the Care Clinic in Bellingham? Or Eisenhower Medical Center in Rancho Mirage, California?
6. What generic categories of information are in patient medical records as of 12/12/12?
7. What patient medical information categories are to be added to records in 2013?
8. Why not promote an annual day (week) for citizens to update their healthcare records, especially where there are new forms and revisions? Healthcare providers are diligent about updating records for payment and release from liability.

FINANCIAL SERVICES AND BILLING

1. Do hospital Financial Services and Billing communicate with each other about patient accounts? For instance, if the patient disputes a bill, the dispute is handled by Financial Services, but Billing continues dunning the patient with threats of collection while the dispute is being processed.
2. What treatment provider is responsible for dealing with state-mandated insurance and pharmacy services on behalf of the insured?
3. Patients would like to know about cost and insurance coverage before treatment, but no one will say. Financial ruin is a bigger fear than disease, but never addressed in clinical setting. I was frequently told that if a procedure was not denied it was approved. Why negative instead of positive affirmation?
4. What treatment provider is responsible for dealing with state insurance care management contractors? For example, Uniform Medical Plan's use of MedImpact in determining when and whether prescriptions can be refilled on a certain date?
5. What role does legal counsel play in Community Hospital's promulgation of legal and financial forms presented to patients by providers for signature and compliance?

For the record, I spoke to persons in the following Community Hospital positions seeking clues to who might answer the above questions:

- Social Worker Clinical Specialist
- Patient Records Clerk
- Administration Assistant
- Administration Secretary
- East Tower Reception Desk Receptionist

- Risk Management Specialist
- Privacy Officer
- Patient Experience Coordinator
- Clinical Social Worker Supervisor
- Medical Librarian
- Human Resources Staff
- Public Relations Aide
- Financial Services Representative

Senior healthcare providers were unavailable and inaccessible to me.

Washington State Health Care Authority Q&A

As a state university professor, Shearlean was an employee of the state of Washington. Her (and my) health insurance at the time of her cancer diagnosis was through the Public Employee Benefit Board (PEBB) program under the state's Health Care Authority. See the Health Care Authority organization charts, Exhibit 7, for a diagram of how pharmacy benefits are administered under Washington state's PEBB program. Note that the PEBB is not shown on the organization chart and so its relationship to other parts of the organization is unfortunately unclear.

As far as I knew, no Health Care Authority organization chart or functional description of the Health Care Authority was available during the time of Shearlean's care. And I was unable to find a diagram such as Exhibit 7 on the Internet on my own. I could only guess how the organization was structured and intended to function.

I obtained the information provided here in February 2013 as part of my fact-checking effort to verify the contents of this book. As Shearlean's caregiver I worked with the system daily for the 18 months I cared for her. I didn't understand it then and understand it now only slightly better. The disconnection between the Health Care Authority and patient is exemplified by pharmacy benefits administrator ODS's following statement: "The Uniform Medical Plan is not an insurance company." I was stunned when I read this. Until I read this I, and everyone I spoke to about Uniform Medical Plan, spoke of it as "my insurance company." Asked by a provider for my insurance card, I produced a card on which was printed Uniform Medical Plan. Under "insurance" on every form I completed I entered "Uniform Medical Plan." That Uniform Medical Plan was, in the vernacular, "my insurance company" was never questioned, refuted or rejected.

Visiting the Health Care Authority Web site on April 11, 2013, under the "About Us" tab, under the subheading Uniform Medical Plan I found the following statement:

"The Uniform Medical Plan (UMP) is a self-insured, ***preferred provider health insurance plan*** (author's emphasis) available to PEBB enrollees worldwide."

Well, if it quacks like a duck, walks like a duck and looks like a duck it might be a duck.

This kind of hair-splitting between "insurance company", "insurer" and "insurance plan" merely undermines patient and caregiver efforts to understand the system they must rely on. Multiply this dozens of times by state employees and agencies, and you can only pity the poor caregiver and patient trying to use such a system to get care and treatment.

I submitted the following questions to Washington state's ODS, a self-described Pacific Northwest health company, in an attempt to understand how the state's health insurance worked. I contacted ODS for this information because I was unable to get the information from the Health Care Authority's communications office. As far I have been able to determine, ODS is a commission sales company offering health plans purchased by Washington state. It also administers Washington State Rx Services. ODS once stood for Oregon Dental Services, but long ago outgrew that definition and ODS is merely a symbol and not an abbreviation for anything.

You can read the ODS replies to my questions for yourself and determine whether I got useful answers to my questions. My reaction to the answers is contained in my email to Chandra M. Wahrgren, ODS Vice President, which follows the Q&As below. To maintain continuity and anonymity, I replaced the actual pharmacy names with the symbolic designations used throughout the book.

AUTHOR Q: Is MedImpact still managing pharmacy services for Washington state and/or Uniform Medical Plan? If not, who is doing it or how is it being done?

ODS A: The Uniform Medical Plan (UMP) drug plan operates as Washington State Rx Services and is administered by ODS. It is important to note that Washington State Rx Services is the name of UMP's pharmacy program and is not the name of an organization.

The Health Care Authority hired ODS to provide oversight and to administer the UMP pharmacy plan benefits in 2008. While ODS manages many aspects of the program such as member services, benefit design and development, analytical and clinical services in house, we have subcontracted with MedImpact. ODS partners with MedImpact, a national pharmacy benefit manager (PBM) for prescription claims processing for retail, mail-order and specialty pharmacy network management, manufacturer rebate administration and after hours customer service.

AUTHOR Q: When RxB was Washington state's specialty mail-order pharmacy, one of its pharmacists told me that "the insurance company" had to preapprove all prescriptions? At the time the insurance company we were discussing was Uniform Medical Plan under Harrington's administration.

ODS A: The Uniform Medical Plan is not an insurance company. The Uniform Medical Plan is a self-funded PPO health plan administered by the Washington State Health Care Authority for eligible PEBB members. Harrington Health was the third party administrator contracted by the Health Care Authority through 2010 to administer the medical benefits for the UMP. The UMP pharmacy benefits are administered under a separate Health Care Authority contract with ODS and its subcontractors.

From January 2008 through March 2012, RxB reviewed prior authorization requests for specialty medications that were running through the UMP pharmacy benefit. Washington State Rx Services reviewed prior authorization requests for non-specialty medications that were running through the UMP pharmacy benefit. Beginning April 2012, Washington State Rx Services reviewed all prior authorization requests for both specialty and non-specialty medications.

AUTHOR Q: At the same time as above, Uniform Medical Plan's case manager told me that UMP had no control over RxB. Were both parties probably talking about MedImpact? Who approves filling a prescription covered under Uniform Medical Plan today? 2009?

ODS A: Based on the information provided, it appears that the UMP case manager providing the information may have been a representative of UMP's medical plan administrator (Harrington). If this is accurate, the case manager was correct as the medical plan administration was and remains separate from the UMP pharmacy program and benefit administration. Therefore, as the medical administrator, Harrington did not hold the contract with RxB.

The Health Care Authority hired ODS to administer the UMP pharmacy plan benefits. The program is branded Washington State Rx Services. Washington State Rx Services encompasses all aspects of the pharmacy benefit management contract, including services provided by ODS and its subcontractors. MedImpact (PBM), RxW (mail-order), and RxB (specialty pharmacy) were contracted to provide services to UMP members under the Washington State Rx Services pharmacy program during the dates referenced (2008-2010).

Washington State Rx Services pharmacy benefits are administered in accordance with the UMP plan design and coverage protocols.

UMP follows the Washington Preferred Drug List (PDL). Senate Bill 6088, passed in 2003, requires state-run health care programs to establish a state preferred drug list (the Washington PDL).

The following Washington state agencies follow the Washington PDL: UMP, Medicaid, and Department of Labor & Industries (L&I).

Under state law, the UMP PDL is based on the Washington PDL. The Washington PDL is developed from the recommendations of the Washington State Pharmacy & Therapeutics Committee (P&T Committee). The Washington State P&T Committee is an independent group of practicing health care providers; a list of P&T Committee members and the criteria for selection is posted at www.rx.wa.gov/pt.html. The Washington State P&T Committee reviews scientific evidence, such as how effective a drug has proven to be as compared with other similar drugs, to determine which drugs will be included on the Washington PDL.

If a drug has not yet been reviewed by the Washington State P&T Committee, UMP follows recommendations from the ODS P&T Committee regarding whether the drug will be covered, the tier status, and if a prior authorization, quantity level limits or step therapy will apply.

The above was applicable in 2009 and remains applicable today.

AUTHOR Q: To whom does a Uniform Medical Plan patient appeal for assistance solving Rx problems with state-contracted mail-order pharmacies today? 2009?

ODS A: UMP members can contact Washington State Rx Services/ODS for assistance in answering questions and/or requesting information and aid in filing grievances and/or appeals. Washington State Rx Services' customer service is available to provide support with any aspect of the pharmacy benefit program, including the UMP mail-order pharmacy in 2009 and today. The Washington State Rx Services customer service team is committed to helping UMP members access their prescription drug coverage. This includes working with a pharmacy when issues arise, verifying how a drug is covered, identifying limitations to drug coverage, obtaining a cost estimate for a drug, finding network pharmacies, and following up with prescribers and members when information is requested in order to review coverage. The Washington State Rx Services program includes strict performance standards and expectations to ensure timely responses to all member appeals.

AUTHOR Q: Is there any kind of block diagram or organization chart that describes the components of the Washington State Healthcare System and the parts' relationships to each other? I've spent hours searching the Internet and every state healthcare Web site, but have found nothing—the Washington State Health Care Authority organization chart (revised 11/01/2012) provides no information of use to a consumer or patient.

ODS A: Please see attached organization chart that describes the roles of ODS and its partners in administering UMP's pharmacy benefit.

AUTHOR Q: Does the Health Care Authority or any other Washington state healthcare entity provide healthcare providers with a user-oriented guide to how the Washington state healthcare system functions? For example, how does a clinician write a Rx correctly for a patient? Or, if MedImpact blocks filling a prescription how does a clinician remedy the problem in a timely way?

ODS A: Providers and patients have access to the Washington State Rx Services customer service for assistance and questions on prescription drug coverage. The Washington State Rx Services customer service contact information is printed on the member's UMP identification card, in the UMP Certificate of Coverage and on the UMP website at www.ump.hca.wa.gov.

The claims processing system utilized by the Washington State Rx Services program provides automatic alerts to pharmacies when a prescription requires a prior authorization and clinical review. This notice includes an explanation of the coverage requirement and contact information at the point of service to ensure that pharmacies have the information they need to seek support. Washington State Rx Services provides UMP members, providers and pharmacies with 24/7 access to client services and a pharmacy help desk.

AUTHOR Q: How are the actions of two state-contracted mail-order pharmacies coordinated for cooperation with each other and timely response to patient needs? What agency oversees the conduct and operation of contracted healthcare providers, such as mail-order pharmacies?

ODS A: Procedures are in place to transfer prescriptions between the UMP mail-order pharmacy and specialty pharmacy. When the UMP mail-order pharmacy receives a prescription for a specialty drug, the member will be notified and the UMP mail-order pharmacy will transfer the prescription to the specialty pharmacy. Similarly, when the UMP specialty pharmacy receives a prescription for a non-specialty drug, the member will be notified and the UMP specialty pharmacy will transfer the prescription to the UMP mail-order pharmacy.

MedImpact manages the UMP pharmacy network and establishes contracts with pharmacies. UMP network pharmacies include retail, mail-order and specialty pharmacies. Washington State Rx Services/ODS oversees the services and programs provided by its subcontractors, which include MedImpact.

AUTHOR Q: Does Washington State Prescription Services work with clinicians— prescribing doctors and nurses—to facilitate filling prescriptions on a timely basis?

ODS A: Washington State Rx Services works with prescribers and their office staff to ensure prescriptions are filled on a timely basis. When a drug requires a prior authorization, we will contact the prescriber's office and request the information required to complete the review process. To ensure timely responses to authorization requests, we adhere to a follow-up procedure. If the information is not received after three attempts, we will notify both the provider and member that the drug is not covered due to lack of response for information.

UMP prescription benefits, coverage limitations, preauthorization and notification requirements, and other information are described in the UMP Certificate of Coverage and are available on the UMP website at www.ump.hca.wa.gov.

AUTHOR Q: Does Washington State Prescription Services supervise the performance of state-contracted mail-order pharmacies in filling the medication needs of UMP covered patients?

ODS A: MedImpact contracts directly with the UMP retail, mail-order and specialty pharmacy providers. Washington State Rx Services/ODS oversees the services and programs provided by its subcontractors, which include MedImpact.

AUTHOR Q: If a UMP patient has a pharmacy problem caused by a decision by MedImpact, to whom does the patient appeal the problem for timely (24-48 hours) resolution?

ODS A: UMP members can contact Washington State Rx Services for assistance in resolving any medication-related issue or concern. In 2012, over 95% of the calls received were resolved on the same day. Some calls may require additional research and involvement from the prescriber, member or pharmacy. When this occurs, members are informed on the status until there is a resolution.

AUTHOR Q: How many Prescription Services customer service representatives are presently available to UMP patients today?

ODS A: Washington State Rx Services has 26 dedicated pharmacy customer service representatives and two supervisors available to UMP members.

AUTHOR Q: Would you or someone you know be willing to review and comment on draft Chapter 7 of my book, "Waking Up Dying." The chapter is central to the purpose of my book. The chapter deals in great detail with my year-long problem trying to obtain medication from RxB on time for my wife.

ODS A: Effective April 1, 2012, the RxB contract servicing the UMP pharmacy benefit was discontinued. Appreciating this change and the fact that RxB is no longer operating as a specialty pharmacy, Washington State Rx Services/ODS is not able to support or facilitate a review of the content.

We appreciate having the opportunity to respond to your questions. Please feel free to contact us if we can be of additional support.

Sincerely,
Chandra M. Wahrgren
Vice President, Client Strategies, ODS

The following email was my response to ODS's answers to my questions above:

Good Morning Chandra

Thank you for the thorough and timely reply to my questions about the state's PEBB health insurance system in response to my fact-checking on behalf of my book "Waking Up Dying."

Of all the healthcare professionals I have contacted over the past three months for fact-checking my book, you are the only one to actually respond in a useful and thorough way, and on time.

I salute you.

Unfortunately, it was truly mind-numbing to read the explanations you provided. The language is the epitome of bureaucratic gobbledygook. Despite my 50 years of being a professional writer, one specializing in highly technical and complex subjects ranging from mathematical modeling to computer programming to risk analysis to space craft flight evaluation reports, I doubt I can transform the information you provided into anything that can be usefully comprehended by the readers of my book.

I may have the facts now, but they surpass all understanding. I doubt any of them will make their way into my book because they would detract from comprehension of the subject I am writing about. (Uniform Medical Plan will have to remain my "insurance company" in the book because by the time I related your definition of the insurance company the reader's eyes will have glazed over and he will have closed the book.)

At least now I understand why I have never comprehended the system that I was part of for many years as an insured on my wife's health insurance through her employer, Western Washington University.

I can tell you that I sincerely believe that no one covered by PEBB can even recognize the system intended to serve him from the description you provided.

Shearlean Duke's problems with obtaining care during treatment for glioblastoma brain cancer from August 2009 to February 2011 could not be addressed, let alone solved in a timely way with the system in place as described by your correspondence.

The system your email describes cannot help an acutely ill patient in need of urgent care. It is too vast, too complicated, and too slow for a stricken person to navigate.

I am lobbying for some sort of care or case manager to help such patients to deal with systems such as yours. The system you describe might be fiscally sound, but it is worthless to caregivers and patients in a desperate fight for life. 95% effectiveness looks good on paper, but the remaining 5%—at today's rates of elderly coming into the healthcare system with critical conditions—amounts to thousands not being adequately cared for.

Sincerely
Robert Duke

Heathcare Reform: State and County Level

ORGANIZATIONS AND INDIVIDUALS around the United States are working to transform local healthcare systems by eliminating the problems such as those experienced by patient Shearlean Hamby Duke and caregiver Robert (Bob) Allen Duke featured in this book. Only one organization, though, has undertaken such an all-encompassing and persistent effort to transform healthcare at the grassroots level as Whatcom Alliance for Health Advancement (WAHA). WAHA was founded in 2002 in Whatcom County, Washington state, the locale of "Waking Up Dying."

The following is from WAHA's Web site's brief "About Us" posting, on January 14, 2013:

> Our mission is to connect people to healthcare and facilitate the transformation of the current system into one that improves health, reduces cost, and improves the experience of care. We are powered by our unique, two-part mission of providing local access services while fostering public participation and meaningful system change.
>
> We advance by improving people's lives today, while building a better health system for tomorrow.

ASSUMPTIONS

1. The current healthcare system is broken. As a nation we pay more but receive less than most other industrialized countries. We need to change the way we deliver healthcare, beginning with our local delivery system.
2. Economic forces need to be aligned so providers are paid according to the quality of their treatment, and the extent they help keep people healthy. The people using the service have enough clear information about pricing and payment obligations to effectively manage their own care.
3. Birth, illness and end of life are events far too important to leave only to professionals, regardless how skilled and well intended they may be. Our system of care must foster patient and family participation.

HISTORY AND LEADERSHIP

In 2002 the St. Luke's Foundation convened over 200 Whatcom County community members in order to increase awareness about eroding access to health coverage and care, and to identify potential strategies for developing a community-based response. The creation of WAHA and its strong alliance of providers, consumers, and community leaders is the outcome of that summit. Over the past ten years WAHA has served an estimated forty thousand residents, nearly 20% of our County's population.

WAHA is governed by a Leadership Board that includes community members and representatives from leading healthcare, public health, business and governmental organizations. These leaders, as well as other community partners, serve on advisory committees dedicated to WAHA's mission. Larry Thompson serves as Executive Director and Regina Delahunt serves as the Leadership Board Chair.

WAHA is a non-profit organization located in Bellingham, Washington.

It is significant to compare WAHA's goals to our experience because the story of one is substantially the story of the other. Our story tells of the impact of an indifferent and dysfunctional healthcare system on an elderly patient and caregiver at the most vulnerable time of their lives. WAHA's reports describe what principles must be adopted to guide the transformation of the Whatcom healthcare system (and others) to meet the following community and patient goals:

- Connect people to healthcare
- Facilitate transformation of the current system
- Improve health
- Reduce costs
- Improve the experience of care

I exhaustively document our experience with the Whatcom and Washington state healthcare systems, using our experience as journalists. This book provides detailed examples of the practical consequences and human cost of treatment by a defective healthcare system. WAHA's steering committee's report, below, articulates the principles by which the healthcare system can be improved and fixed. The steering committee comprises members from the community, health department, clinics, hospital, insurers, mental health providers, businesses, and county and regional government. The steering committee represents five other groups consisting of 10 to 18 members each. Principles of change summarized in the following points represent a broad consensus.

Compare WAHA's goals for improving the healthcare system (numbered and bulleted items) with the reality we confronted (in italics) in the system that is being challenged to change.

1. **Care should be organized around patient-centered medical homes.**

   - The medical home is a personal provider who has a whole person orientation.

     Author Duke: We had no personal provider, but desperately needed one. As caregiver, I was the only person with a "whole-person" orientation and I met with obstacles at every turn. It wasn't until May 28, 2010 that patient Shearlean Duke managed to elect a palliative care physician.

- Care in the medical home is team based, i.e. physicians and nurse practitioners provide care in conjunction with care coordinators among others.

  Author Duke: We had to provide much of our own care coordination and assemble our own team. Most telling, there was no one to turn to even when what was missing was identified. In 2012, when I made an effort to identify who among 22 candidates could provide the needed coordination, which I couldn't find in 2009, I came up empty. No one would even talk to me about it.

- All medical homes meet the National Committee for Quality Assurance (NCQA) criteria.

  Author Duke: I recommend trying to define your own criteria for a quality healthcare organization and then see how it matches up with NCQA at www.ncqa.org.

2. **Coordination is a hallmark of the system.**

   Author Duke: Lack of coordination is a hallmark of the existing system, the one I experienced.

   - Those who coordinate care document the care provided with the aim of informing all others in the care system.

     Author Duke: As far as I know this does not exist anywhere. I provided all care documentation.

   - Health information exchange systems are used to ensure that patient information navigates optimally through the whole system.

     Author Duke: All health information exchanged for us was botched beginning to end. It was practically nonexistent. Records were not available.

   - Medical homes consistently arrange and support chronic disease management.

     Author Duke: Why just chronic? Patient Shearlean was acute and urgent for 18 months, so would have benefited from consistent management.

- There is a Community Case Management system that serves as a referral resource for the cohort of patients with the most co-morbid conditions.

  Author Duke: Care and case management were obviously lacking and badly needed. Yet every level and every person at Community Hospital rebuffed every effort I made to identify or discuss such management.

3. **The patients experience care in all settings as collaborative and patient centered.**

   - Care is planned between providers to be seamless.

     Author Duke: Shearlean's care was piecemeal. Everything was wait and see. We were not aware that providers ever talked to each other or developed a plan. I had to fight for even short-range plans.

   - Clinic operations center on meeting the patient's needs.

     Author Duke: Infusion, in particular—either at Community Hospital or Infusioneers—was terribly hard on the patient and totally for the ease and benefit of the provider. Administratively, when the patient was entering for care, operations were self-serving, not patient-serving.

   - Care is coordinated across all settings, including nursing homes, hospitals and clinics.

     Author Duke: This goal could be broader and specify many more sources of stress and difficulties—labs, insurers, pharmacies and administrators.

4. **Care seeks to activate patients.**

   - The system supports and encourages self-management by engaged consumers.

     Author Duke: The current system discourages and penalizes engaged patients and caregivers. Many patients cannot be active due to their symptoms or by choice. Their appointed caregiver or agent must be embraced by the system and accorded the necessary courtesy and authority.

- Patients have access to their own electronic health records.

  Author Duke: I could not find an explanation of what this is supposed to consist of. A request to Community Hospital to simply state what a patient's health record is supposed to contain remained unanswered. It is one thing to have access but another to know whether it is complete and what rights the patient and caregiver have to the information.

- Patient satisfaction is consistently measured and used to improve care processes.

  Author Duke: I received several surveys from Community Hospital while Shearlean was under care there and I refused to answer them and wrote letters of complaint about them. They were obviously structured to elicit responses that would support the hospital's goals and were entirely in its self-interest. The surveys were too long and too late and too generic. They were a waste of precious time. When I made an actual complaint, since it did not conform to Community Hospital's requirements, it took no action.

5. **Patients have access to care when they need/want it.**

   - Doctor's offices know who needs a visit and contact patients to schedule an appointment.

     Author Duke: Patients also know when they want and need care, but providers are only willing to provide care on their schedules and on their terms.

   - Patients have 24/7 continuous access to their medical home via phone, e-mail, or in person visits.

     Author Duke: Even a recent (April 2013) award-winning clinic's Web site was too hard to use and only marginally improved communication with its doctors or practices. In 2009 I could directly email one doctor and now four years later, I still have problems emailing my primary care doctor. Information Technology (IT) systems are still (as always) being designed for the practice, not the patient.

- Patients have online access to support services, including scheduling, medical records, and test results.

  Author Duke: Not yet available in February 2013. It is impossible to even discuss it with Community Hospital.

6. **The care coordination system supports patients and families as they engage in improving their own health.**

   - Evidence-based disease management programs are available in the community for key conditions identified through the analytic system.

     Author Duke: It is unclear what this means, but I think it does not apply to my circumstances.

   - All consumers have made conscious choices about their end-of-life experience and these wishes are respected.

     Author Duke: With the end-of-life documents I had available, prepared before 2009, I was not able to fulfill my responsibilities as caregiver and Shearlean was unable to avoid harassment. Few providers, let alone the patients, understand the basic documents. WAHA workshops are addressing this through community education.

   - Community programs to enable learning healthy behaviors are available and well integrated into the delivery system.

     Author Duke: Not pertinent to my situation.

7. **We seek a delivery system to serve the whole community, inclusive of linguistic and cultural diversity, and all socioeconomic backgrounds.**

Author Duke: This should extend to personal relationships such as marriage vows. I vowed to care for Shearlean in sickness and in health, but my efforts were thwarted by rules and procedures of the providers.

- Our efforts are oriented toward members of our community from all cultural and demographic backgrounds.
- Inclusiveness requires cultural and linguistic sensitivity as well as active efforts in measuring and reducing disparities.

8. **Quality is consistently measured and care is evidence based.**

- Quality is consistently measured, adjusting for risk where feasible, and rapid response occurs when discrepancies are noted.

Author Duke: I never witnessed a rapid response to an urgent need. Where would the patient or caregiver find comparisons or signs of improvement or performance measurements?

- Providers know how they compare to others within their practice and nationally.
- Providers are supported as they aim to improve the quality of the care they provide.
- Quality performance is also measured at the population level.

9. **The financial structure of the system must create aligned incentives to achieve its aims.**

Author Duke: Presently the financial structure obscures visibility and punishes patients who seek information. If a bill is disputed to gain visibility to charges and services, it goes to collection while in dispute, punishing the patient who asks for information.

- Payment reinforces accountability for: 1) quality care and 2) cost reduction.

- Payment will transition from fees-for-service to new methods.

10. **The future system will be accountable, transparent, and function in a culture of continuous quality improvement.**

    Author Duke: I wonder what will be the enforcement mechanism?

    - Data will be used to measure progress toward system goals.
    - Governance will be transparent and inclusive of consumer needs.

About the Author

ROBERT A. DUKE is a retired corporate communications executive with more than 50 years experience as a technical writer, feature journalist and public relations practitioner. At age 71 he was the sole caregiver for his wife, Shearlean, for 531 days until her death February 2, 2011 from glioblastoma brain cancer. Duke resides in Bellingham, WA. He enjoys cruising his boat in the Pacific Northwest's Inside Passage in British Columbia and Southeast Alaska. This is his fourth non-fiction book.

Waking Up Dying Blog

The blog, Waking Up Dying, at robertaduke.com, supports and supplements this book. It exists to encourage healthcare reform and to be a source of information and encouragement for patients, caregivers and reformers, especially those dealing with acute diseases requiring urgent care. It is dedicated to the caregivers who are in a race against the imminent end of life, caring for patients for whom there is no tomorrow.

Public comments are welcome on the blog, and constructive ones will be posted to share with everyone.